Irish Regiments During The Great War

Irish Regiments During The Great War
Two Linked Accounts of the Fighting During the First World War 1914-1918

The Irish at the Front

The Irish at the Somme

Michael MacDonagh

LEONAUR

*Irish Regiments During
The Great War
Two Linked Accounts of the Fighting
During the First World War 1914-1918*
The Irish at the Front
and
The Irish at the Somme
by Michael MacDonagh

First published under the titles
The Irish at the Front
and
The Irish at the Somme

Leonaur is an imprint of Oakpast Ltd
Copyright in this form © 2010 Oakpast Ltd

ISBN: 978-0-85706-322-9 (hardcover)
ISBN: 978-0-85706-321-2 (softcover)

http://www.leonaur.com

Publisher's Notes

The opinions of the authors represent a view of events in which he was a participant related from his own perspective, as such the text is relevant as an historical document.

The views expressed in this book are not necessarily those of the publisher.

Contents

The Irish at the Front   7

The Irish at the Somme   139

The Irish at the Front

Michael MacDonagh

Contents

Prefatory Note	11
A Dauntless Battle Line	13
Introduction	17
The Retreat From Mons	27
Battle of the Rivers	37
Contest For the Channel Coast	44
Asphyxiating Gas and Liquid Fire	51
The Immortal Story	59
The 10th Irish Division in Gallipoli	71
In the Rest Camp	79
Fight For Kislah Daght	85
For Cross and Crown	94
The Great Push at Loos	107
The Victoria Cross	114
"For Valour"	127

Prefatory Note

This narrative of the more signal feats of the Irish Regiments in France, Flanders, and at the Dardanelles, is based on letters of regimental officers and men, interviews with wounded soldiers of the battalions, and those invalided home, and, also, in several cases, on the records compiled at the depôts.

The war is the greatest armed struggle that the world has ever seen, and when we think of the heroism and resolution shown in it, the trials and the sufferings, the victories and the disasters, and then turn to the bald and trite official despatches, the dissimilitude of things, the contrast, is most abrupt and jarring. But so it is, and probably we must continue to rely upon the accounts given by the men in the fighting line for any real appreciation of the nature of the war.

Michael MacDonagh.

A Dauntless Battle Line

The Irish Regiments and Their War Honours

Ireland is represented in the fighting forces of the Empire by a regiment of Foot Guards, eight regiments of the Line, each of two Regular battalions, and with several linked battalions of the Special Reserve, or old Militia, and many Service battalions raised for "Kitchener's Army." Altogether, these various battalions of the Irish regiments number fifty-four. There are two Dragoon regiments and one regiment each of Hussars and Lancers. The Volunteer or Territorial system has not been extended to Ireland.

Still, the country is not without representation in the Auxiliary Forces. She has raised two Yeomanry regiments, the South Irish Horse, and the North Irish Horse, and in England there are two predominantly Irish Territorial battalions, the London Irish Rifles (18th Battalion of the London Regiment) and the Liverpool Irish (8th Battalion of the King's Liverpool Regiment), both of which have "South Africa, 1900-02" as a battle honour. There are also tens of thousands of Irishmen in the English, Scottish, and Welsh regiments, the Artillery, the Engineers, the Army Medical Corps, as well as in the Royal Navy.

The following are the Irish Infantry and Cavalry regiments, with their badges and battle honours:—

Irish Guards.

In acknowledgment and commemoration of the brave and honorable part taken by the Irish troops in the Boer War an Irish regiment of Foot Guards was added to the Brigade of Guards in 1900 by command of Queen Victoria. Unlike the Scots Guards, which are largely English, the Irish Guards are almost exclusively Irish. Badges: the Cross of the Order of St. Patrick and the Shamrock. Recruiting area: all Ireland.

Royal Irish Regiment.

The Harp of Ireland, with the motto *Virtutis Namuriensis Præmium* ("The Reward of Bravery at Namur"), surmounted by a Crown and enwreathed with Shamrocks. Recruiting area: the Munster Counties of Tipperary and Waterford, and the Leinster Counties of Kilkenny and Wexford. Depôt: Clonmel.

The Sphinx, superscribed "Egypt." The Dragon, superscribed "China"; "Namur, 1695"; "Blenheim"; "Ramillies," "Oudenarde"; "Malplaquet"; "Pegu"; "Sevastopol"; "New Zealand"; "Afghanistan, 1879-80"; "Tel-el-Kebir"; "Egypt, 1882"; "Nile, 1884-85"; "South Africa, 1900-02."

Royal Inniskilling Fusiliers.

A grenade with the Castle of Inniskilling flying the flag of St. George inscribed on the ball. Motto: *Nec aspera terrent* ("The harshest trials do not affright us"). Recruiting area: the Ulster Counties of Donegal, Derry, Tyrone, and Fermanagh. Depôt: Omagh town.

The Sphinx, superscribed "Egypt." "Martinique, 1762"; "Havannah"; "St. Lucia, 1778, 1796"; "Maida"; "Badajoz"; "Salamanca"; "Vittoria"; "Pyrenees"; "Nivelle"; "Orthes"; "Toulouse"; "Peninsula"; "Waterloo"; "South Africa, 1835, 1846-7"; "Central India"; "Relief of Ladysmith"; "South Africa, 1899-1902."

Royal Irish Rifles.

The Harp and Crown, with the motto *Quis Separabit?* ("Who shall divide us?") on a scroll beneath, and a bugle with strings, the symbol of a rifle regiment. Recruiting area: the Ulster Counties of Antrim and Down, including the City of Belfast. Depôt: Belfast.

The Sphinx, superscribed "Egypt." "India"; "Cape of Good Hope, 1806"; "Talavera"; "Bourbon"; "Busaco"; "Fuentes d'Onor"; "Ciudad Rodrigo"; "Badajoz"; "Salamanca"; "Vittoria"; "Nivelle"; "Orthes"; "Toulouse"; "Peninsula"; "Central India"; "South Africa, 1899-1902."

Royal Irish Fusiliers.

A grenade with a French Imperial eagle and a wreath of laurel on the ball, surmounted by the Gaelic motto, *Faugh-a-Ballagh* ("Clear the Way"), the whole being set in a wreath of Shamrocks and surmounted by the Plume of the Prince of Wales. Recruiting area: the Ulster Counties of Armagh, Monaghan, and Cavan, and the Leinster County of Louth. Depôt: Armagh town.

The Sphinx, superscribed "Egypt." "Monte Video"; "Talavera";

"Barrosa"; "Java"; "Tarifa"; "Vittoria"; "Nivelle"; "Niagara"; "Orthes"; "Toulouse"; "Peninsula"; "Asia"; "Sevastopol"; "Tel-el-Kebir"; "Egypt, 1882, 1844"; "Relief of Ladysmith"; "South Africa, 1899-1902."

CONNAUGHT RANGERS.

The Harp and Crown, with the motto, *Quis Separabit?* Recruiting area: all the Counties of Connaught—Galway, Roscommon, Mayo, Sligo, and Leitrim. Depôt: Galway.

The Elephant. The Sphinx, superscribed "Egypt." "Seringapatam"; "Talavera"; "Busaco"; "Fuentes d'Onor"; "Ciudad Rodrigo"; "Badajoz"; "Salamanca"; "Vittoria"; "Pyrenees"; "Nivelle"; "Orthes"; "Toulouse"; "Peninsula"; "Alma"; "Inkerman"; "Sevastopol"; "Central India"; "South Africa. 1877-8-9"; "Relief of Ladysmith"; "South Africa, 1899-1902."

LEINSTER REGIMENT.

The Plume of the Prince of Wales, encircled by a wreath of maple leaves, and surmounted by a Crown. Recruiting area: the Leinster Counties of Longford, Meath, Westmeath, King's County, and Queen's County. Depôt: Birr.

"Niagara"; "Central India"; "South Africa, 1900-02."

ROYAL MUNSTER FUSILIERS.

The Shamrock and a grenade with the Royal Tiger on the ball. Recruiting area: the Munster Counties of Cork, Kerry, Limerick, and Clare. Depôt: Tralee.

"Plassey"; "Condore"; "Masulipatam"; "Budara"; "Buxar"; "Rohileund, 1774"; "Sholinghur"; "Carnatic"; "Rohileund, 1794"; "Guzerat"; "Deig"; "Bhurtpore"; "Ghunzee, 1839"; "Afghanistan, 1839"; "Ferozeshah"; "Sobraon"; "Chillianwallah"; "Goojerat"; "Punjaub"; "Pegu"; "Delhi, 1857"; "Lucknow"; "Burma, 1885-87"; "South Africa, 1899-1902."

ROYAL DUBLIN FUSILIERS.

A grenade with the motto, *Spectamur Agendo* ("We are known by our deeds"), surmounted by a Crown; also the Arms of the City of Dublin set in a wreath of Shamrocks. Recruiting area: the Leinster Counties of Dublin, Kildare, Wicklow, and Carlow. Depôt: Naas.

The Royal Tiger, superscribed "Plassey"; "Buxar." The Elephant, superscribed "Carnatic"; "Mysore"; "Arcot"; "Condore"; "Wandiwash"; "Pondicherry"; "Guzerat"; "Sholingbur"; "Nundy Droog"; "Amboyna"; "Ternate"; "Banda"; "Seringapatam"; "Kirkee"; "Maheidpoor"; "Beni Boo Alli"; "Asia"; "Aden"; "Mooltan"; "Goojerat"; "Punjaub"; "Pegu"; "Lucknow"; "Relief of Ladysmith"; "South Africa, 1899-1902."

4TH (ROYAL IRISH) DRAGOON GUARDS.

The Harp and Crown, and the Star of the Order of St. Patrick.

"Peninsula"; "Balaklava"; "Sevastopol"; "Tel-el-Kebir"; "Egypt, 1882."

6TH (INNISKILLING) DRAGOONS.

The Castle of Inniskilling with the St. George's flag, and the word "Inniskilling" underneath.

"Dettingen"; "Warburg"; "Willens"; "Waterloo"; "Balaklava"; "Sevastopol"; "South Africa, 1899-1902."

5TH (ROYAL IRISH) LANCERS.

The Harp and Crown with the motto *Quis Separabit?*

"Blenheim"; "Ramillies"; "Oudenarde"; "Malplaquet"; "Suakim, 1885"; "Defence of Ladysmith"; "South Africa, 1899-1902."

8TH (KING'S ROYAL IRISH) HUSSARS.

The Harp and Crown with the motto *Pristinae virtutis memores* ("We are mindful of our ancient glory").

"Leswarree"; "Hindoostan"; "Alma"; "Balaklava"; "Inkerman"; "Sevastopol"; "Central India"; "Afghanistan, 1879-80"; "South Africa, 1900-02."

Introduction

"Though I am an Englishman, I must say the Irish soldiers have fought magnificently. They are the cream of the Army. Ireland may well be proud of her sons. Ireland has done her duty nobly. Irishmen are absolutely indispensable for our final triumph."—Letter from Brigadier-General W.B. Marshal, of the 29th Division, on service at the Dardanelles.

"Your Irish soldiers are the talk of the whole Army. . . . Their landing at Suvla Bay was the greatest thing that you will ever read of in books. Those who witnessed the advance will never forget it. . . . God! the men were splendid."—Captain Thornhill, of the New Zealand Force.

"As you know, I am not Irish. I have no Irish connections whatever. In fact, I was rather opposed to the granting of Home Rule; but now, speaking honestly and calmly, after having witnessed what I did—the unparalleled heroism of these Irishmen—I should say nothing is too good to give the country of which they are, or rather were, such worthy representatives. My God! it was grand.

It filled one with admiration and envy. . . . I have no religion, but it was most charming and edifying to see these fine chaps with their beads and the way in which they prayed to God. We are all brothers, but to my dying day I bow to the Irish."—Letter from a Scottish soldier at Gallipoli.

"Tell Ireland she may well be proud of the Irish Division. No men could have fought more gallantly or achieved better results. More of our countrymen are required to beat the Germans. I am certain that Ireland will respond as enthusiastically now as she has always done throughout her past history. *Eire go brath!*"—Lt.-General Sir Bryan Mahon, Commanding the 10th (Irish) Division.

It is these soldiers of ours, with their astonishing courage and their beautiful faith, with their natural military genius, with their tenderness as well as strength; carrying with them their green flags and their Irish war-pipes; advancing to the charge, their fearless officers at their head, and followed by their beloved chaplains as great-hearted as themselves; bringing with them a quality all their own to the sordid modern battlefield; exhibiting the character of the Irishman at its noblest and greatest—it is these soldiers of ours to whose keeping the Cause of Ireland has passed today.

It was never in worthier, holier keeping than that of these boys, offering up their supreme sacrifice of life with a smile on their lips because it was given for Ireland. May God bless them! And may Ireland, cherishing them in her bosom, know how to prove her love and pride and send their brothers leaping to keep full their battle-torn ranks and to keep high and glad their heroic hearts!

I find it hard to come within the compass and key suitable for a Preface when I am asked to write a few pages to introduce a book about our Irish soldiers. Too many things surge up demanding expression—gratitude, appreciation of the significance of what they are doing, anxiety that Ireland may play the part to them that history has assigned to her. I must only do the best I can and select a few points to remark upon.

And, first, let me remark upon this point about which there is now universal agreement. The war has brought into view again what had been somewhat obscured of late: the military qualities of the Irish race. There are now, throughout the armies in the field and throughout the world which follows their fortunes, no two opinions upon this point. I quote among the words at the head of this Preface the tribute of an English General at the Dardanelles which I have seen in a recent letter, because it is typical of the military opinion one hears on every hand, and because for his generous praise he has found an expression which well sums up the general verdict. The Irish soldiers, he says, are "the cream of the Army." On the Western front I heard the same idea put in another pointed phrase; "We always look upon an Irish regiment as a *corps d'élite*."

The war, in short, is proving anew the experience which other wars—and other armies under other flags—have so often tested, and which makes it a maxim with British Generals, as it was in Sir Ralph

Abercrombie's day, always to try and have some Irish troops included in their commands, if possible, to be on hand for work about which no risks of failure can be taken and for which an inspiring lead is essential. It is proving again that the Irish people, like their racial kinsmen the French, are one of the peoples who have been endowed in a distinguished degree with a genuine military spirit, a natural genius and gift for war which produces born soldiers and commanders, and which is the very reverse of the brute appetite for slaughter. Irish soldiers may be few in comparison with the scale of modern armies. They bulked larger in the armies of Wellington, of which they formed the backbone, when the proportions of population were different. They may be comparatively few, but their quality is admittedly precious. As the English General above quoted says, they are an "absolutely indispensable" ingredient.

I shall have to talk about the Irish soldiers in this Preface; and I want any comrade of theirs who is not Irish who may chance to see these lines, and any other reader who is not Irish, to bear in mind that it is about Irish soldiers I am intended to talk here, and not about others; that that is my business here; and I would beg them to understand that in fulfilling this duty I am not overlooking for a moment the renown of English, Scottish, Welsh, or Dominion soldiers.

Also, I would like to tell them this: that it is from the Irish soldiers—and I have listened to it from their lips again and again—you will hear the heartiest and warmest tributes to the valour and staunchness of their British and Dominion comrades. These gallant comrades, I know, will be the last to begrudge us the pious task of making some record of the Irishmen's work who have fought and died by their side, and of trying to add, as her sons would wish, to Ireland's honour through their deeds. The official record has not been copious, and Ireland may be pardoned the watchfulness of a mother's pride.

Let me turn from the soldiers themselves for a moment to look at the significance of the part they are playing before history. It is important for Ireland, and I am sure it is also important for the British Empire, and perhaps for America as well, to appreciate the part taken by the Irish troops in this war. The war, which in a night changed so many things, offered to Ireland a new international place, and her brave sons, not hesitating, acting upon a sure and noble instinct, have leaped forward to occupy it for her. After long struggles the Irish people had won back from England a series of rights—ownership of the land, religious equality, educational freedom, local self-government—

an advance which had coincided with and been helped by the emancipation and rise of British democracy.

The culmination was reached when in the session of 1914 the Imperial Parliament passed the Act to establish national self-government. Ireland had said, "Trust me with this, and I will wipe out the past and be loyal to the Empire"; and the answer—somewhat long delayed, no doubt, but still it came—was the King's signature to the Government of Ireland Act. Thus when the war arrived Ireland had at once a charter of rights and liberties of her own to defend, and, like Botha's South Africa, her plighted word to make good. The war by a most fortunate conjunction united in a common cause the defence of England against a mighty danger and the defence of principles for which Ireland, to be true to herself, must ever be ready to raise her voice or draw her sword.

Besides her honour and her interest—her interest, always the last thing to move her, but now happily involved in the same cause—human Freedom, Justice, Pity, and the cry of the small nationality crushed under the despot's heel appealed to her. These things she has followed throughout her history, mostly, up to now, to her bitter loss, but not to the loss of her soul; in that is her distinction now. Her sons, fighting for her honour and her interest, are fighting for these things too. It is for these things—Honour, Justice, Freedom, Pity—she will stand in that new place of influence she is winning in the world's councils.

There, acting with and through her sister democracies, Canada, Australia, New Zealand, South Africa, and Great Britain—in all of which, as in the great Republic of the West, her children are a potent leaven—her spirit will help to bend the British Empire to a mission of new significance for humanity. That is the heritage of her tradition. It was in that spirit her sons went throughout Europe influencing the world of a thousand years ago. That is the spirit her sons are illustrating upon the field of war today.

Ireland has chosen this path. I would pause for a moment further to ask people to think a little on this: suppose she had, as well she might with her history, and as some of her sons both at home and in America have wanted her to do, chosen a different alternative? Ireland's strength as an international factor is not to be measured only by her political position at the heart of the Empire or her strategic position in the Atlantic, or by the size of her population at home, but also by the millions of her kin throughout the Empire and America, whose deep and enduring sentiment for her, linked as it is with their distinguished and never-tarnished loyalty to the new lands of their adoption, is one of the striking facts of modern history. Germany understands this factor; and keeps on making unceasing and ingenious efforts, especially in the United States, to make her account with it.

For Ireland to have chosen the opposite alternative, or to be flung into it by the fortune of war, would in my opinion be for her an unmixed calamity, the worst in her history. Her fate as a possession of Germany, as Germany's western fortress, naval base, Heligoland of the Atlantic, would from the nature of the case be far worse than that of Prussian Poland, Schleswig, and Alsace for the last forty years. Only those who are ignorant of Prussianism and its most recent methods—methods followed long ago by every tyrannical Power, including the England of the past, but which Prussia still maintains as a menacing anachronism in the age of democracy—have any illusions upon this matter.

The Irish people, with a few insignificant exceptions, have no such illusions. They have, for the first time in their history—a memorable fact—put a national army into the field, a glorious army! And they have put that army in the field for the express purpose of defending Ireland from such a fate and of doing their share in helping to rescue the unfortunate and heroic peoples who have already fallen under it.

With the Irishmen already serving, or who obeyed the call as reserves when war was declared, and those who have volunteered since the war, the Irish army in the field has amounted to 154,038 men to this date, and this number is being increased and replenished at the rate of about a thousand men a week. More than a hundred thousand have volunteered since the war, and before the year is out it is our hope that at least half another hundred thousand will have followed their example. To these may be added for Ireland's credit the officially acknowledged Irish units in Great Britain, such as the "London Irish," the "Liverpool Irish," the "Tyneside Irish" (a brigade).

But account cannot be taken, though their existence may be noted, of the many thousands of Irish in English and Scottish regiments and in the Canadian and Australian forces. There are some special Irish Colonial units, too, apart from the Irish, in practically every Colonial battalion, such as the Vancouver Irish Fusiliers and the Quebec Irish Regiment. A short time ago General Botha's wife at Capetown presented green flags to a South African Irish regiment. But it is the army raised in Ireland itself which is our more special concern here, for that is the army which it is Ireland's privilege and duty to maintain at its full strength in the field; and that consists of the regular battalions of the historic Irish regiments and of three specific new Irish Divisions with "service" battalions of the same regiments. Each of the new Divisions is under the command of a distinguished Irish General. The three together would constitute an Army Corps. The formation of these three Irish Divisions is a fact of great note. It is the first time Ireland is officially represented in the field by a larger unit than the regiment.

It is to be noted that this book only deals with the achievements of the old Irish regiments, and one of the new Irish Divisions, namely, the 10th. The 16th Irish Division, the 36th Irish Division, and the Tyneside Irish Brigade have only recently gone to the Front.

From letters home from men and officers, from the speeches of Generals delivered immediately after an action, and sometimes sent home in a letter or an order of the day, from the spontaneous testimony of onlookers of other corps rather than from official reports, the record, so far, of these Irish levies, old and new, is put together. Official mentions are scant. The official account given by Admiral de Robeck of the landing and taking of "V" Beach, with its sunken wire entanglements, one of the most extraordinary of deeds, and valuable in results in spite of the appalling cost to the Irish battalions who accomplished it, for it rendered the landing of the troops that arrived later safe—a feat which General Sir Hunter Weston next day declared to be "without parallel in the history of feats of arms"—did not even mention the names of the glorious Irish regiments—although the names of the regiments concerned in all the other landings were given with eulogies.

General Hamilton, in explanation of his meagre references to the Tenth Division at Suvla, says he found it difficult to obtain "living human details." I do not refer to this by way of complaint, though I hope this omission may yet be officially set right. The thing is past, and there is going, we hope, to be a great change in such matters in future. Besides, the facts get known. Such deeds cannot be hidden—they are too great. I refer to the matter to explain why it is that books like this, imperfect as it is, have to be compiled.

Other volumes like it will have to supplement the tale. We Irish are determined that henceforth the doings of our armies in the field shall not be in vain in any sense. Piously shall we glean the record, whether official or unofficial, and what our men, our officers, and our Generals think ought to be known shall no longer, so far as we can help it, remain unknown. Our brave lads in the battle-line may rest assured that their country is lovingly and proudly watching them, and that the sacrifice they make in her name will, as they wish it—for their wish is the same as the dying Sarsfield's on the field of Landen—go to her profit.

The record so far brings Ireland great honour. And this excites no jealousy in the Army—for it is from the other corps in the Army itself comes the most generous testimony to the work of the Irish soldiers and the most comrade-like regret where it is thought there has been lack of recognition. What stands out is that on every front, and whether new levies or regulars, the work of the Irish troops has not only been of great merit in every instance, but of exceptional merit, and they have to their credit some of the most splendid and astonishing achievements. The Irish Guards at Mons, the Royal Irish Regiment at Ypres, the London Irish at Loos (dribbling a football before them as they charged—the boys in the trenches, before the charge, holding out the matches with which they had lit their cigarettes to show each other that their hands were not shaking), the regular battalions at "V" Beach, the new "service" battalions of the Tenth Division at Sulva, I name out of a long list to illustrate this statement.

To General Mahon's Division, composed exclusively of new levies who were civilians when the war began—thousands of Nationalist families in Leinster, Munster, and Connaught represented its ranks—the terrific open fighting at Suvla Bay (which began with the shelling of the lighters at the landing and the bursting of chains of contact mines as they set foot on shore) was their first experience of being under fire. Undismayed, their coolness undisturbed, they formed for attack as if on the parade ground. These were the "freshies" spoken of in the letter partly quoted above of Captain Thornhill, himself a representative of those magnificent Australian and New Zealand troops whose prowess has been another of the revelations of the war.

"The Empire can do with a heap more 'freshies' of the Irish brand," he writes. "Their landing at Suvla Bay was the greatest thing you will ever read of in books by high-brows. Those that witnessed the advance will never forget it. Bullets and shrapnel rained on them, yet they never wavered. . . . God! the men were splendid. The way they took that hill (now called Dublin Hill) was the kind of thing that would make you pinch yourself to prove that it was not a cheap wine aftermath. How they got there Heaven only knows. As the land lay, climbing into hell on an aeroplane seemed an easier proposition than taking that hill."¹

It may be well to point out, for it bears upon one of the popular fallacies about Irish character, that it is not only in the desperate charge or the forlorn hope that Irish soldiers have proved their worth in this or other wars. They have shown it equally in the tenacity, grim yet cheerful, with which for days and weeks and months difficult positions are held and bitter hardships borne. Again, let it be noted what this whole young Tenth Division proved itself fit for after its months at Gallipoli. When it was decided to occupy Salonika and to march to the aid of the Serbian army it was to the Irish Division, under their splendid Irish commander, General Sir Bryan Mahon, that the place of honour for this desperate enterprise was given.

Coming straight from their hard service in the Peninsula, they performed in the Serbian mountain passes above Lake Doiran what General Sarrail, the eminent French Commander, the vanquisher of the Crown Prince's Army at Verdun, has pronounced to be one of the most striking feats of arms of the whole war. Acting as a rearguard against an army ten times their number, they did what was neither expected nor counted upon. But their instinctive military genius, as well as their courage and determination, came into play, and they held up the overwhelming enemy for so long and with such skill that the entire French and British forces were able to withdraw safely to their defensive positions without the loss of a single gun or a single transport wagon.

One seems to be verging on exaggeration in these accounts, but the thing is bare truth, and I am striving to bring out what has been

---

1. One is reminded of tributes to Meagher's Brigade at Fredricksburg in the American Civil War. "Braver men," writes Horace Greely, in his "American Conflict," "never smiled at death. Never did men fight better or die, alas! more fruitlessly than did Hancock's corps, especially Meagher's Irish Brigade, composed of the 63rd, 69th, and 88th New York, 28th Massachusetts, and the 116th Pennsylvania, which dashed itself repeatedly against those impregnable heights, until two-thirds of its numbers strewed the ground" (vol. ii., p. 345). In the same book Greely quotes the following from the correspondent of the London *Times*, watching the battle from the heights, and writing from Lee's headquarters: "To the Irish Division commanded by General Meagher was principally committed the desperate task of bursting out of the town of Fredricksburg and forming under the withering fire of the confederate batteries to attack Marye's Heights. Never at Fontenoy, Albuera, or at Waterloo was more undoubted courage displayed by the sons of Erin than during those six frantic attacks which they directed against the almost impregnable position of the foe."

done for Ireland by the character of these troops. I have indicated their martial quality. But they have brought another quality into the field which is equally characteristic and therefore should at least be mentioned here, and which, perhaps, in the circumstances of the time, deserves a special reference. That is, their religious spirit. Everybody has remarked it. The Irish soldier, with his limpid faith and his unaffected piety, his rosary recited on the hillside, his Mass in the ruined barn under shell-fire, his "act of contrition" in the trench before facing the hail of the assault, his attitude to women, has been mostly a singular impression. And his chaplain! The Irish battalion must have its chaplain as well as its colonel, and both must be of the best. The chaplains of every denomination and of every corps have made a noble name for themselves in this war; but I am speaking here only of the Irish chaplains—of the men like Father Finn, killed at "V" beach, refusing to stay behind on the ship because, as he answered, "The place of the chaplain is with the dying soldier"; and like Father Gwynn, of the Irish Guards, killed at the French front, of whom his battalion commander, a Protestant Irishman, writes these words:

> No words of mine could express or even give a faint idea of the amount of good he has done us all out here, or how bravely he has faced all dangers, and how cheerful and comforting he has always been. It is certainly no exaggeration to say that he was loved by every officer, N.C.O. and man in the battalion. The Irish Guards owe him a deep and lasting debt of gratitude, and as long as any of us are left who saw him out here, we shall never forget his wonderful life, and shall strive to lead a better life by following his example.

This quality of our soldiers appears to have impressed observers, as well as their fighting quality. It is referred to again and again, and the same transference of thought from the character of the men to the cause of their country, as appears in one of the letters above quoted from a Scottish soldier, a spectator of "V" beach, occurs repeatedly: "The race that can produce such men, who did such glorious work for the Empire, has the most perfect right to get the freedom of its country and the right to rule it.... There is not a man in the service but who would willingly do anything now for the Irish people—yes, the Irish Catholics."

Thus we see that our Irish troops in this war are fulfilling a mission. As I said at the outset, it is into their keeping, with the eyes of the world upon them, that the cause of their country for the time being has passed. The influence of their action upon her fortunes will extend far beyond the immediate effects which will appear the moment the war is over. No people can be said to have rightly proved their nationhood and their power to maintain it until they have demonstrated their military prowess; and though Irish blood has reddened the earth of every continent, never until now have we as a people set a national army in the field.

I have written vainly if I have not shown, moreover, that never was a people more worthily represented in the field than we are today by these Irish soldiers. It is heroic deeds entering into their traditions that give life to nations—that is the recompense of those who die to perform them—and to Fontenoy, Cremona, Fredericksburg, and the rest, these soldiers of the Irish people to-day have added Mons, Ypres, Loos, "V" beach, Suvla Bay, Lake Doiran. How do the Irish people regard their armies in the field? How do their brothers at home regard these brothers in the battle line, who, at the call of danger and national opportunity, by passing into the soldier's panoply have lifted the name of Irishmen to a new plane in the world's eyes, and opened to their country's cause a new outlook? To themselves the same opportunity of ennoblement comes. The ranks of their brothers in the field are thinning under the wastage of war.

Will they keep them filled? Aye, will they! I have given my lifetime, such as it has been, to the service of Ireland in a deep faith in the essential nobility and wisdom of the Irish people. I should be untrue to that faith if for a moment I had any doubt on this matter—if I could harbour for a moment the idea that the young men of Ireland could think unmoved of the wistful bewildered faces of their noble brothers while they held back, could watch the ranks of the Irish armies thinning, and the glorious regiments, brigades, and divisions gradually filling up with others than Irish soldiers until their character as Irish armies finally vanished and ceased to exist—and something, I fear, would go with that character which Ireland might never get back.

No, the Irish race has not changed, as these very soldiers have proved. Chivalry is of its essence, and nations who do not want to die, but to live, as Ireland does, must act through their essential qualities. Those brave sons in the field need not fear for the honour they have won for their country. Their brothers are coming to them. Ireland's armies will be maintained.

J.E. Redmond.

February, 1916

Chapter 1

The Retreat From Mons

Regular battalions of all the Irish regiments were included in the British Expeditionary Force which left for France, at the outbreak of war, in the early weeks of August, 1914. For its size it was the finest Army that the world has ever seen, in equipment, discipline, and martial ardour. It was commanded by Field-Marshal Sir John French, the scion of an Irish family long settled in Roscommon, of which Lord De Freyne is the head, and a soldier who made a brilliant reputation as a cavalry leader in the South African War.

On the morning of Sunday, August 23rd, two of the three Army Corps which composed the Force were extended along a front of twenty-five miles east and west of Mons, a Belgian town of 25,000 inhabitants and the centre of coal mining, iron, and glass works. In the First Corps, under Sir Douglas Haig, were the 1st Irish Guards, the 2nd Munster Fusiliers, and the 2nd Connaught Rangers. The Second Corps, under Sir Horace Smith-Dorrien, included the 2nd Irish Rifles and the 2nd Royal Irish Regiment. The 4th Royal Irish Dragoons were with the cavalry. An Irish trooper of that regiment on outpost duty had the distinction of opening the Great War between England and Germany by firing the first shot, which brought down a Uhlan officer, in the early hours of Saturday, August 22nd, fifteen miles beyond Mons, on the road to Brussels.

The Battle of Mons, the first encounter in force between the British and the Germans, commenced at twenty minutes to one o'clock on Sunday, August 23rd. Not a German was then in sight. But an enemy aeroplane hovered overhead, like a hawk peering for prey in the fields and hedges, and there was a burst of shrapnel over the British lines, followed by the booming of distant artillery. An attack so soon was unexpected. The bells of Mons had been ringing for the Sunday services, as usual, all the morning, and the Cathedral was crowded with worshippers at the High Mass when the sound of the German guns broke startlingly in upon their devotions.

It was a beautiful day, and many of the men in one of the Irish regiments billeted in a farmyard close to the town were bare but for their trousers—availing themselves of the warm sunshine to wash and dry their shirts and socks after their long tramp in France and Belgium—when the bugles rang out "Stand to arms." The Germans were unseen, but having on Saturday beaten the French at Charleroi—to the British right—they were advancing in overwhelming numbers, under Von Kluck, in the cover of the woods, railway embankments and hedgerows. Soon the sharp crackle of musketry was added to the cannonading of the guns, and the sabre and lance of cavalry gleamed in the sun.

The first of the Irish regiments to exchange shots with the enemy's infantry were the 2nd Rifles, who suffered severely, holding a position in the suburbs of Mons. The 2nd Royal Irish Regiment defended a village behind the town, and on the main road leading south. A Gordon Highlander named Smiley says the Irish were "fearfully cut up" when his company, about two miles behind, were directed to advance to their relief. The Gordons crept up the road, and reached the trenches of the Irish at dusk. Another Gordon says:—"When we got to the trenches the scene was terrible. The Irish were unprepared for the sudden attack. They were having dinner when the Germans opened on them, and their dead and wounded were lying all around."

The Irish Guards, who lay to the east of Mons, on the British right, had, as the regiment's first experience of warfare, to meet the shock of a cavalry charge. One of the most popular recruiting posters in the early days of the war was a picture of a comical-looking Tommy on the field of battle. He was represented striking a match to light his pipe, and saying, with a devil-may-care glint in his roguish eye, "Half a mo', *Kaiser*," while German horsemen in the background were charging towards him. The idea was suggested to the artist by an incident in the encounter between the Irish Guards and the Germans at Mons. "I am told," says an English newspaper correspondent, "that when the German cavalry were only 200 yards away one Irish Guardsman momentarily put down his rifle and begged a cigarette of a comrade, which he coolly lit."

Then they 'prepared to receive cavalry,' and did it in better order and with much less excitement than if they had been about to witness the finish of a St. Leger." In this we have an example of the easy bearing in the presence of the advancing foe for which, by all accounts, the Irish are remarkable. Such imperturbability springs not so much from contempt of the enemy, as from confidence in their own prowess. The two front ranks were kneeling, and presenting a double row of steel. Their virgin bayonets, seen now for the first time on a field of battle, glittered as sharp and terrible as if they had around them the halo of a hundred victories. Standing behind were two other ranks who poured a stream of rifle fire into the German horsemen. So the Irish Guards met the whirlwind of galloping horses and flashing swords, and drove back the survivors in a ragged, straggling line. They were eager to start winning battle honours for their banners, and Mons is a brilliant opening of a list that promises to be lengthy and crowded before this Great War terminates.

Then came the order for a general retreat of the British forces. In the evening Sir John French found out that he was vastly outnumbered in men and guns—250,000 Germans to 82,000 British—and saw that if his Army were to escape being outflanked and annihilated they must retire until they got behind some substantial line of natural defence which they could hope to hold against such fearful odds.

The retreat lasted twelve days. It was one long drawn-out rearguard action. The fighting took place along a line of about twenty-five miles and backwards for a distance of about eighty miles, which was covered by forced marches at night as well as by day. Hardly for an hour were the British permitted any rest or respite. They were continually harassed by enormous masses of the enemy who by thundering at their heels and striking at their flanks sought to turn the retreat into a rout. In that the Germans completely failed. The retirement was a splendid military achievement. It was also an episode of intense dramatic interest, and though I am necessarily concerned only with the part taken by the Irish regiments in the ordeal, it was made memorable for all time by feats of unparalleled heroism and endurance by every arm of the Service, and each and all of the nationalities represented in it.

The British rearguard frequently gave battle to their pursuers, holding them in check or sending them staggering back with the vehemence of the blow. On Wednesday, August 26th, the first stand was made on the Cambrai—Le Cateau—Landrecies line. Here it was that the 2nd Connaught Rangers gave the Germans another unpleasant taste of the fighting quality of the Irish.

"It was a grand time we had, and I wouldn't have missed it for lashin's of money," says a private of the regiment in a racy account of the episode. "The Germans kept pressing our rearguard all the time. They were at least five to one, and we were in danger of being cut off. At last the Colonel could stand it no longer, so the word was passed round that we were to give them hell and all. 'Rangers of Connaught,' says he, 'the eyes of all Ireland are on you today, and I know you never could disgrace the old country by allowing Germans to beat you while you have arms in your hands and hearts in your breasts. Up, then, and at them, and if you don't give them the soundest thrashing they ever got you needn't look me in the face again in this world—or the next!' And we went for them with just what you would know of a prayer to the Mother of Our Lord to be merciful to the loved ones at home if we should fall in the fight. We charged through and through them until they broke and ran like frightened hares in terror of hounds."

That same day one Division of the Third Army Corps was brought hurriedly up by train to Le Cateau. In it were three other Irish regiments—1st Irish Fusiliers, 2nd Dublin Fusiliers, and 2nd Inniskilling Fusiliers. They went straight into action to protect one of the flanks of the resumed retirement. In a fight near Le Cateau the Inniskillings lost many officers and men. The Dublins were at Cambrai. They appear to have been uproariously and outrageously Irish. A few weeks later the London correspondent of the *Manchester Guardian* gave some interesting extracts from a letter written by an English officer of the Dublins.

He said that while the men were waiting for the Germans they sang "The Wearing of the Green" and "God Save Ireland." One of the officers remarked, by way of a joke, "We have heard enough all day of your damned Fenian songs, boys; give us something else." The boys then struck up, the officer says, a song called "Dear Old Ireland." This ballad, by T.D. Sullivan, tells in stirring verses and chorus, set to a rousing air, of some of the habits and customs of Ireland, and of the affection she inspires. One verse runs:—

> *We've seen the wedding, and the wake, the pattern and the fair,*
> *The well-knit frames at the grand old games in the kindly Irish air;*
> *The loud 'Hurroo,' we've heard it, too; and the thundering 'Clear the way!'*
> *Ah, dear old Ireland, gay old Ireland, Ireland, boys, hurrah.*

It was not the first time that the song was heard on a field of battle. On that night in December, 1863, in the American Civil War, when the Federals and Confederates were bivouacked on the banks of the Rappahannock awaiting the dawn to commence the bloody fight for Fredericksburg, an Irish regiment in the service of the North sang the song as they sat by their camp fires. Was that a tremendous echo that came across the river?—

For Ireland, boys, hurrah; for Ireland, boys, hurrah!
Here's dear old Ireland; fond old Ireland—
Ireland, boys, hurrah!

The Irishmen of the North listened intently. Then it came upon them with wild surprise that the chorus had been taken up by an Irish regiment in the service of the South!

The officers of the Dublin Fusiliers at Cambrai were not scandalised, nor did they put on a severe air, when they heard these rebelly songs, survivals of a dead past, and yet deeply moving for the national memories clustering round them. On the contrary, like good regimental officers, they welcomed them, as they would probably have welcomed anything that helped to raise the hearts of their men in their hour of trial. "As my old brother-officer observes," says the writer of the letter, "'These confounded Fenians can fight. Four times within one hour my blackguards drove a charge home with the bayonet.'"

That day was a most critical one for the British. The Second Army Corps was streaming southwards. But Von Kluck was making a determined effort to outflank and envelop the First Army Corps. The Corps escaped the net with the loss of one of their finest regiments, the 2nd Munster Fusiliers, killed, wounded, and made prisoners. It was the most tragic event of the retreat. A day or two previously the Munsters were entrenched behind six guns of Field Artillery. Uhlans swept down upon the battery and killed the gunners. Then two companies of the Munsters charged with fixed bayonets, and put the Germans to flight.

But what was to be done with the guns? All the horses had been killed, and time was pressing. Were the guns to be lost after all? The thought never entered into the heads of the Munsters. By putting themselves into harness, with a few light cavalry horses which they had captured from the Uhlans, they pulled the guns away. "As we had not enough horses," said a wounded Munster in hospital at Tralee, "we made mules of ourselves, for we were not such asses as to leave the guns to the enemy." The guns were brought back five miles, where horses were available to relieve the Munsters.

On the night of August 26th the regiment were rearguard to the retiring First Army. They held two cross-roads between Chapeau Rouge to the north, and Fesney to the south, and had orders to keep watch over these important positions until they got word to fall back. It is said the word was sent not once, but thrice—the first during the night—but only one reached them the following afternoon, and then it was too late. The other despatch-riders lost their way, or were shot or made prisoners. The result was that the Munsters were left in the lurch while the mass of the First Corps, unaware of their comrades' desperate position, were hurrying away to the south.

At dawn, as the regiment lay concealed behind the hedgerows and in the beet fields of the farmsteads and in the orchards laden with fruit, they were discovered by a German patrol. The enemy at once surrounded them on three sides and attacked with vastly superior forces. "The Germans came at us from all points, horse, foot and artillery and all," said one of the survivors, "and the air was raving with shouting, screaming men waving swords and rifles and blazing away at us like blue murder." To add to their troubles the rain was falling in torrents, drenching the men to the skin.

The officers decided to withdraw to the village of Etreux, a few miles back, where they hoped to find the shelter of a position of defence which might help them to hold up the Germans, despite the terrific odds on the side of the enemy. The battalion retired by companies—two companies covering the withdrawal of one another in turns. In fighting these rearguard actions the men sought cover wherever they could find it—crouching in farm buildings, and behind wagons, walls, and heaps of stones, firing at the ever-advancing Germans. The Munsters were grimly silent until it came to bayonet fighting between khaki and grey, and then the air was rent with yells of rage and hate, shrieks of pain, and the low wailing sobbing of the Irish keen.

During the retirement a despatch-rider reached the Munsters. He had a message for them to retire "at once." It was not timed, but it was probably the last of the three orders sent from Headquarters, and was therefore written hurriedly. It seems also to have been written many hours before it was delivered, as the bearer said he had been compelled to hide for a long time from the Germans. But it was too late. The Munsters were encircled by a ring of fire. The enemy had worked round to their rear and now barred the way to the village of Etreux. Major Paul Charrier, described as a hearty, genial Kerryman, was in command of the Munsters. Three times he gallantly led his men in an attack upon the key of the German position, a large mansion that was loopholed and turned into a fortress. He was twice wounded, yet he continued to lead, and in the last assault he fell to rise no more with a bullet in his head.

Eight other officers were also dead. Six of the survivors were disabled. Between four and five hundred of the rank and file were killed or wounded. Ammunition was run out. Not another cartridge was to be found by the men in the bandoliers of their dead and dying comrades. It was then 9 p.m. The men listened for sounds of approaching relief, but none was heard. There was nothing left for the remnant of the battalion, reduced to four officers and 256 non-commissioned officers and men, but to surrender. Only 155 men got out of the trap, and most of these belonged to the regimental transport. It came out afterwards that the Munsters had been engaged against seven battalions of German infantry, three batteries of artillery, many cavalry, and many Maxim guns.

So impressed were the Germans by the bravery of those Irish lads that they paid every respect to the living and the dead. Captain H.S. Jervis, the senior surviving officer, in letters written to the bereaved wives and mothers of his fellows, states that the next day the Germans allowed him to send out a burial party of his own men. "They found Paul Charrier lying as he had fallen, head towards the enemy," he tells Mrs. Charrier. "The sergeant told me he looked as if he were asleep. They buried him, with eight other officers of the regiment, in a grave separate from the men." More than that, when the Germans learnt that their prisoners were Irish and Catholic they sent for one of their own Catholic chaplains to read the service for the dead at the graveside of the rank and file.

Sir Conan Doyle, in a lecture on *The Great Battles of the War*, delivered in London, made the remark: "If ever surrender was justifiable it was so in these circumstances." That was said before full and authentic reports of what happened, including the composition of the overwhelming forces that surrounded the Munsters, had come from the officers imprisoned in Germany, which will be found in a little pamphlet called *The Munsters*, written by Mrs. Victor Rickard, the widow of a brave man who afterwards commanded the battalion and fell at Rue Du Bois. The military lesson of the episode, in the opinion of Conan Doyle, is that great attention should be paid to making known the real situation to troops operating at a distance, and the miscarriage of the messages sent to the Munsters makes pertinent the telling here of a story, on the authority of a wounded corporal of the Gloucestershire Regiment, of a splendid example of Irish resolution and endurance in the operations on the Aisne later on in September:—

Orders had to be given to a battalion holding an advanced position to fall back. The only way was to send a man with orders through a murderous fire. Volunteers were asked for from the Royal Irish Fusiliers. All wanted to go, but by tossing for it a selection was made at last. He was a shock-headed lad who did not look as if there was much in him, but he had grit. Ducking his head in a way that made us laugh, he rushed into the hail of shot and shell. He cleared the first hundred yards without being hit; but in the second they brought him down. He rose again and struggled on for a few minutes, was hit once more, and then staggered a bit before finally collapsing.

Two more men of the Irish Fusiliers dashed into the fire and rushed across while the Germans were doing their best to pink them. One picked up the wounded lad and started back to the trenches, and the other, taking the despatch, ran ahead. Just as the wounded man and his mate were within a few yards of our trenches and we were cheering them, there came another hail of bullets, and both went down dead. Meanwhile, the man with the despatch was racing for all he was worth. He got through all right till the last lap, when he was brought down. He was seen from the other trenches, and half a dozen men ran to his aid. They were all shot; but the man with the message was now crawling towards the battalion in danger. With assistance he reached them and the object was gained; they were withdrawn to a new position before the Germans succeeded in their plan of cutting them off.

By August 29th the British had fallen back to the line Compiègne-Soissons, before the German hordes. The weather generally was intensely hot, making the retreat still more trying to the Army. The situation was further complicated by the flight southwards of almost the entire population, thronging and blocking the roads. When the British fell back the inhabitants had just commenced the saving of the harvest which, undreaming of war, they had tended with solicitude and saw growing with joy. But the corn and grass were to be garnered by a dissolute and predatory foreign soldiery whose hands, in many instances, were red with the innocent blood of those who had sown them. So, accompanied by tens of thousands of fugitives—wailing women and children for the most part, distracted by the dread and terror of this calamity which had so incomprehensibly fallen upon them—the British hastened on towards Paris.

On Tuesday, September 1st, the 4th Guards Brigade—Grenadiers, Coldstreams, and Irish—had to sustain at Villers-Cotterets the brunt of another of these fierce onslaughts which the Germans delivered against such of the British troops as attempted to stem the pursuit. The Brigade had had little rest since the commencement of the retreat with the enemy ever at their heels. Only the day before, August 31st, the Irish Guards had the longest and most trying of their forced marches. Hardy, wiry, and fleet-footed, they covered thirty-five miles with very little food, as their transport had to keep far in advance of the column to avoid capture.

At a parade of the battalion on the roadside at Villers-Cotterets on the morning of September 1st, the commanding officer, Lieutenant-Colonel Morris, addressing them on horseback, congratulated his men on their grit and vitality. He made the very interesting statement that whilst a substantial percentage of the other regiments in the Guards' Brigade had succumbed to the heat and fatigue of the march, only five men of the Irish Guards had fallen out from exhaustion.

Then all of a sudden, as the tale is told by Private Stephen Shaughnessy of Tuam, the men got orders to "Fix bayonets." The news was brought that the Germans were approaching under cover of the woods which abound in this part of France. Colonel Morris rode through the ranks, shouting, "Irish Guards, form up! Remember you are Irishmen!" The Irish Guards entered one of the woods and almost immediately caught sight of the Germans. Both sides blazed away at one another with the rifle, through the trees and undergrowth, and frequently came into grips at the point of the bayonet.

Sergeant Patrick Joseph Bennett, in a letter to his sister at Thurles, gives another instance of the unruffled mood and quiet confidence of the men during the three hours of fighting in the wood. "The Irish boys," he says, "were very cool when the shots were flying round us. They were calmly picking blackberries."

n the end the Germans were beaten off, but at the heavy loss to the Irish of 150 of the rank and file and several of the officers. Morris was among the fallen. The last that Private Shaughnessy saw of the Colonel was on the road beside the wood giving orders, mounted on horseback and smoking a cigarette. He was the younger son of Lord

Morris and Killanin, a famous Irish judge and humorist, and brother and heir-presumptive of Lord Killanin. He left a son, Michael, who was born ten days before his father left for the Front, and was just a month old when his father fell on the field of honour. Colonel Morris was of the finest type of soldier, and was long mourned by the regiment.

A good idea of the dangers and hardships of the retreat, apart from the fighting, and also the humours which relieved it, is given by a private of the 2nd Irish Rifles:—"It wasn't the fault of the Germans if we got away alive. They were after us night and day," he says. The greatest trouble of the regiment was to find their way through woods and strange country by night. "We got on like the Babes in the Wood, holding each other's hands, so as not to lose touch with each other. We dare not light a match or make a sound that would betray our presence, and when we saw lights in the distance twinkling like will-o'-the-wisps, we had to send our scouts to find out the meaning before we approached."

Sometimes it was the Germans, and then the scouts did not get back, and the regiment had to dodge the enemy as best they could. "Once when they were looking for us their searchlight played in the open just where we were, only we were in the shade, and if we had moved another inch our shadows would have been seen. We heard them talking and shouting to each other, but they gave no chase, thinking we had got away in another direction. We had no food for hours, except such fruit as we could pick up on the way." Does it not read as if the pursuers and the pursued were playing some monstrous game of hide-and-seek?

By September 3rd the Marne was crossed, and the long retreat of the British was brought to an end without any grave disaster. French had out-generalled and out-marched Von Kluck. But the Germans were also over the river by the 5th and practically at the gates of Paris. The British Army then fell back upon the Seine. So black did the prospect appear that the French Government and Legislature thought it prudent to remove from Paris to Bordeaux.

Chapter 2

Battle of the Rivers

The British Expeditionary Force was driven through Northern France before a mighty and irresistible wind of steel and lead, but the tempest did not overtake and disperse them, as it might have done—such was its roaring fury—any less disciplined and stubborn troops. At the end of it all the British were weary from want of sleep and plenty of hard fighting, but not badly shaken, and certainly with spirits undaunted. So marvellously quick did they recover that on September 7th, within a few days of the end of the retreat, they had the great joy of joining with the French in turning upon the Germans and rolling them from the gates of Paris back over the rivers Marne and Aisne.

The Battle of the Rivers consisted of a series of almost continuous engagements, lasting till the end of September, principally with strong rearguards of the enemy who were holding the fords and bridges of the Marne and Aisne, and their tributaries, the Grand Morin and the Petit Morin, and the villages, farmlands and orchards of the intervening countryside. Between the different British regiments there was an emulation to outshine each other. It was a splendid vanity, for everything done to realise it tended to the confusion of the common enemy. This phase of the war was therefore crowded with incidents showing the bravery of the soldiers of all the nationalities within the United Kingdom. From the Irish point of view the most remarkably dramatic was the rallying of the Irish Guards round the green flag.

It is only a square piece of cloth, but its colour is green, and on it is the Harp of Ireland and inscribed in a wreath are the words: 'Eire go brath,' once bright and clear, but now faded and obliterated almost beyond recognition. That is the flag the Irish Guards obtained when they received information that they were for the Front, and from the moment they set foot on foreign soil that treasured emblem of Irish nationality has been displayed at the head of the battalion, the pride and admiration of the regiment.

So writes Corporal Michael O'Mara of the Irish Guards. The first occasion upon which the flag was produced was when the Marne was crossed, and on September 9th the Irish Guards had to advance for miles across rather open country, swept by shot and shell, to dislodge the Germans from a commanding position south of the Aisne.

The Irish as soldiers have two qualities which, though widely different in nature, are really each the concomitant of the other. The first is imperturbability, springing from indifference to danger, of which the Retreat from Mons supplied some choice examples, as I have recorded. This attribute is displayed while they are waiting for the shock of an advancing attack, or for the command to launch themselves upon a foe shooting at them from behind entrenchments. The clash comes or the order to charge is given; and then it is that, showing the other quality, they give vent to the fire and force of their passionate temperament, which, as often as not, impels them to attempt strokes more daring and rash than the occasion quite demands.

In the course of the advance between the Marne and the Aisne on September 9th the changeful fortunes of the conflict seemed to make the final issue doubtful. The line of the advance of the Irish Guards was a hill upon which the Germans were strongly posted with several machine-guns, each pouring forth a terrible stream of 600 bullets a minute. Men were dropping on all sides. Then it was that the towering form of an Irish Guardsman was seen running well on in front of the first line flourishing the green flag, which he had tied round the barrel of his rifle, and shouting "Ireland for Ever."

The men roared at the sight. On they swept, with redoubled speed, after the darling flag, in one of their furious, overmastering Irish charges, made all the more terrible by their vengeful yells. A thunderstorm was raging at the time. The gleam on their bayonets may have been the flash of the lightning, but it was more suggestive of a glint of the flame of love of country that glowed in their eyes.

"It was all over in ten minutes," writes Private H.P. Mulloney to his sweetheart in Ireland. "They absolutely stood dumfounded, with white faces and knees trembling. I shouldn't like to stand in front of that charge myself. Our men were drenched to the skin, but we didn't care; it only made us twice as wild. Such dare-devil pluck I was glad to see. 'Back for those guns,' roared an officer, 'or I'll have every one of you slaughtered.' The men didn't want telling twice. We proceeded to line up the prisoners and collect the spoils, which amounted to about 150 prisoners, six Maxim guns, and 38,000 rounds of ammunition."

Even in these rude passages we find expressed the rapture of the Irish Guardsmen with the tumult and the passion of the fight.

The hill was surmounted and the machine-guns taken. Afterwards the advance was continued for five miles, over a country covered with dead Germans and horses, and blazing homesteads. The Irish rested for a time in a field, and then pushed on again until they reached the banks of the Marne. They captured 600 Germans, including many officers and eight machine-guns. But if the advance was swift, sure, and triumphant a bitter price had to be paid for it, as is the way of war, for many a fine and stalwart Irish youth found his grave between the rivers.

The man who produced the green flag was Corporal J.J. Cunningham from Dublin. He bought it in London before the Irish Guards left for the Front. It became a prized possession of the regiment. "You may be surprised to hear that the Irish flag I bought from the pedlar before parting with you I have still got," Cunningham, who was made a sergeant, says in a letter to a friend in London.

> It has been carried through all our engagements, and with God's help I will carry it back to England. Clay from the trenches has made the harp on it very dirty, but, thank God, that is the only disgrace it has suffered. I did not think when we were buying it that it would go through so much.

I am told, indeed, that in a far later stage of the war, at another critical moment, it was flourished by the Earl of Cavan, an Irishman, then in command of the Guards' Brigade, to egg on the Irish to an enterprise before which other units had excusably quailed. He knew of the episode between the Marne and the Aisne. He had probably heard also a story of the American Civil War. An Irish regiment on the side of the North carried a green flag bearing a harp in the glow of a sunburst, and so noted were they for their wild and reckless daring that a Confederate general, seeing the dreaded colour surging forwards, and borne proudly aloft through the battle smoke and the hail of bullets, cried out to his men, "Steady, boys, steady. Here's that infernal green flag again." The Germans, on the day that Lord Cavan waved the improvised flag of the Irish Guards had reason also to curse it if they but knew—for the loss of valuable trenches.

On September 13th the main forces of the Germans retired to the high ground two miles north of the Aisne and entrenched themselves. As the British also dug themselves in, this was the beginning of trench warfare. But the combatants did not settle themselves down to it entirely for some months afterwards. There were still surprise attacks and counter-strokes, in which cavalry took a part, as is seen from an adventure of the 2nd Irish Fusiliers as told by Lance-Corporal Casement. "One night," he says, "after a very hard day in the trenches, when we were wet to the skin, and had lighted fires to dry our tunics, we heard firing along our front, and then the Germans came down on us like madmen. We had to tackle them in our shirt-sleeves. It was mainly bayonet work, and hard work at that. They were well supported by cavalry, who tried to ride us down in the dark, but we held our ground until reinforcements came up, and then we drove the enemy off with a fine rush of our horsemen and footmen combined."

One of the most inspiring of the deeds of self-sacrifice which the war has produced was done by an Irish soldier. In the churchyard of a village near the Aisne is the grave of a private of the Royal Irish Regiment marked by a cross without a name, but with the arresting inscription—"He saved others; himself he could not save." The story of how this unknown hero gave his life to save others was told by a wounded corporal of the West Yorkshire Regiment in an hospital at Woolwich. On September 14th, in the concluding stage of the struggle for the Aisne, the battalion was sent ahead to occupy a little village near Rheims.

"We went on through the long, narrow street," says the narrator, "and just as we were in sight of the end of it a man in khaki, to our great surprise, dashed out from a farmhouse on our right and ran towards us shouting a warning. Immediately we heard the crackle of rifles in front, and the poor chap fell dead before he reached us."

The West Yorkshires ran to cover, and ultimately drove the Germans out of the houses they occupied at the outskirts of the village. Then they discovered that an ambush had been prepared into which they would have moved to their doom but for the warning given by the man in khaki at the cost of his life. He was a private of the Royal Irish Regiment—2nd battalion—who was taken prisoner the day before and confined in the farmhouse, but his identification disc had been removed by the Germans, and there was no means of discovering his name. "We buried him with military honours," concludes the narrator; "and there was not a dry eye among us as we laid him to rest."

At this early period of the war, while the cavalry—not yet transformed into infantry by the adoption of trench warfare—were still being used as horsemen, Irish troopers were distinguishing themselves. I have noticed in the newspapers, from time to time, disputes as to which unit of the auxiliary forces was the first to come under fire. The honour had been claimed by the London Scottish, who entered the field at Neuve Eglise in the first days of November, and allowed until it was established that the Northumberland Yeomanry had been in action before the London Scottish left home. But the Northumberland Hussars have in turn to yield to the South Irish Horse.

This section of the Irish Yeomanry went to France early in August, 1914. They were attached to the Guards' Brigade, and were with the Irish and Coldstreams when they turned in the little town of Landrecies to hold back the Germans on August 25th, the second day of the retreat from Mons. The North Irish Horse arrived in France on August 20th, and pushing forward at once reached the French and Belgian frontier in time to relieve the pressure on the retreating forces. They had their baptism of fire near Compiègne on September 1st, and fought again a few days later at Le Cateau. These little side details or footnotes of history are not without their interest. Often, indeed, they excite the mind even more than the big, decisive events.

During the Battles of the Marne and the Aisne both the North and the South Irish Horse were employed rounding up parties of Uhlans in the woods, and scouring the isolated villages and deserted farmhouses for stragglers. The Uhlans, by all accounts, were contemptible as foes.

"They run like scalded cats when they see you," writes Captain N.G. Stewart Richardson, of the North Irish Horse, to a friend in Belfast, "and are always in close formation as if afraid to separate. I had a grand hunt after twenty (there were five of us), and we got four dead, picking up two more afterwards. We came on them round the corner of a street, and they went like hunted deer."

The duties were discharged with varying good luck and bad. Corporal Fred Lindsay tells how the North Irish Horse discovered one of those minor tragedies of war and lost Troopers Jack Scott of Londonderry and W. Moore of Limavady.

With a Sergeant Hicks they were sent to patrol as far as a ford in the river which, unknown to us, was held by a German force with a machine gun. When the three reached the ford they found a British officer dead across his motor-car and some of his men dead around the car. They were about to dismount to investigate when the machine-gun fired upon them, instantly killing the two troopers. Sergeant Hicks escaped on Moore's horse, his own being shot under him.

On another day, the same troop came upon a force of Uhlans in a wood near a village, and succeeded in killing some, taking a good many prisoners, and capturing a number of horses. "In this action," Corporal Fred Lindsay relates:

Trooper M'Clennaghan, of Garvagh, accounted for three Uhlans and took two horses single-handed; and two others and myself, firing simultaneously at an escaping Uhlan, brought both horse and rider down at 900 yards' distance. Sitting on the roadside later eating biscuits and bully beef with the rest of us Viscount Massereene complimented us, saying, 'Boys, you have done a good day's work. If we only had an opportunity like this every day!'

Subsequently the North Irish Horse had the distinction of forming the bodyguard of Sir John French. The South Irish Horse took service, like the cavalry, in the trenches.

There is also to be told a story of a clever ambush and capture of a long scattered line of German transport wagons loaded with food by a party of the 5th (Royal Irish) Lancers after the Battle of the Marne. Commanding a bridge over a stream, by which the convoy had to pass, was a coppice in which the Lancers were able to conceal themselves and the horses. They waited until the head of the column was straggling across the bridge, and then they emptied their carbines into them along a wide front that gave the impression of a great force being engaged in the attack.

One who was there thus describes what followed:—

The Germans were taken completely by surprise. Their horses started to rear and plunge, and many men and animals went over into the stream, being carried away. The motor wagons could not be stopped in time, and they crashed into each other in hopeless confusion. Into this confused mass of frightened men and horses and wagons that had run amok the Lancers now charged from two separate points, setting up the most awful cries in English where they didn't know any other language, but as some knew a little French and others more Irish they joined in, and all that added to the confusion of the Germans, who must have fancied that the whole Allied Army had come down on them. The lancers made short work of the escort at the head of the column, and the officer in command agreed to surrender all that was under his direct control, though he said he couldn't account for the rearguard.

CHAPTER 3

Contest For the Channel Coast

It had become evident that the design of the Germans, then hacking their way through Belgium, was to reach Calais and Boulogne so as to cut the direct communication of the British with the Channel coast of Belgium and France. With the view of frustrating these plans, Sir John French, early in October, withdrew his forces from the orchards and woodlands by the banks of the Aisne to French Flanders, on the north-west, a mingled industrial and agricultural country. The British Commander had also hoped to be in time to outflank the right wing of the enemy, but in this he was disappointed by the fall of Antwerp, which enabled the Germans to sweep quickly round to Ostend, higher up the Belgian coast.

The British lines now ran, first from the historic French city of St. Omer in a south-easterly direction to the smaller towns of Bethune, Givenchy, and La Bassée, towards the great French manufacturing city of Lille, prominent on the landscape with its forest of tall chimneys; and, secondly, from St. Omer again north to Ypres, the ancient and beautiful capital of Flanders. Here, for months to come, many most desperate and critical battles were to be fought, in an extraordinary tangle of railways, canals, roads, industrial villages, mills, breweries, dyeworks, machine-shops, brick-fields, lime-kilns, and intervening patches of intensive agriculture—the most densely crowded area in the world—with the ultimate result that the advance of the Germans to the Channel coast was stopped by impregnable lines of British trenches.

In these operations both the 1st and 2nd battalions of the Leinsters, the Connaught Rangers, the Irish Rifles, the Irish Fusiliers, and the Irish Regiment took part, with the 2nd battalions of the Dublins, Munsters, and Inniskillings, whose first battalions—as we shall see later—were destined for more terrible enterprises against the Turks at the Dardanelles. It is not easy to get from the official despatches the correct proportion of the main events in France and Flanders, not to speak of being able, by the impersonal generalities of these documents, rightly to estimate the worth of the services of particular battalions. My purpose, therefore, is to attempt to depict the war on the Western Front, as seen through the eyes, not of the commanders, but of the men in the ranks and the regimental officers, and in doing so I confine myself necessarily to episodes happening here and there over the far-spreading field of conflict in which Irish regiments and individual Irish soldiers distinguished themselves.

There were two tremendous and prolonged struggles for the possession of Ypres. The chief battle, that of Ypres-Armentières, lasted from October 17th to November 15th, 1914. One of the first movements of the British was to dislodge the enemy from positions they held near Lille. In these engagements national impetuosity led to the advance of two Irish battalions too far without supports, and their practical annihilation. On October 18th the 2nd Leinster Regiment was part of a Division which chased the Germans out of the French town of Hazebrouck, about twenty-five miles north-west of Lille, and pursued them beyond Armentières, a town on the river Lys, within nine miles of Lille.

The Leinsters were about a mile in advance of the main body. They pushed on to a French village called Premesque, still nearer to Lille, and there entrenched, when the Germans surrounded them. For a day and a half the Leinsters held out until they were relieved by French troops. The French commander thanked them for saving the village, but it cost the battalion more than 500 men and officers.

At the same time another Irish battalion was engaged on a similar enterprise in the same field of operations with more disastrous results. "On October 19th," says Sir John French in his despatch on the battle of Ypres-Armentières, "the Royal Irish Regiment, under Major Daniell, stormed the village of Le Pilly, which they held and entrenched. On the 20th, however, they were cut off and surrounded, suffering heavy losses." As the possession of Le Pilly threatened their communications between La Bassée and Lille, the Germans made a determined effort to capture it. It was evident to the Royal Irish that their position was most precarious. They held on, however, and beat off a succession of attacks, hoping that assistance would come before they were completely isolated. German riflemen crept up and ensconced themselves in farm buildings on the outskirts of the village on one side; and machine-guns were brought to a little wood on the other, so that the Royal Irish were enfiladed to the left and right.

The fight was still going on when darkness fell. "All night we could hear the firing up there," writes Gunner P. Hall, Royal Field Artillery, who was with his battery on a hill some miles from Le Pilly; "and desperate efforts were made by our tired troops to regain the ground the Royal Irish had left uncovered, but the job was too big for men so exhausted as they were." What exactly had happened was but a matter for surmise. For hours after the village had been surrounded by the Germans the crackle of rifles and the rapid volleying of the machine-guns told that the Royal Irish were yet unsubdued. Then there came an ominous silence; and in the early hours of the morning a few survivors of the battalion staggered more dead than alive into the British camp.

"They got a rousing cheer, for we had given them all up as lost," says Gunner Hall. For the rest, some weeks later, a long official list of names of the Royal Irish Regiment appeared under the heading "missing." But the vast majority of them will never be found until the Day of Judgment.

The Royal Irish Regiment had ceased to exist as a fighting force. The battalion may be said to have been defeated. The enemy, no doubt, boasted of it as such. But they set thus early in the war a shining example of dash, resolution, and endurance in facing fearful odds which must have had as much moral effect as a victory to our arms.

The most terrific phase of the great battle was from October 29th to November 2nd, immediately to the south of Ypres, east and west; and the most critical hours were, as Sir John French says, on October 31st when the Germans broke through the British lines at Gheluvelt, a village on the road leading from Ypres south-east to Menin. On November 2nd the Germans were everywhere repulsed. The Brigadier-General, Lord Cavan, commanding the 4th (Guards) Brigade, paid the following remarkable tribute to the work of the Irish Guards on that momentous occasion in a letter to the Officer Commanding the battalion, Colonel Proby:—

> I want you to convey to every man in the battalion that I consider that the safety of the right flank of the British section depended entirely on their staunchness after the disastrous day, November 1st. Those of them that were left have made history, and I can never thank them enough for the way in which

they recovered themselves, and showed to the enemy that Irish Guards must be reckoned with, however hard hit.

Lord Cavan, in a report dated November 7th, further states:—

> On October 31st, November 1st and 6th, the Irish Guards lost 16 officers and 597 other ranks in disputing 200 yards of ground with superior forces.

Private Stephen Shaughnessy supplies an account of the incidents of November 6th, when the Irish Guards were overwhelmed. He says:—

> At this time the enemy's strength was two to one. We endeavoured to hold the enemy by machine-guns and rifle fire, until they succeeded in penetrating the French line about two or three miles on our right, and managed to come behind our rear line.

Then he gives an instance of the desperate duels that were fought between the slowly retiring Irish and the hotly pressing Germans.

"While retreating," he says, "Captain King-Harman was the only officer I saw alive. He was then standing up and firing with his revolver on the Germans, who were only 60 yards away. I, or anyone else in our battalion, did not see him alive afterwards." He adds:—

> The only comrade I found within reasonable distance was Private Birmingham, of Clonmel, formerly of the Royal Irish Constabulary. We discussed the situation. He got over the trench to fall back to the troops reforming in our rear. As I was getting out of the trench, a rifle bullet came through my great coat, penetrated my cardigan jacket without touching my body. We formed up again, and were reinforced by the Life Guards, notwithstanding which we were unable to regain our lost territory. When darkness came, we were brought back a mile behind the line for a rest and refreshments. The roll was called, and only 47 of the battalion answered.

The worst was over; and Sir John French indirectly, at least, extols the Irish Guards for helping to avert a disaster, by his praise of their Brigade Commander, Lord Cavan. In his despatch on the Battle of Ypres-Armentières, the Field-Marshal says:—

> The First Corps Commander (Sir Douglas Haig) informs me that on many occasions Brigadier-General the Earl of Cavan, commanding the 4th Guards Brigade, was conspicuous for the

skill, coolness, and courage with which he led his troops, and for the successful manner in which he dealt with many critical situations.

Another Irish regiment to obtain one of these rare and therefore much coveted recognitions by a commander of an army corps was the Royal Irish Rifles, who were fighting round the village of Neuve Chapelle, to the south, from October 25th to October 27th. "During an attack on the 7th Infantry Brigade," runs an order issued by Sir H. Smith-Dorrien, the Commander of the 2nd Corps, "the enemy came to close quarters with the Royal Irish Rifles, who repulsed them with great gallantry with the bayonet. The Commander wishes to compliment the regiment on its splendid feat, and directs that all battalions shall be informed of the circumstances of his high appreciation of the gallantry displayed."

On October 27th the Germans gained possession of the northern part of the village, but towards evening the British had partially recovered the lost ground when fresh hostile reinforcements were brought up, and the entire village was captured by the enemy. The Germans would have made a bigger advance were it not for the gallant stand of the Irish Rifles against overwhelming odds.

A sergeant of the battalion supplies some details of the feat:—

One morning after we had had several days of awful shelling in the trenches the Germans came to attack us. They advanced into view through the rain and mist, and though they were ten times our strength we held our ground until the necessary dispositions could be made in other parts of the field to withstand their onslaught.

As will be seen from many an incident in the course of this narrative the Irish fight best when it comes to the real crisis—the two antagonists engaged in close and relentless contest, man to man and bayonet to bayonet. At first it was furious smithing, gleaming thrust and parry, stab and hack, hack and stab, with the Irish in the trenches and the Germans above; and, in the end, it was the Germans running away and the Irish speeding their departure with rifle fire.

"We did not think there was anything very wonderful about what we did," says the sergeant modestly, "but everyone went wild about it. One staff officer said we ought all to have two Victoria Crosses each, and we had the satisfaction of being splendidly praised by the General in Command."

"Nothing," says Napier in his *Peninsular War*, "so startled the French soldiery as the wild yell with which the Irish regiments sprang to the charge." We are also told by Napier that at Barrosa and Bussaco the heroes of Marengo and Austerlitz reeled before the thunder shout of *Faugh-a-Ballagh* ("Clear the Way") raised by the Royal Irish Fusiliers and the Connaught Rangers. What is more likely is that the French gave way before the irresistible bayonet charge that swept like a flame in the thunder of that haughty battle-cry. The Great War shows that both these historic regiments maintain the ancient tradition of raising a wild, terrific yell when they dash forward, a yell which sends the creeps down the back, and impels the foe irresistibly to turn and fly for fear of what is to follow.

The Irish Fusiliers were the first to enter Armentières (on the occasion that the Leinsters impetuously pushed forward to Premesque), and they did so shouting their old Irish slogan, *Faugh-a-Ballagh*, and enforcing it by driving the enemy from their positions behind every tree and at every turn on the road leading into the town. Private H. Dawson, a West port boy in the 1st Connaught Rangers, tells how a company of the battalion frightened a big force of Germans out of their trenches, and out of their senses also, no doubt, by the blood-curdling yells they gave vent to as they advanced with the bayonet. It was on the night of November 4th, 1914, in the neighbourhood of Neuve Chapelle. The company was ordered to attack the German trenches, two platoons to do the fighting and the two others to follow after with shovels, to fill in the trenches, if they were taken.

"At midnight," writes Private Dawson, "we moved forward with such cheers, shouts, and cries that the Germans, thinking that a whole brigade was advancing, evacuated the trenches and fled. The moon was shining, and when the Germans afterwards saw the handful of men that routed them they returned in greatly increased numbers and made a murderous onslaught on us."

They can sing, too, as they advance, these Connaught Rangers, as Private Robert McGregor of the Gordon Highlanders relates in a graphic letter to his father at Parkhead, Scotland. On December 26th, 1914, the Germans attacked the trenches in front of them at a particular point. The Gordons who held the trenches got out to meet the enemy as they came on in the open. There was a close fight with varying fortunes, but the Germans were reinforced, and as there were only about 170 of the Gordons left it seemed as if they were bound to be annihilated.

"But just at that moment," writes Private McGregor, "we heard the sound of singing, and the song was 'God Save Ireland.' It was the Connaught Rangers coming to our relief. Well, I have seen some reckless Irishmen in my time, but nothing to match the recklessness and daring of these gallant Rangers. They took the Germans on the left flank. The Germans now probably numbered about 2,000 against 800 Connaughts and 170 of us, but were they 50,000 I don't believe in my soul they could have stood before the Irish. The Connaughts simply were irresistible, and all the time they kept singing 'God Save Ireland.' One huge red-haired son of Erin having broken his rifle got possession of a German officer's sword, and everything that came in the way of this giant went down. I thought of Wallace. Four hundred and seventy Huns were killed and wounded, and we took 70 prisoners. Had it not been for the Irish I wouldn't be writing this, and when it comes to a hand-to-hand job there is nothing in the whole British Army to approach them. God save Ireland and Irishmen."

CHAPTER 4

Asphyxiating Gas and Liquid Fire

Many a desperate engagement has been fought from Ypres in the north to La Bassée in the south. Neuve Chapelle, St. Eloi, St. Julien, Festubert, Givenchy, Hooge—to mention a few of them—are places that will stand for all time in history as the scenes of most bloody and tragical battles. They do not all spell British victories; but every vowel of them represents British bravery, suffering, endurance, resolution; and linked with them in enduring fame are the Dublins, Munsters, Inniskillings, Leinsters, Connaughts, Irish Fusiliers, Irish Rifles, and the Irish Regiment.

An Irish battalion of another kind makes a splendid entry into the history of the war at this stage—the Liverpool Irish. They all had to face the new and most infamous methods of fighting introduced by the Germans, clouds of asphyxiating gas and sheets of liquid fire, the opening, literally, of "the mouth of hell" in warfare. But these horrors were encountered and overcome by the Irish battalions with the same valour as had previously rendered vain the more legitimate weapons and methods of the enemy.

Neuve Chapelle is a rural village, with many enclosed gardens and orchards, four miles to the north of La Bassée, and on the road between Bethune and Armentières. Fierce engagements for its possession were fought in October and November, 1914. The Germans were driven out of it on October 16th. It was retaken by them at the beginning of November; and though strongly entrenched and barricaded by the enemy it was finally captured by the British on March 11th and 12th, 1915.

The 2nd Royal Irish Rifles took part in the severe fighting around the village at the end of October, 1914, and, as I have already stated, were highly praised by Smith-Dorrien for their valiancy in holding up a big German attack. They lost heavily on that occasion, but their dead were avenged by the help the battalion gave in inflicting so serious a defeat upon the enemy as the victorious reoccupation of Neuve Chapelle. The first glimpse we got of the Royal Irish Rifles in the battle is in a letter written by an officer of a battalion which was closely co-operating with them, Captain and Adjutant E.H. Impey, of the 2nd Lincoln Regiment. "The Irish Rifles came through us," he says, referring to proceedings on March 10th, "and we cheered them lustily. Lieutenant Graham was rallying his men round him with a French newsboy's horn, giving a 'view-hallo' occasionally just as a master collects his pack."

Captain Impey states that on the next day, March 11th, the Lincolns were ordered to support the Irish Rifles, "Owing to some mistake," he says, "the Irish Rifles attacked before their time, and so got no artillery support. They lost very heavily in officers and men." It was on this day that the battalion suffered the grievous loss of their commanding officer, Lieut.-Colonel George Brenton Laurie. On the first day Colonel Laurie seemed to have had a charmed life. "He deliberately walked up and down, giving orders and cheering the men on amid a flood of fire," says Sergeant-Major Miller of the battalion. "He seemed unconscious of the fact that a great bombardment was taking place. It was a wonderful sight to see him there, his big military figure standing out boldly in presence of his soldiers."

Colonel Laurie was killed by the terrific shell fire which the Germans poured on the advancing British. "It was brutal. We were lying in a wood. The bullets were whistling over us in millions, and the screeching of the shells was terrific," says Bugler Jack Leathem in a letter to his mother at Downpatrick. "The trees were flying about like chaff and the fellows getting blown to pieces. I do not know how some of us escaped. Someone must have been praying for us. You know I am not very nervous, but I was not sorry when it was over. It was four very hard days, fighting both day and night, with no sleep and no trenches to protect us, only the ones we dug ourselves with our entrenching tools. They saved us from the bullets, but it was impossible to get out of shell-fire."

"You would hardly credit it," adds Bugler Leathem, "but every time we lay down to take cover out came our pipes and 'fags.' You would have thought we were on a manœuvre parade at home instead of in one of the fiercest of battles." This was the spirit that brought the battalion to Neuve Chapelle. About one o'clock in the afternoon of

March 11th the 2nd Lincolns proceeded up the road into the village, or, as Captain Impey says, "the ruins of what was once a very pretty village," and found the Irish Rifles there before them.

"We lay in support in this village," Captain Impey writes, "while the Irish Rifles fought the enemy in front. A company was sent in close support just behind them along a hedge."

One of the most interesting documents relating to the Irish regiments in the war is a letter written by Father Francis Gleeson, chaplain of the 2nd Munster Fusiliers. In it he states that each of the four companies of the 2nd Munsters carries a green flag with a golden harp in the corner, the Royal Tiger in the centre, and "Munster" inscribed underneath. "The Irish flags are being highly honoured," he says. "The French people are awfully kind to and fond of the Munsters, because they are so Irish and Catholic. It is really true to say that in us, the 'Munsters,' they recognise the children of the men who fought for them at Fontenoy and Landen. They know that we are old, old friends, indeed.

Their histories tell of Ireland's brave sons having died for their country here." Moved by these memories of the Irish Catholic Brigade in the service of France from the fall of the Stuarts in England until the fall of the Bourbons in France—and regularly recruited for a hundred years from Ireland—the French people recognise the distinct and separate nationality of the Irish regiments. "We are '*Les Irlandais,*' and not '*Les Anglais*'" says Father Gleeson. "Our flags have done that." "The French priests are very fond of us," he goes on to relate, "and give us the use of their beautiful chapels. The people wept after the Munsters the other day when we left a village where we were billeted for a rest." He proudly adds, "On all sides the Munsters are being congratulated for their magnificent behaviour. This is due to the men's faith! They are the best conducted battalion of all the Armies engaged in this world-war, because they are the most Irish, the most Catholic, and the most pure."

The 2nd Munsters have been in the thick of the fighting ever since the outbreak of war. Of the men who landed in France in August, 1914, there are but few survivors. The bones of many are mouldering in the soil of France and Flanders. Others are prisoners at Limburg-an-Lahn in Germany, captured in the rearguard actions during the retreat from Mons. The gaps in the ranks have been filled up by other lads from Limerick, Cork, Kerry and Clare. Always uncertain are the chances of life, but how strange and fantastic they sometimes appear!

Who of these boys ever imagined in 1914 that within a year they would be serving in the British Army, much less fighting against Germany on the Continent? Fresh from the towns and villages of Munster, and new to soldiering and warfare, their racial qualities were put to the test at Rue de Bois, close to Neuve Chapelle, on Sunday, May 9th, 1915, when the Third Infantry Brigade were ordered to attack the trenches that had been held by the Germans since October.

The story of the fight brings out the services of the chaplain of the battalion; and the sustaining courage which the men derive from their religious observances and their green flags, the embodiment of that ancient Irish inspiration—"Faith and Fatherland." I have compiled my narrative from the accounts written by Mrs. Victor Rickard, widow of Colonel Rickard, the officer in command of the regiment, who was killed gallantly leading his men on that memorable day; and Sergeant-Major T.J. Leahy, of Monkstown, Co. Cork, who took part in the engagement.

It is worthy of note that Sergeant-Major Leahy, in an earlier letter, mentions that he served Mass for the chaplain, and was known to Father Gleeson as his "altar boy." He corroborates what Father Gleeson has written of the high moral conduct of the battalion by saying, "Prayers more than anything else console me, and every fellow is the same, so the war has been the cause of making us almost an army of saints."

In his description of the battle, Sergeant-Major Leahy states that on the preceding day, Saturday, May 8th, close on 800 men received Holy Communion at the hands of Father Gleeson, and wrote their names and home addresses in their hymn books. When evening came the regiment moved up to take their places in the trenches in front of Rue de Bois. "At the entrance to Rue de Bois," writes Mrs. Rickard, "there stands a broken shrine, and within the shrine a crucifix. When the Munsters came up the road, Major Rickard halted the battalion. The men were ranged in three sides of a square, their green flags—a gift from Lady Gordon—placed before each company. Father Gleeson mounted, Colonel Rickard and Captain Filgate, the adjutant, on their chargers, were in the centre, and in that wonderful twilight Father Gleeson gave a General Absolution."

Sergeant-Major Leahy supplies other particulars of that moving scene. "On the lonely, dark roadside," he says, "lit up now and then by flashes from our own or German flares, rose to heaven the voices of 800 men, singing that glorious hymn, 'Hail, Queen of Heaven.' There were no ribald jests or courage buoyed up with alcohol; none of the fanciful pictures which imagination conjures up of soldiers going to a desperate charge. No, there were brave hearts without fear; only hoping that God would bring them through, and if the end—well, only a little shortened of the allotted span. Every man had his rosary out, reciting the prayers, in response to Father Gleeson, just as if at the Confraternity at home, instead of having to face death in a thousand hideous forms the following morning." He mentions also that after the religious service Father Gleeson went down the ranks, saying words of comfort; bidding good-bye to the officers, and telling the men to keep up the honour of the regiment.

At dawn the German position was bombarded for seven minutes in order to cut gaps in the barbed-wire entanglements through which the Munsters might pass to the enemy's trenches. Then, as Sergeant-Major Leahy relates, the order was given by the officers—"Are you ready, lads?" "Yes," came the response. "Then over the parapet, like one man, leaped 800 forms, the four green company flags leading." The intervening plain measured three hundred yards. It was swept by the close-range fire of the Germans, like rain from thunder-clouds. Hundreds of the Munsters fell in the charge; but "The green flag was raised on the parapet of the main German trench, and in they went," says Sergeant-Major Leahy.

Mrs. Rickard states that the regiments on the left and right, being unable to get near the line where the Munsters were fighting, the position became that of a forlorn hope; and the battalion was ordered to retire. "You were the only battalion attacking to penetrate and storm the German trenches, although under a hellish fire," said the Commander of the Brigade, subsequently addressing the Munsters. "You have added another laurel to your noble deeds during the present campaign. I am proud to command such a gallant regiment."

"So the Munsters came back after their day's work," writes Mrs. Rickard; "they formed up in the Rue de Bois, numbering 200 men and three officers." "It seems almost superfluous to make any further comment," she adds.

Father Gleeson was in the trenches during the answering bombardment by the Germans. "It was terrible," said Private Danaher; "houses, trees, and bodies flying in the air. Still, Father Gleeson stuck to his post attending to the dying Munsters, and shells dropping all around him. Indeed, if anyone has earned the V.C., Father Gleeson has. He is a credit to the country he hails from, and has brought luck to the

Munsters since he joined them."

The Liverpool Irish leaped into fame and glory at the first chance afforded them. That was at Festubert on June 16th, 1915. The battalion, then in reserve, was rushed up to the trenches. A big surprise movement by the French was arranged for that night, and the Liverpool Irish were to create a diversion by an assault on the enemy's trenches that fronted them, so as to attract reinforcements to the spot in the hope that the lines to be attacked by the French, away to the right, might thereby be weakened. It was what used to be called "a forlorn hope" in ancient warfare, such as the storming of a breach, from which the chance of a safe return was small, but which, if it did no other good, would weaken the arm of the enemy in encountering the main onslaught.

The detachment of the Liverpool Irish selected for this desperate enterprise had an ideal leader in Captain Herbert Finegan, dashing, combative, and resolute. The son of the late Dr. J.H. Finegan, a well-known Irish physician in Liverpool, he was educated at Stonyhurst, had a brilliant career at Liverpool University, and, with his uncommon gifts of mind and tongue, seemed destined for distinction in the law courts and the House of Commons, when war broke out and diverted him to a wholly different arena of activity. He was given charge of the attack. His company was the first over the parapets. "Come on, Irish. Show them what we can do!" he cried in his impetuous way as he thrust forward his head menacingly towards the German lines. When the men were out of the trenches, a sergeant of the company exclaimed, "It's sure death, boys, but remember we are Irish." He was immediately blown to bits. The Germans, seeing the movement, met it by scourging the advancing lines with shell fire.

Lord Wolseley has said that almost every officer who has led a storming party across the open in full view of the enemy would acknowledge that his one anxiety from first to last was, "Will my men follow me?" Captain Finegan had no misgiving of the kind. He did not need to look over his shoulder to see if his men had rallied to his cry. They pressed round him as he ran across the open, these Liverpool Irish, most of whom had never seen Ireland, and yet were as eager to maintain her reputation for valour as the Irish Guards, the Munsters, the Dublins, or the Connaught Rangers, born and reared at home. Capt. Finegan was shot dead at the edge of the German trenches. Fired by this example, the men pressed onward, and did not stop or stay even when they had done what they had set out to do. "It was a job to make them come back when we got the order to retire," said one of the officers.

The forlorn hope had unexpectedly blossomed into a victory. The Liverpool Irish took a German trench for themselves, along with helping the French to make a rapid advance which resulted in the capture of three miles of trenches of the enemy's lines. They got congratulations on their achievement from the commander, Sir Henry Rawlinson. Many of them shared the fate of their gallant leader. It was a fate that Capt. Finegan had anticipated. "I will either go home with the Victoria Cross, or stay here with a wooden one," he once remarked to Sergeant MacCabe, of his company.

At Festubert also the 2nd Inniskilling Fusiliers carried through with complete success an enterprise notable for wild daring and stern valour. One attack on the German trenches had failed. The ground between the opposing lines was strewn with the British dead. A second attack was ordered under cover of darkness. The 2nd Inniskillings were to lead the van in the principal sector. In spite of the pitchy blackness of the night, it was certain that the German machine-guns and rifles would take heavy toll before their trenches were reached.

But the Inniskillings mix brains with their bravery. So soon as night fell, about 8 p.m., they crept over the parapet, one by one, and squirmed on their stomachs towards the German lines. Slowly and painfully they crawled through a sea of mud, from dead man to dead man, lying quite still whenever a star-shell lighted up that intervening stretch of 200 yards. By this method, platoon after platoon spread itself over the corpse-strewn field, until the leading files were within a few yards of the German trenches.

Then came the hardest task of all—to lie shoulder to shoulder with the dead until at midnight a flare gave the signal, "Up and into the German trenches." But the Inniskillings held on with steady nerves through all the alarums of the night. Occasionally bullets whistled across the waste, and some who had imitated death needed to pretend no longer. But the toll was not heavy. At least it was infinitesimal by comparison with the cost of an open tumultuous charge from their own trenches. When at last the flash blazed up the leading platoons were in the German trenches before the enemy had time to lift their rifles.

The Inniskillings caught the Germans in many cases actually asleep. Many of the grey-coats woke up just in time to find British bayonets at their throats. The entire force was confused and demoralised by this sudden appearance in their trenches of khaki and the deadly bayonet, and were quickly overthrown. The Inniskillings paid less for the capture of the first and second lines of trenches than they might have done by an open attack for the first alone. They made it possible for the whole division to sweep on and to score a victory where another division had previously found defeat.

CHAPTER 5

The Immortal Story

The most terrific thing in the bombardment of the southern end of Gallipoli by the British Fleet, from the Ægean Sea, on Sunday morning, April 25th, 1915, was the roar of the *Queen Elizabeth*—the mammoth vessel of the Navy and armed with the mightiest guns—sending forth at each bellow and flash a ton of high explosives. It inspired awe and dread to the uttermost, that concentration of fire from all the ships of the Fleet. What living being, or work of nature or man, could survive it? Those on the ships who were searching the peninsula with the most powerful telescopes could see no sign of life. Houses and walls disappeared, and clouds of sand and earth and smoke arose where the Turks were supposed to be entrenched. There was no reply to the cannonade, not even the crack of a rifle.

The allied Fleets of England and France had failed to batter open the gates of the Dardanelles from the sea in March; and now there was to be an attempt to invade Gallipoli by making a number of separate but simultaneous landings of British troops on the southern and western sides of the peninsula. The object was to seize the Turkish positions defending the Straits, which was to be followed, if all went well, by an advance to Constantinople by both land and sea, and the dictation of terms to the paralysed Ottoman Empire at St. Sophia. English, Scottish, Australian, New Zealand, and Indian troops, as well as Irish, were engaged in this grand enterprise.

They all acquitted themselves nobly, especially the Lancashire regiments, with their very large Irish element; and the Dominion forces, in which Ireland was also well represented; but to the Irish regiments was allotted what proved to be the most desperate part of the invasion, as will be found fully admitted in the official despatches of Sir Ian Hamilton in command of the Army and Admiral de Robeck of the Navy. The British troops consisted of the 29th Division under Major-General Hunter-Weston. In it were battalions of three Irish regiments, 1st Dublin Fusiliers, 1st Munster Fusiliers, and 1st Inniskilling Fusiliers. They had been brought from India and Burma to England at the outbreak of the war, and having rested for some months in the Midlands, around Coventry, left Avonmouth for the Near East on St. Patrick's Day, 1915.

Along this western side of Gallipoli, washed by the Ægean Sea, the yellow cliffs of sandstone and clay, clothed in scrub, seem to rise, in an undeviating line, clear out of the waters to a height of from two to three hundred feet. But there are points where the line is really shoved back, as it were, and here and there, at these places, flat semicircles of sand lie between the water and the base of the cliffs. It was on half a dozen of these small beaches that the troops were to be landed under the cover of the bombardment by the Fleet. The Dublins and the Munsters were to land at "Beach V" immediately below the castle and village of Sedd-el-Bahr, strongest of the Turkish positions.

In this particular landing very remarkable use was made of a steamer called the *River Clyde*, turned into a troopship. She had about 2,500 troops on board, all Munsters and Dublins, save two companies of the Hampshire Regiment, who formed part of the same brigade, the 86th. So closely packed were the men that they could scarcely move. The plan was to run her ashore, full steam ahead, and when she was beached the troops were to emerge through openings cut in her sides, on the lower deck, and passing down narrow gangways make a dash for the shore over a bridge to be formed of some lighters which accompanied her.

The *River Clyde* was beached about 400 yards from the castle of Sedd-el-Bahr, which rose above the high ground to the right; and the bridge of lighters was also successfully run in towards the shore from the gangways jutting from the improvised doors in the port and starboard bow of the vessel.

While the preparations were in progress three companies of the Dublins were being brought ashore in open boats drawn by steam pinnaces, five or six boats in each tow, and over thirty men in every boat. No sign had yet been given that any of the enemy were about on the cliffs and hills, shrouded by the dust and smoke caused by the shells of the Fleet; and it looked almost as if the landing would be unopposed. But the enemy were there in their thousands, lying low with rifles and machine-guns. The Turks have shown on many a field of old their fine fighting qualities. They had been trained in all the newest tricks of warfare by German officers.

They were animated also by two of the most powerful emotions—defence of their native land against unbelieving dogs of Christians; and the firm conviction that death in such a cause was but the opening of the gates to the sensuous delights of Paradise. So they were biding their time, and the hour for action struck when the boats crowded with the Dublins were about twenty yards from the shore. The furious reception they gave to the landing parties was astounding, having regard to the terrific preliminary bombardment by the Fleet which had lasted several hours. The Turks were as ready for the invaders as if the explosives of the *Queen Elizabeth* had gone wide of the mark, or else as if she had contented herself with pelting the entrenchments with boiled potatoes or roasted apples.

The scene of the landing was, in configuration, like an amphitheatre with the beach as a stage. The beach itself is a strip of powdery sand about three hundred yards long and ten or twelve yards wide. Behind it is a steep rising ground of sandstone and clay grown with prickly scrub. Sir Ian Hamilton calls it a "death trap." He could not have given it an uglier nor yet a truer name. Barbed wire entanglements were cunningly concealed in the shallows of the foreshore. The Turks were posted with artillery on the heights, and had sharpshooters and also machine-guns ensconced in holes made in the face of the cliff less than a dozen yards from the sea.

When the picket-boats, or steam pinnaces, got to within two hundred yards of the shore they cast off; and the cutters, with the Dublins, continued on their way towards a narrow strip of rock jutting out from the beach, which made a natural landing-place. Then it was that the Turks concentrated upon the boats a most destructive fire of rifles, and machine-guns from the amphitheatre, and shrapnel from the fort at Sedd-el-Bahr. The attacking party was practically wiped out. Only a few passed through this tornado of lead unscathed. Colonel Rooth, of the Dublins, the adjutant, Captain Higginson, and the chaplain, Father Finn, were killed. Sergeant J. Colgan, who was in the boat with these officers, says:—

> Only six of us got away alive out of a boat-load of thirty-two. One fellow's brains were shot into my mouth as I was shouting to them to jump for it. I dived into the sea. Then came the job to swim with my pack, and one leg useless. I managed to pull out the knife and cut the straps and swim ashore. All the time

bullets were ripping around me.

Here is another individual experience supplied by a private of the Dublins:—

> I jumped into the sea with my gun, and made towards the shore. When I got up on the rocky place I had my first bullet in the side. I felt as if I was struck with an iron bar in the back. It knocked me down. I put up my right hand to my head with the pain, when I got a bullet through that also. I had thus two narrow escapes. The first bullet just missed my lung and spine; it made a big hole in my back. The second one just missed my head.

Extremely rare were such miraculous deliverances from death. Many of the Dublins who got safely out of the boats and attempted to swim or wade to the shore were entangled in the barbed wire and drowned. The few who reached the shore crawled on their stomachs, or ran, reeling and staggering, to the shelter of a narrow ridge of sand, about four feet high, which fortunately stretched across the beach not far from the cliff. Most of the boats were destroyed. Others, with their ghastly loads of dying and dead, drifted out to sea, where they were picked up by the Fleet. An officer of the Dublins who was in one of these boats says:—

> Shrapnel burst above our heads and before I knew where I was I was covered with dead men. Not knowing they were dead, I was roaring at them to let me up, for I thought I was drowning. The guns still played on us till we got back to a mine-sweeper. I was simply saturated all over with blood, and I could feel the hot blood all over me all the way across. When they pulled these poor fellows off me they were all dead, and the poor fellows under me were dead also. The boat was awful to look at, full of blood and water.

Meanwhile the landing of the Munsters from the *River Clyde* was about to commence. Three of the lighters were placed in position to serve as a pier from the vessel to the shore. They covered but a part of the distance. Then out of the holes cut in the sides of the steamer were thrust wooden gangways leading to the lighters.

The Munsters caught glimpses from the lower deck of the appalling scenes of tumult and slaughter attending the landing of the Dublins. They saw the boats drifting by loaded with the mangled bodies of their fellow-countrymen. They saw corpses floating on the sea. They saw the waters, as smooth as glass, turned from blue to crimson. As the Dublins set out for the shore they cannot have had any adequate conception of the withering tempest of lead that awaited them. The Munsters witnessed the whole horrid tragedy. The task before them was every whit as desperate, and fearsome, and knowledge of its nature added to its terrors. It was enough to make the blood curdle in the veins, and fear to clutch at the heart with an icy grip.

Man clings to life tenaciously. Many of these hitherto gay and irresponsible young Munsters had become very serious, and their eyes had a deep, inward look as if they were pondering over some great thing. Were they sad for their shattered dreams of a safe return to Ireland; and of a peaceful home life with a girl of blue eyes, red lips, and black hair as its alluring central figure? An officer passed among them saying, "Our time has come, boys, and we must not falter. Remember we are Munsters; and, above all, remember Ireland."

The men were thrilled by this double appeal to pride in their gallant regiment and love for their dear native land. At the words their spirits mounted high. So that when it was discovered that one of the gangways had been shot away by a shell, and a delay was suggested in order to see if it could not be rigged up again, and one of the officers stepped forward, and shouted, "Volunteers for the first dash," there was an instant response, "We are ready, sir." I am told one of the Munsters made the racy reply:—"Let us at them, sir; sure it's as aisy a job as we can strike." It is the way of the Irish to make light of troubles. "There's nothing so bad but it could be worse," runs one of their sayings. They will seek to pluck contentment from the most desperate of situations.

The officer stepped through the hole on to the gangway, with the men pressing close behind him. At the moment the bullets were rattling like diabolic hailstones against the steel sides by which the hull of the vessel were strengthened. What happened then is graphically described by Private Timothy Buckley, of Macroom, County Cork. Lying wounded in a military hospital in England, he said:—

> The captain of my company asked for 200 volunteers, and as I was in his company I volunteered. We got ready inside on the deck, and opened the buckles of our equipment, so that every man might have a chance of saving himself if he fell into the water. He gave the order to fix bayonets when we should get ashore. He then led the way, but fell immediately at the foot of the gangway. The next man jumped over him, and kept go-

ing until he fell on the pontoon bridge. Altogether 149 men were killed outright and 30 wounded. I was about the twenty-seventh man out. I stood counting them as they were going through. It was then I thought of peaceful Macroom, and wondered if I should ever see it again. When my turn came I was wiser than some of my comrades. The moment I stood on the gangway I jumped over the rope on to the pontoon. Two more did the same, and I was already flat on the bridge. Those two chaps were at each side of me, but not for long, as the shrapnel was bursting all around. I was talking to the chap on my left, and saw a lump of lead enter his temple. I turned to the chap on my right. His name was Fitzgerald. He was from Cork, but soon he was over the border. The one piece of shrapnel had done the job for the two.

Thus men in khaki poured out of the side of the *River Clyde* and raced down the gangway or jumped from it at once on to the first lighter. Two men out of every three fell. The commanding officer of the Munsters, Colonel Monck-Mason, was wounded and put out of action early in the proceedings. Soon the first and second lighters were piled high with wounded and dead, twisted into all sorts of horrid shapes, and the men who escaped being instantly shot were to be seen stepping and jumping and even walking over the bodies of their fallen comrades. Many of these flung up their arms, spun round, and, with a cry of agony, went splash into the sea never to rise again. Then the horrors of the situation were added to by a most unfortunate mishap.

The lighter nearest to the beach gave way in the current and drifted backward into deep water. The men in it jumped out in the hope of being able to swim and wade to the shore. Most of them were drowned by the weight of their equipment. But the Munsters never quailed. All the time they continued emerging from the *River Clyde*, in an unbroken stream, two men out of every three still dropping on the gangway or on the bridge, and the survivors still pressing forward with their faces dauntlessly set for the land. Those who got to the shore rushed to join the Dublins under the scanty cover afforded by the low sandy escarpment. The first of the Munsters to gain the beach was Sergeant Patrick Ryan. He swam ashore in his full kit; and got the Distinguished Conduct Medal for "showing under heavy fire the greatest coolness and powers of leadership."

Mr. H.W. Nivenson, one of the newspaper correspondents with the Mediterranean Expeditionary Force, mentioned in a lecture on the operations which he delivered in London, that he and others saw the landing through their glasses from a ship some miles out at sea. One of the party, seeing the men who had landed dropping on the beach, and not understanding the tragic nature of the scene, remarked to Mr. Nivenson: "Why are our men resting?"

The beach was, in fact, strewn with maimed men, or men on whose sufferings the oblivion of death had mercifully fallen. Pinnaces which had towed the boats of the Dublins hung about picking up the dead and wounded from the sea, and members of their crews heroically landed on the beach to carry off the disabled living. Officers and bluejackets suffered death while engaged on this work of mercy. Consequently most of the wounded could only be removed when it was dark. They lay on the beach all day, in the hot sand under the broiling sun, in agonies of pain and thirst, till nine o'clock at night.

Surgeon Barrett, of the Royal Navy, a Cork man, who was on the *River Clyde*, says:—

> I had some of the wounded back on board—chaps whom I had seen half an hour before well and strong—now wrecks for life. It was awful. They were very cheery and dying to be back again at the Turks. It was very strange. I would see a poor chap dying, and asking him where he came from, the answer would be 'Blarney Street, Cork'; another 'Main Street,' and one poor sergeant, who had five bayonet wounds in his stomach, came from 'Warren's Place.' He died that night, and was cheery to the last. They are fine fellows, and won the admiration of everyone.

Surgeon Peter Burrows, R.N., another Irishman, though severely wounded, remained on the *River Clyde* until April 27th, succouring the injured. He attended to 750 disabled men while suffering great pain himself, and being quite incapable of walking during the last twenty-four hours of his continuous duty. The Distinguished Service Order was given to Surgeon Burrows.

Altogether more than 1,000 men had left the *River Clyde* by 11 o'clock in the morning. Two-thirds of them had been shot dead, drowned, or wounded. The landing was then discontinued. It was resumed under the shelter of darkness, when, strange to say, the 1,000 men remaining on the *River Clyde* got ashore without a single casualty. In fact not a shot was fired against them. But before they were landed a night attack was made by the Turks on the remnants of the Dublins and Munsters crouching on the beach under the protection of the bank.

Lieutenant Henry Desmond O'Hara, of the Dublins, took command, all the senior officers having been killed and wounded. He was awarded the Distinguished Service Order and promoted to be captain for his initiative and resource in restoring the line when it had been broken by the Turks, and organising a successful counter-attack which caused great loss to the enemy. Captain O'Hara died soon afterwards of wounds received in action. He was the only son of Mr. W.J. O'Hara, resident magistrate, Ballincollig, Co. Cork, and a nephew of Dr. O'Hara, Bishop of Cashel.

In the morning an assault was made upon the fort and village on the heights. The Dublins advanced, with the Munsters on their right and the Hampshires on their left. Through the prickly scrub or brushwood of the hill ran three lines of trenches and a network of entanglements made of barbed wire of an unusually strong and vicious kind. Out of these entrenchments the machine-guns poured a devastating stream of lead. To attack such a position seemed almost to match in madness the landing of the day before. I do not think there is any sound of battle more appalling to the soldier who has to face it than the devil's tattoo of the machine-gun sending forth its six hundred bullets by the minute.

"It was up the hill and back again, up and back," writes a Kildare man in the Dublins, "till we began to wonder if the Turks would not drive us into the sea."

Lord Wolseley said that one of the most difficult things for an officer to do is to induce a line of men who, during an advance under fire, have found some temporary haven or shelter, or have lain down, perhaps, to take breath, to rise up together and dash forward in a body upon the enemy's position. Here, however, there were deeds of bravery of the highest order. Corporal William Cosgrave got the V.C. for pulling down, single-handed, the posts of the high wire entanglements.

In order to give encouragement to his men Sergeant C. Cooney, of the Dublins—afterwards awarded the Distinguished Conduct Medal—freely exposed himself in the open, though the Turks were lying within seventy yards of him. This conspicuous contempt of danger had the effect the gallant sergeant desired. The men charged with a daring and fury that swept the Turks out of the trenches, at the point of the bayonet, and had them back in the village by 10 o'clock. In the streets the Irish were held in check for hours and suffered more heavy losses from the fire of the Turks strongly posted and concealed in the ruins of the houses.

But at noon the final rush was made, and the Munsters and Dublins stood triumphant within the captured fort. Most of the Turks had retired during the last stages of the attack; but in the fort were captured 200 of the enemy with several machine-guns. The first man to enter the fort was a Dublin Fusilier, Private T. Cullen, who got the Distinguished Conduct Medal for conspicuous gallantry.

The landing at "Beach V," Gallipoli, is one of the most terrible and heroic episodes to be found in the annals of the British Army. The Turks and the Germans were amazed at its audacity and mad recklessness. By all the rules of war it was doomed to disastrous failure. Von der Goltz, the German general, who designed the defences, boasted that the landing was impossible. It succeeded because of the unconquerable bravery, determination, and self-sacrifice of the troops. Yet the part taken by the Irish regiments is meanly ignored altogether by Admiral de Robeck, and but scantily recorded by Sir Ian Hamilton. Ten lines to the Dublins; less than twenty to the Munsters!

How inadequate and bald the account of the general appears in the light of the full immortal story! But tributes to the magnificent bravery of the Irish have been paid by others. Major-General Hunter-Weston, commanding the 29th Division, made a stirring speech to the 1st Dublin Fusiliers on their relief from the firing line after fifteen days of continuous fighting. "Well done, Blue Caps!" he cried. The Dublins are known as "Blue Caps." During the Indian Mutiny a despatch of Nana Sahib was intercepted in which he referred to those "blue-capped English soldiers that fought like devils." These were the predecessors of the Dublins.

"Well done, Blue Caps!" said General Hunter-Weston, "I now take the first opportunity of thanking you for the good work you have done. You have achieved the impossible. You have done a thing which will live in history. When I first visited this place with other people of importance, we all thought a landing would never be made, but you did it, and therefore the impossibilities were overcome—and it was done by men of real and true British fighting blood. You captured the fort and village on the right that were simply swarmed with Turks with machine-guns, also the hill on the left, where the pom-poms were. Also the amphitheatre in front, which was dug line for line with trenches, and from where there came a terrific rifle and machine-gun fire. You are indeed deserving of the highest praise. I am proud to be in command of such a distinguished regiment, and I only hope, when you return to the firing line after this rest (which you have well earned), that you will make even a greater name for yourselves. Well done, the Dubs! Your deeds will live in history for time immortal. Farewell."

Brigadier-General W.B. Marshal, of the 29th Division, writing in November, 1915, to his friend Mr. James O'Regan, Grand Parade, Cork, says:—

> I am now one of the very few survivors of those who landed with the 29th Division on April 25th, 1915. Nearly all the rest have been killed, wounded, or invalided, so that I may count myself very lucky after eight months of strenuous work, I should be glad of a change.

He adds some very striking passages:—

> Though I am an Englishman, I must say the Irish soldiers have fought magnificently. They are the cream of the Army. Ireland may well be proud of her sons. Ireland has done her duty nobly. Irishmen are absolutely indispensable for our final triumph. If I am spared to return at the end of the war I shall make my future home in 'Dear Old Ireland,' which has always had a warm corner in my heart, for in no part of the world have I met more generous, warm-hearted, or braver people than in the Emerald Isle.

Trooper Brennan, of the Australian Light Horse, writing from Anzac to his father in Kilkenny, says he received an account of the Landing of the Dublins and Munsters from men of the Royal Scots; and goes on to make this comment:—

> Somehow, it's a funny thing how nearly every account of an Irish regiment's prowess comes from a Scotchman—I remember it was a Highlander who told of the Munsters at Mons. At any rate, I tried to get some particulars from a few of the Dublins and Munsters themselves, and I failed miserably. They were all talking of poor Johnny this and that who got shot, or Paddy something-or-other, or the bad water, or the failure of the rum issue, so I came to the conclusion that an Irishman's fighting is somewhat like his temper or dislikes—no sooner dispensed

with than forgotten.

Here, sure enough, is a Scot who was at Gallipoli, and saw the landing, writing in glowing terms of the Irish in a letter published in January, 1916, by *The Tablet*, who took it from a Scottish paper:—

> I am astonished that Glasgow folks—and I have met quite a number since my return from that 'hell' out there—seem to be unaware of the extraordinary bravery which was displayed by the Irish soldiers, especially the Munsters and the Dublins. As you know, I am not Irish, and have no Irish connections whatever—in fact, I was rather opposed to the granting of Home Rule; but now, speaking honestly and calmly, after having witnessed what I did—the unparalleled heroism of these Irishmen—I say nothing is too good to give the country of which they are, or rather were, such worthy representatives.
>
> My God, it was grand! It filled one with admiration and envy; because certainly no soldiers could show greater daring and bravery than these fine boys did in face of an awful fire and destruction. Aye, the race that can produce such men, supermen, as those chaps were, to do such glorious work for the Empire has the most perfect right to demand and, what is more, to get the freedom of its country and the right to rule it. Yes, it is but the merest truth to state that there would be no Dardanelles campaign heard of today if it had not been for the extraordinary services of these Irish troops, white men every one, and I have no doubt but that God has taken them to Himself.

The Scottish soldier then goes on to bear remarkable testimony to the deep religious fervour of the Irish troops:—

> Oh, but they deserve a rich reward! What surprises me is that the papers have not been full of their praises. I would have expected that it would have been made widely known that the Irish boys had at least saved the situation and displayed a bravery the like of which was never equalled. It is a shame and a scandal, because I can tell you there is not a man in the Service who is aware of the great gallantry but who would willingly do anything now for the Irish people—yes, the Irish Catholics. I have no religion, but it was most charming and edifying to see these fine chaps with their beads and the way in which they prayed to God. We are all brothers, but to my dying day I bow to the Irish.

Many an Irish home was made desolate. Ireland mourned for her young men; but there is an uplifting sorrow, the sorrow that is mingled with pride, and of that kind was the sorrow of Ireland.

CHAPTER 6

The 10th Irish Division in Gallipoli

At the dawn of Saturday morning, August 7th, 1915, the Ægean Sea and the Gulf of Saros, to the north-west of Gallipoli, were swarming with the most variegated collection of shipping, of all sorts and conditions—transports, cruisers, torpedo-boat destroyers, trawlers, barges, ocean liners, steam pinnaces, rowing boats, and tramp steamers. A fresh landing, at Suvla Bay, had been in progress all through the night. The first great landing, on April 25th, at Sedd-el-Bahr, at the toe of the Peninsula—in which the first battalions of the Dublin and Munster Fusiliers won imperishable renown—had secured a foothold in Gallipoli, but the hills and forts which guarded the passage up the Dardanelles to Constantinople, on the east, were still held by the Turks. Now a new and stupendous effort was about to be made to break the enemy's grip on the Peninsula.

The date, August 7th, 1915, should be ever memorable in the history of Ireland, and also in that of the whole United Kingdom. On that day a Division of the New Armies raised for the war—"Kitchener's Armies," as they are popularly called—was brought under fire for the first time, and collectively engaged in battle. These citizen soldiers were Irish. Irish professional soldiers have always fought most gallantly for England in all her wars. But on that day, for the first time in the long and embittered relations between England and Ireland, a distinctively Irish Division (the 10th), voluntarily raised in Ireland and composed of 20,000 young men of fine character and high purpose, representative particularly of the Nationalist and Catholic sections of the community, were found on the side of England.

The 10th Irish Division was formed in the autumn and winter months of 1914. They left Ireland at the end of April, 1915, to complete their training in the great camp of Aldershot. At the end of June they embarked from England as part of the Mediterranean Expeditionary Force. On Friday evening, August 6th, they parted from the olive groves and vineyards of beautiful islands in the Ægean, off the coast of Asia Minor, where they had been stationed a couple of weeks, and were brought up to Gallipoli.

Here, then, were clerks from offices and counting houses, assistants from drapery and grocery shops, civil servants, public school boys, artisans, labourers, farm hands—a heterogeneous collection of youths from all walks in life—and officered chiefly by barristers, solicitors, engineers, and University students, who had only been a few months in training, and who before this call to arms suddenly rang through the Empire, seemed destined for peaceful and secure careers in civil life. Now, within a few hours of hearing, for the first time in their lives, a shot fired in anger, they were to be plunged right into the fiery and bloody whirlpool of war.

Gallipoli, as it looked from the decks of the troopships, even in the wonderful dawn of that August Saturday morning, had a mysterious and sinister appearance. The men saw yellow clayey cliffs, rising almost sheer from intensely blue water, and beyond these a huddle of pointed and desolate hills, to which no access seemed visible. To their right they could see Achi Baba—a head and shoulders, with two arms extending on each side to the sea—dominating the end of the Peninsula, like a Chinese idol, inscrutable, and disdainful of the shells from the battleships which raised clouds of smoke and dust about its face.

The general objective of all the troops engaged in this new enterprise—English, Scotch, and Welsh Territorials, as well as the Irish Division of the new Armies—was the capture of the Anafarta Hills, a network of ravines and jungles to the north of the high mountain of Sari Bair, the key of the situation in this upper part of the Peninsula. The Australians, New Zealanders, and Maoris had been attacking Sari Bair since dark on Friday night, from their position at Anzac, lower down the Peninsula.

The 10th Division was wholly Irish, save for one English battalion, the 10th Hampshire Regiment. The 29th Brigade, composed of the 5th Connaught Rangers, 6th Leinsters, 6th Irish Rifles, and the 10th Hampshires, was detached from the Division, and landed at Anzac, to co-operate with the Dominion Forces. But the other two Brigades were entirely Irish. These were the 30th, consisting of the 6th and 7th Dublin Fusiliers, 6th and 7th Munster Fusiliers; and the 31st, consisting of the 5th and 6th Inniskilling Fusiliers, and the 5th and 6th Irish

Fusiliers. In addition, there was the Pioneer Regiment, the 5th Royal Irish Regiment (Colonel, the Earl of Granard, K.P.), the purpose of which was to facilitate the progress of the troops by removing obstructions, but which also took part in the fighting.

These two brigades had orders to clear the Turks out of the heights of Karakol Dagh, a long ridge fronting the Gulf of Saros, to the north; and to take a particular hill a few miles to the south, about three or four miles inland from Suvla Bay. This hill is known to the Turks as Yilghin Burnu. It was called Chocolate Hill by the invading army as part of its surface had been burnt a dull brown by shell fire. The division was under the command of General Sir Bryan Mahon, a Galway man, who saw much service in Egypt and the Soudan, and in the South African War led the column which relieved Mafeking.

In a way, it is a pity that things were not so arranged as to have brought these unseasoned and unhardened Irish troops gradually to the great and searching test of war, that they were not afforded the opportunity of feeling the land of the foe under their feet, and becoming somewhat familiar with its extraordinary geographical conditions and climate, before they had to rush into battle. In warfare all that depends, usually, upon unforeseen circumstances, and the chance disposition of the forces. But it may have happened by special direction in this case; and, if so, it was a compliment to the 10th Division. "It is true they are new and untried, but they are Irish," it was probably said at Headquarters, "and being Irish, they may be relied upon, however hard and tough their job." In any case, both brigades were successful in the enterprises to which they were set.

The disembarkation was carried out under fire from the Turkish batteries on the hills. The men were taken from the transports in steam-driven barges, and though the barges had sheltering sides of steel, several men were killed and wounded by exploding shells even before they reached the shore. Half of the 30th Brigade, consisting of the two battalions of the Munsters, to whom was allotted the task of capturing Karakol Dagh, were landed to the north of Suvla Bay, just under the ridge.

"How I wish that their fathers and mothers could know more of how these brave fellows fought and died!" writes the commanding officer of one of the Munster battalions in a letter to his relatives. "They, alas! for the most part just see the names of their dear ones in a casualty list, and can learn nothing further. The beach on which we landed was sown with contact mines, and as we crossed it to form up under cover of a small hill, many a poor chap was blown to bits—not very encouraging for those approaching in other boats. But they never wavered, but landed, and formed up as quietly and steadily as they used to do on the parade ground at the Curragh. I asked one poor chap who was slightly injured how he had got through, and he said, 'All I could think of, sir, was how anxious you must be to see how we would behave.' That is the spirit that one likes to see in a battalion."

The landing place of the other half of the 30th Brigade, the 6th and 7th Dublins, with the Inniskillings and the Irish Fusiliers, was to the south of Suvla Bay, at Niebruniessi Point, under the hill, Lala Baba. The men climbed the cliffs to the sand dunes. Leaving their packs behind them, they carried nothing but what was absolutely necessary—a rifle and 200 rounds of ammunition per man, a water bottle, and rations for two days in a bag, consisting of two tins of bully beef, tea, sugar, biscuits, and tablets of compressed meat.

Thus equipped, with loosened girths and wearing their big brown sun-helmets, the troops advanced in eight or ten long lines, with two paces between each man. The 7th Dublins, the famous "Pals," flower of the youth of Dublin, were in the van. Colonel Geoffrey Downing, in command of the 7th Dublins, as the senior colonel of the battalions in the attacking line, got a message from Headquarters that it was imperative that Chocolate Hill should be taken before sunset. His reply was: "It shall be done."

As the crow flies Chocolate Hill is no more than four miles from the sea line. But to reach it the Irish troops had to make a wide enveloping movement, so that the ground actually covered in the advance was from ten to twelve miles. To the north of the point where the landing took place is a long and broad but shallow lagoon, called Salt Lake. The intense summer heat had dried it up and turned its bottom into a flat stretch of sand and dust, covered with a slight crust of salt which glistened in the sun. The Irish troops first proceeded a considerable distance ahead between the sea and Salt Lake, moving thereby parallel to Chocolate Hill, which lies east of the lake.

At one point they had to pass over a long spit of sand, not twenty yards wide, that divided the sea and Salt Lake. The enemy had its exact range. Many a man was brought down as he attempted to cross it at a run. Then Colonel Downing, of the 7th Dublins, came upon the scene. He paused, lit a cigarette, and walked over the narrow ridge as coolly as if he were doing Grafton Street, Dublin. After this experience the troops wheeled to the right, and marching south-east across

Salt Lake faced the rear flank of their objective.

Crossing Salt Lake in the open, they presented a clear target to the enemy, and were raked with machine-gun fire, shrapnel and high-explosive shells. It is an ordeal that strains to the uttermost all the physical and mental qualities. One of the most common experiences of men who go through it for the first time is a distracting indecision whether to advance, halt, or retreat. But the successive lines went steadily on in short rushes, the men falling on their stomachs between each rush. There was no shelter. The expanse was unbroken even by a rock. The men sank almost to their knees in the soft sand. Very heavy, slow and tiring was the going.

All the time Turkish explosives were bursting on every side, and comrades were dropping out of the ranks killed or disabled. One instance will show the steadiness and resolution of the troops. A shell burst in the middle of a platoon that was marching in rather close formation. Five men were blown to pieces. The platoon opened out and continued their advance. High over their heads the shells from the British cruisers and monitors out at sea went shrieking on their way to find the Turks. The land seemed to tremble with the din and vibration caused by this long-range artillery duel. The men were bodily shaken. But they were also greatly heartened to see, now and then, clouds of earth thrown into the air, telling how the explosive shells from the ships were rending the entrenchments behind which the enemy lay concealed.

After this ordeal in the open sandy plain, the Irish reached a totally different kind of country—an inextricable jumble of hills and gullies, strewn with boulders, overgrown with a thick prickly scrub, and wholly trackless. Here some shelter was afforded from the high explosives of the Turks, but not from their machine-guns and rifles, and the progress was still more slow and difficult. The nature of the country gave a tremendous superiority to the enemy, on the defensive behind their entrenchments. What a hopeless, heart-breaking task it seemed to get free of this entanglement of rocks and scrub, which tore the clothes and lacerated the flesh, and force a way up these steep hills, on hands and feet to the Turkish positions.

Men were falling on all sides. How soon would the end of the fiery furnace be reached? Would anyone get safely through? Such were the thoughts that occupied the mind of many a man, expecting that the next bullet or shell would strike him down. The battalions were broken up into unrelated sections, or else were mixed together. The nature of the ground, the gullies and ravines, the scrub and the rocks, split them up into fragments, each with its independent command. This kind of fighting was quite to the liking of the Irish troops. It gave play to individual personal courage and qualities of leadership.

What they all desired was to get into close grips with the Turks. How they hungered for the wild exultation of the bayonet charge, the shock of man to man in deadly encounter, the pursuit of a vanquished foe! The evening was well advanced before the end came in sight. Major Harrison gallantly led the 7th Dublins and men of other units in the final attack. "Fix bayonets, Dublins, and let's make a name for ourselves," was his cry. The hill had not only natural advantages for defence in rocks, scrub, and trees. It was also a network of trenches. From behind this double cover the Turks threw hand grenades at the Irish, now approaching with a rush and yelling fiercely. Soon they got a taste of bayonet and clubbed rifle administered by Irish hands. The Turks are brave fighters, but they quailed before the Irish onslaught and sought safety from it in precipitate flight. At half-past 7 o'clock, just as it was growing dark, Chocolate Hill was taken.

There is some dispute, I understand, between the Dublins and Inniskillings and Irish Fusiliers as to which battalion the men first in the Turkish trenches belonged. But does it really matter? Are they not all Irish? Probably men of all the battalions were in the last overwhelming rush. There is no doubt that the Dublins get most of the credit for the feat. The battalion was specially complimented by Headquarters for their heroism and endurance. And well they deserved it. What a baptism of fire it was for those inexperienced Irish lads! And what a confirmation of suffering. Over ten hours of continuous open fighting against machine-guns and artillery, and on a day of scorching heat!

"We have gained a great name for the capture, and for the splendid regiment which I have the honour to command," says Colonel Downing. The General of the Division, Sir Bryan Mahon, speaking of all the battalions, said he had never seen better work by infantry. The fact that the hill was widely known afterwards among the troops in Gallipoli as "Dublin Hill" tells its own tale.

But there is another side to war, and tragic though it be, it must not be ignored, even now that the victory has been won. At the last phase of the fight the hills and ravines were flooded with crimson and purple and yellow, as the sun, in regal splendour, went down into the western sea. Those vivid colours were appropriate to the scene—the raging hearts of the opposing forces of men engaged in a death-grapple, the bitter humiliation of the defeated, and the glory of the victor's triumph. Then the night fell and the darkness was softly lit by a multitude of stars in a cloudless and almost blue sky. It seemed to speak most soothingly to the exhausted men of peace, silence, tranquillity, and the lapping coolness of running streams.

Oh, to be able to get away from this terrific din, this intimate contact with throngs of fellow-men, these devilish instruments of death hurtling through the air—away into loneliness and quietude, only for a little while. But there was no respite. The enemy were still close at hand. It would be dangerous to succumb to the almost irresistible inclination to lie down and sleep. There might come at any moment a counter attack by the enemy. Most of the men, therefore, had to "stand to arms" through the night.

The wounded had also to be attended to. Some of them, totally disabled, had lain where they fell, out on the open sandy plain under the burning sun. They were tortured by thirst. As their comrades in the reserve lines passed them by they could be heard moaning in pain, calling for mother or wife, craving for a drink to moisten their parched mouths. It was forbidden the men to fall out of the lines for the purpose of succouring the wounded. That is the duty of the stretcher-bearers, following behind, and to them, the orders are, it must be left. But the 10th Division were new soldiers, and humanity had not been quite suppressed by discipline in the ranks.

The cry of stricken comrade was irresistible. "Water; a drop of water for the Blessed Virgin's sake," they gasped, with mouths open and eyes starting from their heads, as if startled by the sight of something dreadful. So the men stopped for a minute to put a water-bottle to the lips of a mangled friend; and often the murmured thanks stiffened out into rigidity and silence.

Some of the wounded succeeded in crawling into the rocky gullies. Others lay in the thickets of scrub. They were sheltered from the fierce rays of the sun, but were in danger of the equally terrible fate of death by burning. On every side, throughout the day, fires were blazing. The dry scrub and bushes were set alight by petrol bombs. As a line of the Inniskilling Fusiliers were moving forward behind the Dublins, news was brought to them that there were some wounded men in an extensive patch of scrub that had just caught fire. Signaller John Wilkinson and another member of the battalion plunged into the thick smoke and brought out seven men. There was a burst of shrapnel, and Wilkinson, at the crowning point of his noble display of humanity, was killed.

When the wounded were brought down to the beach for conveyance in lighters and mine-sweepers to the hospital ships anchored about a mile and a half from the shore, the dead awaited reverent disposal. Of all the tasks that had to be performed that night in the starlight this was the pitifulest and most poignant. They were buried side by side, at the foot of Dublin Hill. With the death of these young lads in Gallipoli the light went out in many a home in far away Ireland. Mothers were weeping in sorrow and disconsolation. The country was torn by the conflicting emotions of pride in her sons and grief for their loss. It can be truly said that these young Irishmen gave their lives for civilisation and the freedom of Nationalities.

But the immediate inspiration of their bravery was love of Ireland, and the resolve which sprang from it, that there should be no occasion for a word to be spoken in prejudice of the fighting qualities of the race, of the valour which Irish regiments have displayed on the battlefield at all times and in every clime.

Chapter 7

In the Rest Camp

For five days and nights the Irish troops who took Chocolate Hill, or Dublin Hill, on Saturday, August 7th, lay in the captured Turkish entrenchments before they could be relieved. The men were in the highest spirits over their exploit. But they felt stiff and sore and very, very dirty. They had sand in their clothes, sand in their hair, sand in their eyes, sand in their mouths and nostrils, and their faces and hands were black with the grime of powder and the smoke of the bush fires. And now, upon all that, they had to endure the particular discomforts and hardships which attend a campaign in a dry and torrid land.

The greatest trouble arose from the scarcity of fresh water to mitigate the tropical heat. The wells were few and far between, and being within range of the Turkish guns, were, all of them, constantly shelled. The quantity of water that could be brought to Dublin Hill was totally inadequate to satisfy the demand. The supply was strictly reserved for drinking purposes. Water was too scarce and precious to be wasted on personal ablutions. Better a filthy face than a parched mouth. The dirtiest water was drunk with a relish. A Dublin Fusilier sighed for a draught of the cool and crystal water from the Wicklow hills. "Vartry water," exclaimed another; "I'd be quite content with a bucketful from the Liffey, even off the North Wall."

Food was also hard to get. The commissariat had not yet been evolved out of the disorganisation attendant upon the landing. Under such a scorching sun the eating of the bully-beef in the men's ration bags was unthinkable. So their meals consisted chiefly of biscuits. Then there was the pest of myriads of flies. The Gallipoli flies were having the time of the life-history of their species. Big, ferocious, and insatiable freebooters, they would not be denied joining the troops at their meals and getting the bigger share of the scanty rations into the bargain. The worst affliction of all, however, was the stench of the half-buried and rapidly decomposing corpses in the captured trenches.

During the week which thus elapsed between the capture of Chocolate Hill and the still fiercer series of battles for the heights of Kiretsh Tepe Sirt, to the north, and of Sari Bair, to the south, which were to follow, regiments of the Irish Division were constantly engaged with the enemy on the foothills. Sari Bair was the strongest strategical position of the Turks in this part of Gallipoli. Like Achi Baba, towards the lower end of the Peninsula, it commands the Dardanelles, and especially the great military road along the shore of the Straits, over which the Turks were enabled quickly to send reinforcements of men, munitions, and stores from one point to another.

One Irish Battalion actually gained a point on Sari Bair, from which they caught a glimpse of the Dardanelles. This was the 6th Royal Leinster Regiment of the 29th Brigade, which, as I have already mentioned, was separated from the 10th Division and sent south to co-operate with the forces from the Dominions. On Monday, August 9th, a party of New Zealanders had fought their way up to a ridge of Sari Bair, but were unable to hold it; and as they came retreating down to the place where the 6th Leinsters were in reserve, they shouted: "Fix your bayonets, lads; they're coming over the hill."

Sergeant-Major T. Quinlan, of the Leinsters, lying wounded in hospital, tells the story:

> Everyone ran for his rifle and fixed his bayonet, picked up a *bandolier* or two of ammunition, and charged up the hill like a pack of deers, some without boots or jackets. I bet you the Turks never ran so quick in their lives, for our rifle fire and plunging bayonets, as we charged, were too much for them to stand. We regained the lost position in almost twenty minutes.

And down below them, to the east, they could see that narrow ribbon of water which was the object of all this horrible killing—the Dardanelles glistening in the sun.

The positions held by the Irish regiments around Chocolate Hill were regularly bombarded. On August 9th Lieutenant D.R. Clery, of the 6th Dublins (a fine young Dublin man, very popular as a footballer), was missed. Captain J.J. Carroll, of the battalion, writing to a relative, says:

> I know that he was in the very front of the firing line on August 9th, and one of our men told me on the ship coming home of

Dan's magnificent conduct in carrying man after man out of danger. The man I refer to said that in saving others Dan had seemed utterly regardless of danger to himself.

It was also in one of these outbursts of Turkish artillery that on Tuesday, August 10th, Captain James Cecil Johnston, Adjutant of the 6th Royal Irish Fusiliers, was killed. Before the war Captain Johnston—a County Fermanagh man—was Master of the Horse to the Lord Lieutenant of Ireland. Second Lieutenant R.S. Trimble, who was wounded on the same occasion, describes the incident in a letter to his father, Mr. W. Copeland, of Fermanagh. He was standing between his colonel and his adjutant in conversation when a shell came along. It tore the Colonel's arm to pulp, and though it passed Mr. Trimble, who was slightly out of the line of fire, the concussion of it dashed him violently to the ground, and then exploding, it blew Captain Johnston literally to pieces.

The Irish troops were greatly harassed by the enemy's sharpshooters. These snipers assumed all sorts of disguises and occupied every conceivable hiding place—up in the dwarf oak trees, lying prone in the scrub thickets, down in the rocks of the gullies—so that it was very difficult to spot them. Among those discovered was a peasant woman—the wife of a Turkish soldier—who lived with her old mother and her child in a little house near the Irish lines. She was a fine shot, and apparently confined her attention to stragglers, whose bodies she rifled; for several identification discs and a large sum of money were found in her possession.

The daring and resource of the sharpshooters made them a deadly peril. One man caught in a tree wore a head covering and cloak formed of leaves. Another was found in a khaki uniform, stripped from a dead British soldier. The most perplexing feature of the sniping was that shots often came from the scrub behind. One of the victims of these tactics was Lieutenant E.M. Harper, of the 7th Royal Munster Fusiliers, who, while advancing with his company on August 9th, fell from a rifle shot fired from the rear.

The men of all the Irish battalions suffered from this game of hide-and-seek with death as they lay in the trenches on Dublin Hill. Relief came to them in the early hours of the morning of Friday, August 13th. They left at 1.30, and marched seven miles to a rest camp in a gully of Karakol Dagh running down to the Gulf of Saros, which they reached at 4.30, and a footsore, sleepy, haggard, unkempt, bedraggled, hairy, unwashed, and unshaven crowd they were. They owed this bivouac to the success of the Munsters and Royal Irish Regiment in expelling the Turks from part of the ridge.

When dismissed in the camp every man, officer and private alike, flung himself down in the open where he was and as he was, and had his first undisturbed sleep for a week. In the morning they had the luxurious experience of getting out of their clothes and plunging into the sea. How they revelled in it, after that awful week of forced marches, battle, flies, smoke, stench, and sweat! What laughter and splashing! The shouts and the merry jests and their accents made the scene just such a one as might be witnessed at home in a swimming pool under Howth or Bray Head.

Afterwards the chief desire of all was to write home. As the men lay almost naked on the warm sands, under the scorching sun, many a letter was written to loved ones in Ireland, each telling how he got safely through his baptism of fire—the best news he could possibly send—and what a grand name his battalion had made for itself. Words of comfort and cheer are freely used in such of the letters as have been made public. "I'm happier than ever I was; it's just the sort of life I like." "You can't realise what high spirits I am in when I'm fighting. I feel as if it were all one long exciting Rugger match." "Don't you fret, I'll get through it all right; and even if I fall, sure we'll all meet again in the next world after a few brief years."

To call the camp a "rest" camp is, perhaps, a misnomer. It certainly afforded no refuge from the flies. "There is a fellow near me doing nothing but killing them in millions," writes one of the Dublins. "I had ten in a mug of tea as soon as it was handed to me," says another. This place of shelter was not safe even from the Turkish guns. As many as twenty-five men were knocked out by a shell. But such as the camp was, the stay of the Irish in it was very brief indeed.

On the morning of Sunday, August 15th, they were ordered to take up positions on the ridge above them, and wait for the word to go forward and attack. Though "burned like a red herring, and just as thin and thirsty," as one of the officers of the 7th Dublins said, describing himself and giving a comic picture of them all, they were again in good physical condition. And they had need to be. For they were now assigned a task that was to demand of them more fortitude and resolution and a bigger toll of life than even the taking of Dublin Hill.

It was fortunate, then, that on that very Sunday, August 15th, the great Irish Catholic festival of Our Lady's Day, the Catholic members of the forces were able to reinforce themselves with that sustaining power which the Mass and Holy Communion impart. The services were held by Father W. Murphy, one of the chaplains, under the sheltering hill, in the open air, not only within sound of the guns, but within sight of the bursting shells. It was a rudely improvised altar—a stone laid on trestles, a crucifix, and two candles—and the priest in his khaki service uniform under the vestments.

Many of the men thought of the village chapel at home on that fine Sunday morning. They saw the congregation, all in their Sunday best, gathered outside, and while waiting for the bell to stop, exchanging gossip about the war, and inquiring of one another what was the latest from the Dardanelles, about Tom, and Mike, and Joe. The familiar scene was distinct to their mind's eye, and their beating hearts kept time to the measured tones of the chapel bell. After the Mass they were given the General Absolution.

"It was very impressive," says Sergeant Losty, of the 6th Dublins, "to see Father Murphy standing out on the side of the hill, and all the battalions, with their helmets off and holding up their right hands, saying the Act of Contrition and he absolving them."

At this point it is appropriate that I should refer to the cordial and intimate relations which existed between the Protestant and Catholic chaplains of the 10th Division. An officer of the 30th Brigade, consisting of the 6th and 7th Dublins and the 6th and 7th Munsters, gives the following pleasant picture of Father W. Murphy, Catholic priest, and the Rev. Canon McClean, Church of Ireland minister:—

> This morning Father Murphy said Mass in the trenches, where bullets, etc., were falling like hailstones. Oh! he is a splendid man. The Canon, a dear, good Irishman from Limerick, holds his services side by side with Father Murphy. They put a great spirit into the men, who love them both; in fact, almost adore them. I personally think that nothing I know of is half good enough for those two noble gentlemen. Catholic and Protestant are hand-in-hand, all brought about by the gentleness and undaunted courage displayed by these two splendid soldiers of Christ. Never since the landing has the roar of battle, be it ever so ferocious (and God only knows it is bad here at times), prevented these clergymen from forcing their way into the firing line and attending to our gallant sons of Ireland. Canon McClean is over fifty years of age and Father Murphy is forty-eight. You can imagine them, even though of such an age, never off their feet, as they go to and fro daily to their duties.

Both have been mentioned in Sir Ian Hamilton's despatches. Brigadier-General Nicol, in command of the 30th Brigade, writes in the warmest appreciation of their services. "We of the 30th Brigade are never likely to forget your fearless devotion to your duty," he writes to Canon McClean. "With you and Father Murphy we were indeed fortunate; and it was so nice to see you two the best of friends working hand in hand for the common good. You both set us a fine example." Canon McClean is rector of Rathkeale, County Limerick.

CHAPTER VIII

Fight For Kislah Daght

The objective of the new operations was the last crest of Kiretsh Tepe Sirt, or, as some call it, Kislah Dagh—a continuation of the Karakol Dagh, which the Munsters had taken—beyond which it dips and swings southward. Telegraphing from Alexandria, on August 19th, the special representative of the Press Association says, in the vague way then enjoined by the Censor, "The attacking troops were a Division which was almost wholly Irish, and which had already the capture of Chocolate Hill to its credit." The battalions engaged were, as a fact, entirely Irish.

The Munsters and 6th Dublins, advancing from different sides, commenced the attack about midday. "In two hours we had not advanced twenty yards, so heavy and well directed was the fire of the enemy," writes the Colonel of one of the battalions of the Munsters. "Our second in command, most gallant of officers, was mortally wounded, and many others had fallen. Two companies, however, under cover of some dead ground, had managed to get some 200 yards ahead of the rest of the line, and these companies were now ordered to make a strong demonstration up the hill in order to try to weaken the resistance on the top. Fixing bayonets they rushed up with a wild Irish yell, and so great was their dash that they actually reached the crest.

The Turks, appearing from behind every rock and bush, flung down their arms, and held up their hands. Many prisoners were taken, but the charge did not stop. On it swept along the ridge, and the last peak of all was captured before the enemy could make a stand." Here is an equally spirited account of the final charge, written by a man in the ranks, Private Jack Brisbane, of Buttevant, Co. Cork:

The 6th Munsters charged with the bayonet. You often heard a shout in the hurling field. It would not be in it. They were like so many mad men. Go on, Munsters! Up the Munsters! Even the sailors in the harbour heard it, and climbed up the rigging to try to get a view of it, and shouted themselves hoarse. Up the Munsters! It was grand. I am proud to be one of them. Father Murphy, our priest, said the evening after, when he came to give the boys his blessing: 'Well done, Munsters; you have done well,' so says the General. Father Murphy is a fine priest. His last word is: 'Boys, I'm proud I'm an Irishman.'

Lieutenant Neol E. Drury, of the 6th Dublins, who before the war was a partner in a Dublin firm of papermakers, supplies the following spirited account of the action of his battalion in the operations:—

About 4 o'clock everything seemed ready for a charge, so 'Fix bayonets' was the order, and, by Jove, the sight in the sun was ripping. There were several warships lying along the font of the ridge, and all the crews were lining the decks watching the fight. When the flash of the bayonets showed up in the sun a tremendous cheer came up to us. 'Cheer, oh! the Dubs!' Everyone yelled like mad, and charged up the remaining piece of ground as if it had been level. The bhoys put it across the Turks properly, and I can tell you there were not many shining bayonets when we finished. We drove them off the ridge, helter-skelter, and they fairly bunked, throwing away rifles and equipment wholesale. When we got to the top we had five machine-guns playing on them as they ran down the other side, and as our chaps watched them from the summit they cheered and waved their helmets like mad, all the other troops back along the ridge and the ships' crews joining in.

"Throughout the night the enemy, strongly reinforced, delivered counter-attacks, one after another," writes the same commanding officer of the Munsters. "The fighting was severe and bloody, but we held on, and the morning found us still in possession of what we had gained, though our losses had been terribly heavy." He goes on:

I wish I could retail half the acts of individual heroism performed during those hours—how one sergeant and one corporal, the former I believe had been destined for the priesthood, the latter only a boy, threw back the enemy's hand grenades before they could burst one after another, and failing these threw large stones. Alas! before morning they had both paid the penalty of their gallantry. In the morning we were relieved, but the roll call was a sad revelation. My observer, who had been my groom when we had our horses, shot through the body in the charge, refused to be removed until the doctor promised him that he would personally tell me that he was wounded, fearing that I might think he had not followed me. The doctor faithfully fulfilled his promise, though it cost him a long walk at night. Such was the spirit of all ranks. Other units, of course, were equally gallant.

An extract from another letter must be given here, as it reveals one of the little tragedies of war, and the endurance and resolution of the men. Sergeant Gallagher, of D company of the Inniskillings, which was transferred to the Munsters and went into action with them, got a bullet in his right eye and was made stone blind. "I have a confession to make," he writes from hospital to the recruiting officer at Strabane, "I deceived you when you enlisted me. I had a glass eye, and now I have lost the other. I hope to be back in Strabane soon, but I shall never see the glen again, and watch the trout leaping behind the bridge. But I am happy, and we showed these Turks what Irishmen can do. No matter what happens I have done my bit, and I would not exchange with the best man at home."

The casualties among the other units were equally severe. On Sunday, late in the afternoon, the 7th Dublins got the word to push on to the crest of the hill and relieve the battalions that had captured it. They advanced in the mode of progression which alone was possible—slowly, in single file, crawling through the thick prickly scrub, sinking in the sand, stumbling over the rocks. It was laborious and exhausting work. All the time they were harassed by snipers. On the way up their commanding officer, Colonel Downing, was twice hit, and, being disabled, had to be left behind. Gaining the top of the hill, they relieved the Munsters and the 6th Dublins, and entrenched themselves as best they could, under the ridge, on the near side by working hard throughout the night.

At dawn on Monday morning, weary as they were from unremitting toil and want of sleep, they had to meet an attack by a large force of bomb throwers and riflemen. The Turks were at least three to one. Under cover of the night they had crept up the far side of the hill; and hiding, just under the ridge, behind rocks and bushes, hurled hand grenades across the twenty yards of rocky summit. The Dublins could not answer back. Rifle fire was of little use against a concealed enemy.

There were no hand grenades. A few of the Turkish bombs which had not exploded, being wrongly timed, were hurled back, their long fuses still alight. Numbers of the Dublins were falling, wounded or killed. Major Harrison decided to try the effect of a bayonet charge.

This was the action which, at the moment, was just what the men most desired. For them it was maddening to be held behind entrenchments whence they were unable to exchange blow for blow—and more—with those who were dealing death to their ranks. They were aflame with that bloodthirsty rage of men in battle to get at the throats of their opponents, to crush them, if need be to tear them to pieces. So when the order to charge was given the Dublins sprang up into the open.

The first line was led by Captain Poole Hickman, of D company, who came of a well-known Clare family and was a barrister by profession. He never returned from the charge. As the Dublins appeared at the summit there was a splutter of fire along the opposite ridge, which was lined by Turkish marksmen. The men wavered and swayed uncertainly for a minute or two before the shower of bullets. Hickman was well in front, waving his revolver and shouting "On, Dublins!" That was the last that was seen of him alive.

The Turks made a horrid din, shouting and shrieking, as if further to intimidate their antagonists. But the Irish can yell, too, and wild were their outcries as with fixed bayonets or clubbed rifles they scrambled across the rocky summit. Many of them did not go far. As they dropped they lay strangely quiet in clumsy attitudes. Among them was their superb leader, Major Harrison. Others passed scathless over the open ground, only to disappear for ever behind the ridge. These charges and hand-to-hand fights commenced about seven o'clock. The Turks fought with tenacity. It was eleven o'clock before they gave way to the repeated Irish onslaughts.

During those four hours magnificent courage and daring were shown by the officers of the 7th Dublins. Many a young Irishman of brilliant promise was lost that day. They led their companies into the fray and were the first to fall. Captain Michael FitzGibbon, a law student, and son of Mr. John FitzGibbon, the Nationalist M.P., Captain R.P. Tobin, son of Surgeon Tobin, of Dublin—a gallant youth of twenty-one—and Second Lieutenant Edward Weatherill, an engineer, were killed. They were of priceless worth to their country and the beloved of their family circles.

Major M. Lonsdale, of the 7th Dublins, writing to Mr. FitzGibbon, of the death of his son, says he died gallantly, leading part of A company. His death was instantaneous. All the other officers belonging to his company were also killed. "It was a desperate fight," adds Major Lonsdale, "and I do not think any but Irish soldiers could have stood up against the losses we suffered that Sunday and Monday." Lieutenant Ernest Hamilton, of D company, writing to Surgeon Tobin, states that when Harrison and Hickman fell Captain Tobin took command of the company.

"Our men at this time," he says, "were getting badly knocked down. Paddy and I took up a position on the top of the knoll, and from there he controlled the fire and steadied the men. Such gallantry and coolness I have never witnessed. We fought like demons against three times our numbers, and held on, too. Our knoll came in for at least six attacks. During one of these your son was killed, shot through the head. He caught me by the shoulder, and when I turned round he had passed away. I carried him back some distance and placed him under shelter, but had to get back to my position to try to follow his magnificent example. His death affected the men so much that I thought all was finished. They fought for another hour as they never fought before. Then they were relieved."

Similar scenes were being enacted in other parts of the field of operations. The casualties among the officers of all the Irish regiments engaged were very heavy. Captain W.R. Richards, of the 6th Dublins, a Dublin solicitor, and Lieutenant J.J. Doyle, an engineering student of the National University, were killed. So, too, was Lieutenant W.C. Nesbitt, of the same regiment. Before he enlisted Mr. Nesbitt was in the service of the Alliance Gas Company, Dublin. His company had captured a ridge when he was shot in the side. Some of his men ran to his aid and raised him up. At the same instant he was struck a second time and killed.

Among the officers of other regiments who fell was Second Lieutenant Hugh Maurice MacDermot, 6th Irish Fusiliers, eldest son of The MacDermot of Coolavin, Co. Sligo. Writing of the officers of the 5th Irish Regiment, Father Peter O'Farrell, chaplain to the battalion, says: "Nothing could excel, if anything could equal, the conduct of the company and platoon commanders on the 16th. Some stood on the ridge waving their revolvers and pointing out the enemy to their men. Of course they sacrificed their lives, for scarcely a man appeared over the ridge but went down to the well-directed fire of the Turkish snipers. These brilliant men, however, feared nothing. They even sang

Irish tunes and shouted 'Up, Tip,' to encourage the Irish soldiers."

Many gaps were made that day in Irish sporting and professional circles. Only a few more names of the dead can be given out of the many who showed splendid devotion to duty and supreme self-sacrifice: Captain Dillon Preston, of the 6th Dublin Fusiliers; Captain George Grant Duggan, of the 5th Irish Fusiliers; Lieutenant J.R. Duggan, of the 5th Irish Regiment. The 7th Munster Fusiliers lost on August 16th alone four captains and two subalterns killed out of the thirteen officers who had survived the previous engagements.

Among them were two Dublin men—Captain John V. Dunne, solicitor, and Lieutenant Kevin O'Duffy. Lieutenant Ernest M. Harper, of the same battalion, who was also killed, was a demonstrator in chemistry in Queen's University, Belfast. Lieutenant H.H. McCormac, 5th Irish Fusiliers, killed, was on the clerical staff at the Limerick offices of Guinness, the brewers. The famous D company of the 7th Dublins, led by Captain Poole Hickman and Captain Tobin, was practically wiped out. It was composed altogether of young men distinguished in football and cricket and other forms of sport. Many of them had ample private means, all belonged to the professional middle class of Dublin, and they felt it a high honour to serve in the rank and file of the Army.

Sir Bryan Mahon, the General in command of the 10th Division, sent a message to his troops saying that Ireland should be proud to own such soldiers. Ireland, indeed, is proud, though what happened was no more than what she expected. When the 7th Dublins were congratulated upon the stand they had made, their answer was: "And what the blank, blank, did you think we would do?" But with all her exultation in the valour of her sons, Ireland cannot close her ears to the cry of the Colonel of the 7th Munsters on seeing the few officers who returned from the fray: "My poor boys! My poor boys!"

There was a continuous series of desperate fights for the command of Sari Bair until the end of August. On the 21st of the month a general offensive took place on a grand scale, in which the forces of all nationalities that landed at Suvla Bay were engaged. To strengthen the attack of these inexperienced and unseasoned but most gallant troops the veteran 29th Division was brought up from Cape Helles. In that Division were the survivors of the 1st Regular battalions of the Dublins, Munsters and Inniskillings who took part in that most frightful and glorious episode of the campaign—the landing at Sedd-el-Bahr on April 25th, under the murderous fire of the Turkish batteries stationed on the cliffs.

The new Irish battalions again distinguished themselves in the battle of August 21st. The 5th Connaught Rangers made a famous charge for which they were specially thanked by the Australian Commander of their Division. "The Rangers," writes an officer of the battalion, "issued out to attack and capture the Kabak Kuzu wells and the Turkish trenches in the neighbourhood. It did not take them long. The men poured out from a gap in the line, shook out to four paces interval, and with a cheer carried all before them, bayoneting all the Turks in the trenches, capturing the wells, and even capturing some ground on the Kaiajik Aghala. All that night the position was consolidated, and in the morning was still held by the Rangers.

The next day we were thanked by three General Officers and congratulated on the magnificent charge." The 7th Dublins had to advance across an open plain under the heights of Sari Bair. An Australian soldier who stood on a neighbouring hill told me that while English battalions cautiously crossed in a series of rushes—falling flat on their stomachs at each outburst of the Turkish guns—the Dublins made their way over the uneven, hillocky ground at a run. To move slowly, with proper caution, would be torture to their Irish nature, impatient and ardent, in such circumstances.

One of the old Regular battalions in the 29th Division, the 1st Inniskillings, also greatly added to their renown by their dauntless resolution on August 21st. The battalion pushed up to the top of Hill 70, or Scimitar Hill, but were unable to maintain their position, owing, as the Brigadier-General of their Brigade states, "to the unavoidably inadequate artillery support and complete preparedness on the part of the enemy, resulting in heavy cross-fire from shrapnel, machine-guns and rifles."

Again they climbed the hill and again were driven back. They made a third charge up the hill, and after a desperate struggle were compelled once more to yield ground that was now thickly strewn with their dying and dead. The Brigadier-General mentions that the Inniskillings undertook the two further assaults entirely on their own initiative. He adds: "Had there been any appreciable number of survivors in the battalion, and had Captain Pike been spared to lead them for a fourth time, they would have continued their efforts to secure complete possession of the hill."

The operations failed in their main purpose. Sari Bair remained in the possession of the Turks. Mistakes made by some of the Generals of

Divisions are said, by Sir Ian Hamilton, the Commander-in-Chief, to have been largely to blame for things going wrong. But the fighting was not altogether barren of results. The most desperate engagements in the last days of August had for their object the capture of Hill 60, close to Sari Bair. An attack by the 5th Connaught Rangers on August 29th secured its possession.

The battalion was again congratulated on its gallantry by three different General Officers. One of them, General Sir A.J. Godley, in command of the New Zealanders, sent the following message to Colonel Jourdaine, of the 5th Connaughts:—

> Heartiest congratulations from the New Zealand and Australian Division on your brilliant achievement this evening, which is a fitting sequel to the capture of Kabak Kuzu wells, and will go down to history among the finest feats of your distinguished regiment. Personally as an Irishman who has served in two Irish regiments it gives me the greatest pride and pleasure that the regiment should have performed such gallant deeds under my command. Stick to what you have got and consolidate.

But all was in vain. Gallipoli had to be abandoned. The British withdrew from the Peninsula in January, 1916. The cost of the invasion in men, killed, wounded and missing, was 114,555. The casualties in the 10th Irish Division were cruel. At least a third of the forces were killed, disabled, or invalided by bullets, shells and dysentery.

Gallipoli had become a place of shadows and phantoms to the 10th Irish Division. As they looked back upon it they could not but think of the maelstrom of thick and prickly scrub, yielding sand, rocky defiles, and steep hills of that roadless country; of strong Turkish entrenchments, the continuous roar of guns, bullets, shells, concealed snipers; of broiling heat, sweat, thirst, tormenting flies, lack of water, and dysentery, into which they were plunged on August 7th; of scrambling and bloody fighting; and of the want of foresight and imagination in their high commanders that followed. It was a soldiers' campaign, in which the bayonet and the man behind it counted for everything, and the brains of the generals—if indeed there were any—for nothing. The whole network of memories made a horrid nightmare of confusion, agony, and sacrifice of life unparalleled in the history of the British Army, relieved only—but how magnificently relieved—by the endurance and gallantry of the troops, unequalled and unsurpassable.

Yet the 10th Division were loth to leave that dread Peninsula, which, like a fearful monster, had devoured the young men of Ireland.

They were sorry to go, because the purpose of the campaign was unachieved; still more sorry to part from their dead comrades. Because of those dead Gallipoli will ever be to the Irish race a place of glorious pride and sorrow. Well may that huddled heap of hills between Suvla Bay and Sari Bair be haunted by the wraith of Irish tragedy and grief; well may the wailing cry of the banshee be ever heard there.

CHAPTER 9

For Cross and Crown

In which mood do soldiers generally go into battle—devotional or profane? An observer of authority, Mr. J.H. Morgan, professor of constitutional history at University College, London, who had a long stay at the Front, in France and Flanders on Government duty, commits himself to the curious statement that most men go into action, not ejaculating prayers, but swearing out aloud. However that may be as regards the non-religious soldier, it certainly is not true of the Catholic Irish soldier.

By temperament and training the average Irish soldier, like most of his race, is profoundly religious at all times, and the experiences of the chaplains to the Catholic Irish regiments show that at no time is the Irish soldier more under a constant and reverent sense of the nearness of the unseen Powers, and his absolute dependence upon them, than at the awful moment when, in the plenitude of his youth and physical strength, he is confronted by the prospect of sudden death or bodily mutilation.

Of course, if a soldier does swear on the battlefield, that circumstance must not necessarily be accepted as proof either that he is destitute of religious feelings and principles, or that there is any thought of impiety in his mind. Most likely the swearing is done quite unconsciously. At a time when the mental faculties are distraught and the tension on the central nervous system reaches almost to the breaking-point, it is probable that men no more know what they say than they do when they are under an anæsthetic; and that, in the one state as in the other, incongruous expressions—wholly inconsistent with the character of the patient—come to the lips from the deeps of subconsciousness.

There is nothing like constant nearness to death to make men generally turn their thoughts to things serious and solemn. The experiences of Catholic chaplains tell how widely the sense of religion—the vanity of earthly concerns, the importance of eternity, the wish to be at peace with God—has been stirred by the war even in breasts that probably had not harboured in the years of peace a thought that there was any other world but this. Ah, the eagerness of the Irish Catholic soldiers to have sin washed away by confession and the absolving words of the priest!

The Irish are the most religious soldiers in the British Army; and it is because they are religious that they rank so high among the most brave. The two characteristics, religious fervour and fearlessness of danger, have always been very closely allied. In the average Irishman there is a blend of piety and militancy which makes him an effective soldier. Largely for the reason that he is a praying man, the Irish Catholic soldier is a fine fighting man. His religion gives him fortitude in circumstances of unmitigated horror, resignation to face the chances of being mangled or killed at the call of duty; and from this ease of mind spring that bravery and resolution in action which are the most essential characteristics of the soldier.

In order that the Catholic soldier may thus show himself at his best, it is necessary that he should have ready access to the rites of the Church. He wants the priest to be near him, and though the Catholic army chaplains appointed for active service are comparatively few, though their movements are frequently impeded by the ever-changing developments in the military situation, the priest is usually close at hand at his service. Thus the Irish Catholic soldier goes into battle stimulated by the services of his chaplain, praying that God may bring him safely through, or for a merciful judgment should he fall.

Extraordinarily varied and trying as have been the experiences of the priesthood in the mission-field, it is probable that never has it been subjected to so severe a trial of nerve and endurance on its physical side as it is in the present War of Nations. As to the kind of men best suited for the service, the Rev. William Forrest, an Irish Catholic chaplain himself, writes:—

> Priests between thirty and forty, not afraid of some rough and tumble, with, perhaps, an adventurous vein in their composition, and with plenty of zeal and sympathy, would be the most suitable—riders and good horse-masters rather than ponderous theologians and professors, though, indeed, these would have much to learn, and would very greatly profit, by their experience.

Certainly the record of Catholic army chaplains shines gloriously for its zeal, self-sacrifice, and heroism; and its sanctifying light illumines the awful tragedy of suffering and woe that has befallen the human race.

The Catholic chaplain has also various duties to perform when his men are resting in billets, on guard in the lines of communication, or lying wounded or ill in the base hospitals. He goes about in khaki, like the other officers of the battalion to which he is attached, save that he wears the Roman collar and black patches on his shoulder straps. His equipment or kit is usually heavy. It contains the stone for the altar, the vestments, the sacred vessels, the candles, the crucifix, and other requisites for the Mass. On his person he always carries the Holy Oils and the Viaticum for the last sacrament of all, when the soul of the mortally wounded soldier is about to take flight into the eternal.

Services are held in all sorts of places and on every possible occasion. Lieutenant C. Mowlan, medical officer to the 1st Irish Fusiliers, writes:—"We have Mass out in the open, and it is most gratifying to see the long line of men waiting for confession, and at Mass the devotion with which they attend, and tell the beads of our Blessed Lady, a devotion so dear for many reasons, historical as well as devotional, to the heart of the Catholic Irishman. A large crowd attended Communion." A door laid upon two trestles or a packing-case often serves as an altar, with the two burning candles, and a few hastily gathered evergreens for decorations.

Mass is frequently celebrated in the very early hours of the morning before the dawn begins to creep into the sky. And a strange and wonderful spectacle it is! Black darkness, save for the two candles; the priest offering up the Sacrifice at the rudely improvised altar; the soldiers, each with his rifle, and weighed down with his kit and ammunition, grimed with the mud of the trenches and the smoke of battle, kneeling in a circle round the light. They receive the final Blessing with bowed heads, then, crossing themselves, they stand up for the last Gospel, their haggard and unshaven faces all aglow with religious exaltation.

But perhaps the most moving and inspiring scene of all is that of giving the General Absolution to a battalion ordered to advance immediately into action. Father Peal, S.J., of the Connaught Rangers, enables us vividly to see it in the mind's eye. The regiment were in billets in Bethune when one winter's morning at three o'clock they received instructions to make an attack. Before the men left, Father

Peal got the colonel's permission to speak to them. They were drawn up in a large square behind a secular school, called *Collège de Jeunes Filles*, when their chaplain, mounting the steps of the porch, thus addressed them in the dark:

Rangers, once again at the bidding of our King and country you are going to face the enemy. Before you go, turn to God and ask of Him pardon for your sins. Repeat the act of contrition after me." Then the square resounded with the fervent ejaculations of the men. "In the name of the Father, the Son, and the Holy Ghost. Oh, my God, I am heartily sorry for having offended Thee. I detest my sins most sincerely, because they are displeasing to Thee, my God, who art most worthy of all my love; and I promise never to offend Thee again.

"I shall now," says the priest, "give you Absolution in God's name. '*Dominus noster Jesus Christus vos absolvat et ego auctoritate Ipsius vos absolvo a peccatis vestris, in nomine Patris et Filii et Spiritus Sancti.* Amen.' May God Almighty, Father, Son, and Holy Ghost, bless you and lead you to victory. Amen." As the priest blessed them, the men again made the sign of the Cross. No wonder that men of such deep faith and so heartened by the services of their chaplains should fight valiantly.

The tireless care and solicitude of the Catholic chaplain for his men is seen in the fine record, during a long and arduous campaign, of Father Francis Gleeson, of the 2nd Munster Fusiliers, who has been in Flanders and France since the outbreak of the war. If you meet a man of the 2nd Munsters, just mention the name of Father Gleeson, and see how his face lights up.

"Father Gleeson, is it!" exclaimed one whom I encountered among the wounded at a London hospital. "He's a warrior and no mistake. There's no man at the Front more brave or cooler. Why, it is in the hottest place up in the firing line he do be to give comfort to the boys that are dying."

"And, do you know," he added with a laugh, as he recalled the chaplain's playful and sportive ways, "Father Gleeson brought us mouth-organs, and showed that he could play 'Tipperary' with the best of us."

Another man described a meeting with Father Gleeson in a village close to the first line of trenches, where the chaplain was waiting to attend to the wounded. "It got so hot with stray bullets that he gave me absolution as I stood in the street of the ruined village. It was very dramatic, I covered with mud and standing bareheaded, and he blessing me. I'll never forget it."

I gathered, too, that Father Gleeson is the counsellor of the battalion as well as its chaplain. The men go to him with their temporal troubles of all kinds, and never fail in getting sympathy, guidance, and help.

The chaplains of all denominations are equally devoted. But the Catholic priest has a special impulse to self-sacrificing duty for two reasons—first, the desire that Catholics have to die shriven and anointed; and the softening of the bereavement of parents and relations which comes from the knowledge that Paddy, Jamsie, Joe, or Mike had been to his duty before the battle, or had the priest with him when he died. Accordingly, no consideration of danger to himself will deter the Catholic chaplain from going into the firing line to administer the last rites. In the circumstances, it was to be expected that though the chaplains of all the denominations are zealous and brave in the discharge of their sacred duties, the first chaplain of any denomination to give his life for his men should be an Irish priest, Father Finn, of the 1st Royal Dublin Fusiliers, who fell in Gallipoli.

A Tipperary man, serving on the English Mission in the Province of Liverpool, Father Finn joined the 1st Dublins on their arrival in England from India for active service, in November, 1914. The Dublins, with the 1st Munster Fusiliers, took part, as I have already described, in the first landing of British troops on the Peninsula, at Sedd-el-Bahr, on Sunday, April 25th, 1915. On the Saturday morning Father Finn heard the confessions of the men on board the transport, off Tenedos, said Mass, and gave Holy Communion. Then on Sunday morning he asked permission of the commanding officer of the battalion to go ashore with the men.

Colonel Rooth tried to persuade him to remain on the transport, where he could give his services to such of the wounded as were brought back. "You are foolish to go; it means death," said the officer. "The priest's place is beside the dying soldier; I must go," was Father Finn's decisive reply. For these and other particulars of the gallant action of the priest, I am mainly indebted to the Rev. H.C. Foster, Church of England naval chaplain, who was in one of the warships engaged in the bombardment of the Peninsula at the landing, and highly esteemed Father Finn as a friend.

Father Finn left the transport for the shore in the same boat as the colonel. When the boats crowded with the Dublins got close to the beach a hail of shrapnel, machine-gun fire, and rifle fire was showered upon them by the Turks, hidden among the rocks and ragged brushwood on the heights. Numbers of the Dublins were killed or wounded, and either tumbled into the water or dropped on reaching the beach.

This fearful spectacle was Father Finn's first experience of the savagery of war. It terribly upset him. He at once jumped out of the boat and went to the assistance of the bleeding and struggling men. Then he was hit himself. By the time he had waded to the beach his clothing was riddled with shot. Yet disabled as he was, and in spite also of the great pain he must have been suffering, he crawled about the beach, affording consolation to the dying Dublins. I have been told that to give the absolution he had to hold up his injured right arm with his left.

It was while he was in the act of thus blessing one of his men that his skull was broken by a piece of shrapnel. The last thought of Father Finn was for the Dublins. His orderly says that in a brief moment of consciousness he asked: "Are our fellows winning?" Amid the thunder of the guns on sea and land his soul soon passed away. He was buried on the beach where he died, and the grave was marked by a cross, made out of an ammunition box, with the inscription—

To the memory of the Rev. Capt. Finn.

Gallipoli is classic ground. It is consecrated by the achievements of the ancient Greeks over the Persian hordes at the dawn of Western civilisation. It is now further hallowed as the grave and monument of that warrior priest, Father Finn, and the gallant Dublins and Munsters.

The next Catholic chaplain to lose his life on active service was Father John Gwynn, S.J., of the 1st Irish Guards, who was killed in the trenches near Vermelles on October 11th, 1915. Born at Youghal, and reared in Galway, Father Gwynn entered the Society of Jesus in 1884. At the outbreak of the war he was one of the governing body of University College, Dublin, and volunteering for active service he was attached, the first week of November, 1914, to the Irish Guards, as their first war chaplain. A big, handsome man, and soldierly in appearance, Father Gwynn was fitting in every way to be chaplain to so splendid and almost wholly Catholic body of Irishmen as the Irish Guards. His experiences at the Front—the devotion he showed to his duties and the risks he ran—prove more than the truth of the old saying that every Irishman is born either a soldier or a monk, for they establish that often he is born both.

Father Gwynn was the first chaplain of any denomination attached to the British Expeditionary Force to be wounded. That was during the memorable engagement at Cuinchy, on February 1st, 1915, when Michael O'Leary won the Victoria Cross. What a moving picture of piety it presents! The task of the Irish was to retake positions in the brickfields captured by the Germans from the Coldstream Guards. Eager to retrieve the position the Coldstreams first advanced, but being met by a heavy fire from the enemy, they showed signs of wavering. Then a company of the Irish Guards were ordered out. They had received absolution and Communion behind the trenches, a few days before, from Father Gwynn, and their chaplain was still with them at the supreme moment.

Now, before advancing, they knelt in silent prayer for a minute. Then, each man making the sign of the Cross, they sprang to their feet, and dashing in wide open order across the exposed ground, swept by the enemy's fire, they hunted the Germans from the brick-fields. We all know that when the story of Michael O'Leary's achievement that day became known, half the world stood up bare-headed in acknowledgment of his gallantry. I have been told that the incident which was most talked of from end to end of the British lines was that of the Guardsmen kneeling down in prayer before the charge. Nothing like it ever occurred before.

At least it is unprecedented in the history of the English Army of modern times. Those who saw them say that, as the Irish Guards dashed across the plain, they had an expression of absolute happiness and joy on their faces. Surely an episode that will live in the crowded annals of this war. It was then that Father Gwynn was wounded. He said the last thing he remembered was seeing the Irish Guards get to the top of their trench when a lurid blaze seemed to flash into his eyes with a deafening crash. He was hurled back five yards or so and lay unconscious for some minutes. When he came to he felt his face all streaming with blood and his leg paining him. He was suffocated, too, with a thick, warmy, vile gas, which came from the shell.

"A doctor bandaged me up," he goes on, "and I found I was not so bad—splinters of the shell just grazed my face, cutting it; a bit, too, struck me an inch or so above the knee and lodged inside, but in an hour's time, when everything was washed and bandaged, I was able to join and give Extreme Unction to a poor Irish Guardsman who had been badly hit."

I have before me a number of letters written by Father Gwynn. They are all most interesting. In every one of them he has something to say in praise of the Catholicity and valour of the Irish Guards.

"We have to have Mass in a field," he writes in one letter, "the Irish Guards are nearly all Catholics, and we are at present the strongest battalion in the Guards' Brigade. The men then sing hymns at Mass, and it is fine to hear nearly a thousand men singing out in the open at the top of their voices. You have no idea what a splendid battalion the Irish Guards are! You have Sergeant Mike O'Leary, V.C., with you. I often have a chat with him when he comes to see me. But do you know that there are plenty of men in the Irish Guards who have done as bravely as O'Leary, and there's never a word about it." In another letter, written a few weeks before his death, he says:—

> It would have done your heart good to hear them last night in the little village church where we are just for the moment, singing the '*O Salutaris,*' '*Tantum Ergo,*' 'Look Down, O Mother Mary,' and at the end the 'Hail Glorious St. Patrick.' A grenadier officer who happened to be present, having ridden over from where the Grenadiers are, said it was worth coming ten miles to hear. I feared for the roof of the church, especially when they came to the last verse of the hymn to St. Patrick.

Throughout the morning of the day he received his mortal wound, Father Gwynn had had a most arduous and anxious time in the trenches. It was during the fighting round Hill 70, after the Battle of Loos. An Irish Guardsman writes:—

> I saw him just before he died. Shrapnel and bullets were being showered upon us in all directions. Hundreds of our lads dropped. Father Gwynn was undismayed. He seemed to be all over the place trying to give the Last Sacrament to the dying. Once I thought he was buried alive, for a shell exploded within a few yards of where he was, and the next moment I saw nothing but a great heap of earth. The plight of the wounded concealed beneath was harrowing. Out of the ground came cries of 'Father, Father, Father,' from those who were in their death agonies. Then as if by a miracle Father Gwynn was seen to fight his way through the earth. He must have been severely injured, but he went on blessing the wounded and hearing their confessions. The last I saw of him was kneeling by the side of a

German soldier. It was a scene to make you cry.

Shortly after this scene Father Gwynn was at luncheon with four other officers in the Headquarters' dugout when a German shell landed in the doorway and burst. Captain Lord Desmond FitzGerald (brother of the Duke of Leinster) was slightly hit. Colonel Madden was so severely wounded that he died some days afterwards. Father Gwynn received as many as eight wounds. One piece of the shell entered his back and pierced one of his lungs. He was sent to hospital at Bethune, and died there the next morning. In the Bethune cemetery his grave is marked by a marble monument which bears these two inscriptions:—

R.I.P.
REV. FATHER JOHN GWYNN, S.J.
Attached to the
1st Irish Guards.
He Died at Bethune on October 12th, 1915, from
Wounds Received in Action near Vermelles
on October 11th, 1915.
Aged 49 years.
This Monument has been erected by all Ranks of the 1st Bat. Irish Guards in grateful Remembrance of their Beloved Chaplain, Father Gwynn, who was with them on Active Service for nearly twelve months from Nov., 1914, until his death, and shared with unfailing devotion all their trials and hardships.

The wonder, indeed, is that many more Catholic chaplains have not been killed. Father James Stack, of the Redemptorist Order—a County Limerick man—had a narrow escape from being killed by German rifle fire as he was attending to a dying Irish soldier between the opposing lines. The soldier was heard in the British trenches calling for a priest. Father Stack crept out to him, heard his confession, anointed him, and lay by his side praying until he passed away. While he was engaged on this sublime errand of mercy the priest was fired on by the Germans, but he got back unhurt. He was mentioned in Sir John French's valedictory despatch.

A dramatic story is also told of another dauntless Catholic chaplain. One bitter winter's night eight men left a British trench to bomb the Germans. None of them returned. Their comrades wore consumed with anxiety as to their fate. Were they prisoners, were they dead, or were they lying wounded in the mud and the slush? The Catholic chaplain of the battalion volunteered to go out in front and try to learn what had become of them. After some hesitation his request was granted.

"Donning his surplice and with a crucifix in his hand the priest proceeded down one of the saps and climbed out into the open," writes a staff correspondent of the *Central News at the Front*.

With their eyes glued to periscopes, the British line watched him anxiously as he proceeded slowly towards the German lines. Not a shot was fired by the enemy. After a while the chaplain was seen to stop and bend down near the German wire entanglements. He knelt in prayer. Then with the same calm step he returned to his own lines. He had four identity discs in his hand, and reported that the Germans had held up four khaki caps on their rifles, indicating that the other four were prisoners in their hands.

Father J. Fahey, a Tipperary man, made a lasting reputation among the Dominion Forces in Gallipoli by his services as chaplain to the 11th Australian Battalion. The Archbishop of Perth (Australia) got a letter from an officer in Gallipoli which said: "You are to be congratulated for sending us such an admirable chaplain as Father Fahey. He is the idol of the 11th Battalion, and everyone, irrespective of creed, has a good word to say for him." Dr. McWhae, one of the medical officers, puts in a different way the estimation in which Father Fahey is held:

He is one of the finest fellows in the world, and everybody swears by him. He landed at Gallipoli with the covering party, and spends his time in the trenches.

Before the troops left Lemnos Island for the first landing at Anzac on April 25th, 1915, the Brigadier went round and told the chaplains of all denominations that they could go aboard the hospital ships if they wished. Father Fahey and Father McMenamin, a chaplain with the New Zealand Forces, said they would go in the transports with the men and also accompany them into the trenches. And, sure enough, these two priests were the first of the chaplains in the firing line looking after their men.

"The '*Padre*,' as he is called by his battalion," writes the officer in his letter to the Archbishop of Perth, "fills in his spare time carrying up provisions to the men at the front, and helps the wounded back, and I can tell you he is not afraid to go where the bullets fall pretty thickly," Father Fahey has done more in the way of utilising his spare time—he has led the men in a charge against the Turkish entrenchments. On an occasion when all the officers had been killed or disabled he called on the remnants of the company, "Follow me, and though I have only a stick, you can give the Turks some Western Australian cold steel."

Father Fahey himself gives the following racy account of the discomforts which attended the discharge of his duties in Gallipoli:—

> I have had my clothes and boots off only once during the past month. I had a wash twice, and one shave, so I can assure you I do not look a thing of beauty. I am cultivating a beard, and in another month I expect to look as fierce as a Bedouin chief. Water is scarce; we only get enough to drink and cook, but none to wash; so we are not too clean. I have had several narrow escapes, so many, in fact, that I wonder why I am still alive. I had four bullets in my pack, one through a jam tin out of which I was eating, which spoiled the jam and made me very wild. One through my water-bottle; one through a tobacco-tin in my pocket; one took the epaulette off my tunic, and once I had nineteen shrapnel bullets through a waterproof sheet on which I was lying only a few minutes previously. I have lost count of the shells that nearly accounted for me; I hardly expect to get through the business alive, but seeing that I have been lucky so far I may.

The last I heard of Father Fahey was that he was lying wounded in an hospital at Malta. Writing of his work as a priest, he says:

> I have heard confessions in all kinds of weird places, with the shrapnel bursting overhead and bullets whizzing around. I go along the trenches every day in case anyone might want to see me. It is all so strange and uncanny. Passing along the trenches, a soldier with his rifle through a loophole and one eye on the enemy may call me to hear his confession; while it is being done the bullets are plopping into the sandbags of the parapet a few inches away. It is consoling and satisfactory work, if a little dangerous.

The part of the chaplain's work that is most harrowing to him personally, but most consoling to those whom he serves, is that of ministering to the wounded at the hospital clearing stations nearest to the firing line.

"Sometimes when I hold them up on the stretcher to try to get them to take a drink," writes Father L.J. Stafford, one of the chaplains to the 10th Irish Division in Gallipoli, "I think that Christ must have foreseen this awful slaughter and borne it in His Passion as part of the sorrows of mankind, and I try to associate myself with the feelings of His Virgin Mother." The acts and the thoughts of the priest blend together in perfect harmony like the words and music of an inspired hymn to the Almighty. Well might Father Stafford add: "I am in great peril, but doing my duty fearlessly. Could man wish for more?"

As the priest kneels down by these dying Irish youths he receives many last messages to send to the loved ones at home, a sacred trust which he is most scrupulous faithfully to discharge. There are thousands of mothers in Ireland grieving for darling sons lying mouldering in Flanders, France, and Gallipoli. If anything can ease the gnawing pain at the heart of these bereaved mothers, it surely must be the receipt of one of those beautifully sympathetic and healing letters which they receive from the Irish Catholic chaplains. I have had the privilege of reading numbers of them, and happily in none have I come upon any heroics about the nobility of the youth's self-sacrifice and the grandeur of the cause for which he died. To the Irish Catholic mother such phrases bring no consolation. His death tells her that her son has done his duty; that is enough; and her sole concern is with his eternal salvation. It is on this point that the chaplain is at pains to reassure her.

> I saw him last at 7.30 p.m. on July 14th. He was very exhausted, and I could see that he would not last long. He tried to give me his mother's address, but failed. All he could say was: 'Not weep. With God.' I told him I should tell his mother not to weep because he would be with God, and he shook his head in consent. He then said: 'Goodbye, Father. God bless you.'

So does Father Felix Couturier, O.P., describe the death in hospital at Alexandria of Lance-Corporal Wilkerson, 7th Dublin Fusiliers, wounded at Gallipoli. Then there is the consoling letter of Father O'Herlihy, chaplain in Egypt, to Mrs. Kelleher, Cork, telling of the death of her son, Patrick, a private in the 1st Battalion Royal Munster Fusiliers, also wounded in Gallipoli. Here is an extract from it:—

> I've seen many in pain and suffering since the war began, but few have I seen to bear it all so willingly and so patiently as your son, Paddy; for God and His Blessed Mother were helping him a lot. About, a week after the operation his sufferings increased, and on Sunday morning last, when I said Holy Mass at the

hospital, he again asked me to bring him Holy Communion, as he was confined to bed. You could see the happiness in his features, when Our Blessed Lord came to him again to give him new strength and grace to bear up. He said to me after: 'Father, every time you'll say Holy Mass here, you will bring me Holy Communion again, won't you? I don't like to trouble you, but I long so much to receive.' Poor Paddy! He was such a good boy! I know, dear Mrs. Kelleher, you have long since put your son in God's holy hands, leaving him entirely to God. And God and Mary will now, I know, reward you and give you help and grace to bear for the love of them the sorrowful news it's my hard lot to be the first to send you, perhaps. Your poor Paddy passed away to the God whom he loved so much, and for whom he bore all so patiently. Don't fear for Paddy. He is happy now, poor lad, after many sufferings.

Could there be anything more precious to an Irish Catholic mother than such an account of the last hours of the son of her heart—*a vic mo chree*—dying of battle wounds in a far foreign land?

CHAPTER 10

The Great Push at Loos

What a stirring story of Irish gaiety and resolution is that of the charge of the London Irish Rifles in the great advance upon the mining village of Loos, on Saturday, September 25th, 1915! "Hurrah, the London Irish, hurrah!" The shout ran along the British Lines on Tuesday, September 28th, as the battalion, with many gaps in their ranks, returned after the splendid stand against the terrific German counter-attack which followed the charge, when, according to the General of their Brigade, they helped to save the 4th Army Corps.

"The lucky Irish!" That is one of the names they are known by at the Front. They are given posts of difficulty and danger, and so well do they acquit themselves that the company officers get Military Crosses, and the Distinguished Conduct Medal is liberally distributed among the rank and file. Yet their casualties are remarkably low. The jealous and the profane in other London battalions account for it, I am told, by reviving the ancient gibe about the devil always taking special care of his own. It is true the London Irish are up to all sorts of "divilment"—as we say in Ireland—whether in the trenches or in billets.

I have heard no more delicious war anecdote than that which tells of a fine trick they played on the enemy. Their telephone linesmen happened to find two live German cables on the ground behind their trenches. The linesmen, without as much as saying "by your leave" to the Germans, promptly fitted wires to the cables, and for many weeks they had a most serviceable electric installation at the Battalion Headquarters, officers' dug-outs, and dressing-stations, with power "milked" from the enemy.

That is the Irish kind of "divilment," and it is "divilment" that the Devil himself would disown, for it tends to spoil the knavish designs he has in hand when he uses the Germans as his fitting instruments. The London Irish, as a matter of fact, are noted for their religious devotion and practices. I read in the *Spectator* an interesting correspondence round the question whether the Anglican chaplains were of any earthly good at the Front. Nothing was said, I noticed, about their heavenly uses. But a woman sent a remarkable letter she had received from her son in the trenches.

"There is another man who has great influence out here," he wrote. "He is a priest attached to an Irish regiment. He insists upon charging every time with the men, and no one dare protest. He is absolutely the idol of the regiment." This is Father Lane-Fox, the chaplain of the London Irish, who joined in the famous charge of the battalion at Loos, absolving those who were shot as they fell, and arriving in the German trenches with the foremost. And many of the men will tell you that they are "the lucky Irish," because of the comfort and reassurance they derive from the prayers and self-sacrificing services of their chaplain.

The battalion are also able to warm their hearts and fire their blood with the strains of the ancient Irish war-pipes. This old barbaric music has magic in it. It transforms the Gael. It reawakens in the deeps of their being, even in this twentieth century, impressions, moods, feelings, inherited from a wild, untamed ancestry for thousands of years, and thus gives them, more than strong wine, that strength of arm and that endurance of soul which make them invincible.

So the London Irish were ready when the great day came. Three Divisions of the 4th Army Corps took part in the battle of Loos. The London Irish were in a Division exclusively composed of Brigades of London Territorials, and they had the honour of being selected to lead that Division in the attack. As the result of the battle a double length of trenches were carried along a line of four miles, and to a depth, at its greatest, of four miles. The whole of this area, amounting to at least twelve square miles, around the village of Loos, between Hulluch and Lens, was a desperate network of trenches and bomb-proof shelters.

On the night of September 24th the London Irish received their orders and marched out to take up their allotted positions.

"What a sight!" writes one of the men. "Almost pitch dark, as light near the firing line must not be—just a few glimmers here and there to mark cross roads, and those are lanterns, mostly on the ground, in charge of one or more soldiers, according to the importance of the posts, whose job it is to control the traffic. Now and again a more or less lurid illumination comes from the star shells that are used between the trenches while searchlights sweep across the sky. Artillery flashes continuously and the roar of the guns is added to the crash and rattle of the traffic on the roads."

At a point in the march Brigadier-General Twaites was standing to see the battalion go by. He shook hands with the officers and wished them "Good luck." He told the men that he was expecting great things of them. "Remember," he said, "that the London Irish has been chosen to lead the whole Division."

The trenches were reached about midnight. It was an inclement and dreary time. Rain was falling in torrents. For over six hours the men had to wait in sodden clothes in a trench of slush for the order which would mean death to many, to others racking and disabling wounds, and to all who survived the heartache for loved comrades gone forever. Yet how cheerful they were! To say that none of them were afraid would be to convey that each was a bloodless abstraction. Whatever else an Irishman may be he certainly is never that. He is a hot-blooded human creature, with more than his share of the passions and desires which agitate the heart of man, and so he is prone at times to have fits of depression and despair.

It is possible, then, that the minds of some were darkened by gloomy forebodings. But as an instance of the general stout-heartedness of the men, an officer told me that many of them took out cigarettes, and, having lighted them, held the burning match at arm's length to see if their hands were steady as they waited under the shadow of death. Just at the last moment, too, the liveliest interest was aroused by a rumour which ran along the trenches. It was said that some particularly bright spirits in the battalion had arranged to make the coming charge for ever memorable by an act of unparalleled daring. What is it to be? The question was eagerly put. But those in the secret would not say more than the remark that the nature of it no one would ever guess even if he were to sit down and give all his life to it, and work overtime as well.

At half past six o'clock in the morning the signal came from Major Beresford—a shrill note of the whistle and the cry, "Irish up and over." Gas had been turned on some little time before to help in clearing the ground for the advance, and as the wind was slightly favourable it drifted, a mass of dark vapour, towards the German trenches. But as there was a danger that the cloud might be overtaken, if the charge were successful and rapid, most of the men put on their gas helmets, and fearful and wonderful monsters they looked as, in obedience to the company officers' order, "Over you go, lads," they mounted the parapets. Over they went by platoons, with half a minute's interval between each, and though the enemy immediately opened fire they formed up in four splendid lines, with bayonets fixed and rifles at the slope before they charged.

Then it was that the grand secret was disclosed, a thing almost incredible and unthinkable, indeed. A football was dropped by members of the London Irish Rugby Club in the ranks, and as they charged they kicked it before them across a plain as flat, grassy, and bare of cover as the Fifteen Acres in the Phœnix Park, or the upper stretch of Wimbledon Common. A game of football on the border line between life and death! What a fantastic conception! No wonder that the French troops who were watching the advance were astounded by the spectacle. "It is magnificent, but it is not war!" Possibly the French at Loos had the same thought that the French at Balaclava had when they saw the charge of the Light Brigade. But, wait a while. Despite the apparent oddity and inconsequence of the incident, we shall see that behind it there was a grim and dread purpose well befitting the occasion.

On the Rugby playing fields the rush and dash of the Irish are famous. Who that was there will ever forget the glorious international match that was played at Twickenham between England and Ireland the year before the war, with the King and Prime Minister among the tens of thousands of fascinated spectators of the finest game that ever was seen? Several of the grand young fellows who superbly contended for the mastery of the ball on that great day are buried close to where they fell in France and Flanders, gallantly leading their men as company officers (the thought of it is enough to make one weep), and they played the game on these different fields, according to their separate national characteristics—equally clean-handed and chivalrous, both, as sportsmen, incapable of a mean trick or taking an opponent at an unfair advantage; disciplined, resourceful, dexterous, and deft the English; light-hearted, frank, ardent, and dare-devilled the Irish.

So, too, at Loos the London Irish dashed forward with the same rapture in the game that they used to display in a match on their grounds at Forest Hill, shouting their slogan, "On the ball, London Irish!" They kicked the ball before them, not this time in the face of an opposing English, Welsh, or Scottish pack, but against unceasing volleys of shrapnel and rifle fire which brought many of them down, dead or disabled.

One man who was in the charge told me that at first he had a confused sense of a clamorous hubbub and of comrades falling around him. Afterwards he saw dimly—as if still in a bad dream—the football being kicked, and there came vaguely back to his mind the talk in the trenches as they waited for the whistle. Then he had a shock of surprise which brought everything into sharp reality; and the exhilaration of the episode restoring him to normality and confidence, he followed the ball with the others until it was kicked right into the enemy's trench with a joyous shout of "Goal!"

Thus this exhibition of cool audacity—unparalleled, perhaps, in the annals of war—instead of retarding the advance added immensely to its go. It will be historic, that game of football amid the thunders and the lightnings of the field of battle, with the German trenches for the goal; and soaring up from the very depths of the awful tumult of the fight will ever be heard, "On the ball, London Irish!"

So the first line of German trenches was reached. The barbed wire entanglements had been blown to pieces by shell fire before the attack. Another effect of that terrific bombardment, which lasted nineteen days, was the cowed and dazed condition of the Germans. They were so easily and quickly disposed of by the first line of London Irish that the other lines pressed forward, scrambling across the trench over the bodies of killed and wounded enemies; and, as they did so, catching glimpses through the smoke of the haggard and frightened faces of the grey-clad survivors making but a feeble resistance or surrendering without striking a blow.

The advance to the second line of German trenches was not so easy. Here was an inferno of tangled wreckage strewn over mud, smoke-dimmed, and torn with shrapnel, through which the men could advance but slowly, with stumbling feet and gasping breath, while their ears were assailed with horrid noises—screaming, yelling, crashing, pounding, cheering, screeching. Major Beresford, who led the charge, fell with a bullet through his lung on the way to the first German trench. Four officers were killed on the same piece of ground. But the men went steadily on, though bereft of most of their leaders, and at the second line trench of the Germans, more strongly held than the first, were inspired for the ordeal before them by the sight of Captain and Adjutant A.P. Hamilton, who, though shot through the knee and suffering great pain, guided the operations as he moved from place to place, limping heavily.

There was desperately fierce hand-to-hand work here and bomb firing parties were hard at it, clearing out every corner. One man performed a particularly brave act and a shrewd one to boot. He came alone into a German communication trench beyond the reserve line. In a minute a bright thought struck him, and as quickly as possible he bundled the sandbags down into the trench, and so formed a barricade. The Germans came back, just as he had anticipated, and as they clambered over, so he shot them. We got rid of thirteen in this way, and the enemy gave up that passage and retired.

Captain Hamilton remained in this second line trench reorganising and encouraging the men until the consolidation was well advanced. He was awarded the Military Cross for his services. The official record says, "He had to be ordered back for medical attendance." Indeed, the only way that could be found to prevent Captain Hamilton from stubbornly going on till he bled to death was to place him under arrest.

The London Irish had thus magnificently succeeded in the task allotted to them—the capture of a section of the German second line trenches. Carried away by their excessive impetuosity, they also helped to clear the Germans out of the village of Loos, which they were among the first to enter. They were still untroubled and unperplexed. "When the village was about half cleared," says Rifleman T.J. Culley, in a letter to Sister Celestine, of the Homes for Destitute Catholic Children in London, "could you have peered into one of the estaminets which was still inhabited, you would have perceived one of the Irish calmly asking a most attractive and business-like *madame* for a *café au lait*, and being served amid torrents of shot and shell; and when he was finished he slung his arms and calmly walked on to do further death-dealing deeds."

Culley adds that when the village was eventually cleared some of the New Army passed through the thinned ranks of the Territorials to carry on the advance. "You may have noticed in the papers," he says, "that the credit of capturing the village went to the New Army. This is not so. The Territorials, with the London Irish among their leaders, should be given the honour."

But the real trial of the London Irish was now to begin. The Germans on the Sunday launched a tremendous counter-attack. Would the London Irish be able to beat it back, and hold on to the trenches they had taken until relief came? Again and again, there seemed to be no possible escape from the destruction which imminently menaced them.

"All Monday passed and still no relief came," writes a rifleman of the battalion. "Indeed, it was a question whether any minute we should not be blown to atoms and the line swamped with a rush of the enemy. We could hardly stand from fatigue, having been in action steadily since Saturday morning. 'Fight on, lads,' said an officer who was afterwards killed. 'Remember the Division looks to you. This is bound to end sooner or later. Let it be in a way that will never be forgotten when they hear of it at home in London and Ireland.' So we fought on, and never a single German got nearer than a dozen yards from our lines. Soon we got the word that we should be relieved early Tuesday morning under cover of the darkness. The announcement sent a thrill of joy through us, for then we knew we had won." As soon as they got to the back trenches in safety a huge cheer went up from all the others, "The London Irish—Hurroo!"

"They shook us by the hands and took our rifles from our grasp and the kits from our backs in their eagerness to show their gratitude," says the same rifleman.

The general in command of the brigade who stood and watched the battalion on their way to battle on Friday night, addressed the remnant afterwards and said: "Not only am I proud to have had the honour of being in command of such a regiment, but the whole Empire will be proud whenever, in after years, the history of the battle of Loos comes to be written, for I can tell you it was the London Irish who helped to save a whole British Army Corps. You have done one of the greatest actions of the war."

Thus the London Irish raised themselves on the pinnacle of a notable and conspicuous triumph. Thus they earned for themselves the name of "The Footballers of Loos."

CHAPTER 11

The Victoria Cross

That plain Cross of bronze, with the simple motto, "For Valour," is the most honoured and coveted military decoration in the world. It has been won in the present war, down to the end of 1915, by as many as twenty-one Irishmen, who have splendidly sustained their country's inspiring heritage of bravery on the battlefield.

Courage, bravery, valour, are, in a way, mysterious attributes. We all understand what they mean; we all regard them as noble and heroic; we all desire to be possessed of them. Yet we know that only to the few comparatively do they belong; and in a puzzled mood we ask ourselves—Why is it that in the face of death in warfare one man should be fearless and another timid and faint-hearted? It is supposed that most men are naturally cowards. I remember hearing a remarkable statement made by Archibald Forbes, a famous war correspondent of the past, in a lecture on his experiences as a journalist on the field of battle. He said there is infinitely less steadiness in the soldier of any nationality under fire than the civilian imagines. He had watched the conduct on the field of the armies of eight European nations, and there was never an engagement in which he did not see what he called "a stampede," or, more explicitly, soldiers flying in the wild disorder of terror.

Forbes did not attempt to explain why this was so. He simply recorded the fact. To me it seems as if the quality which is commonly called cowardice is but a form of fear, and fear is an instinctive emotion which is to be seen displayed throughout the entire animal kingdom. It shows itself at a very early age in the shrinking apprehensiveness of the infant. The purpose of it appears to be that of self-protection and self-preservation. One of its first impulses is to avoid the danger which threatens by running away from it. We see that in the action of a horse harnessed to a vehicle which, by reason of a sudden fright, breaks from human restraint, and dashes wildly through the streets, endangering itself and everyone that crosses its course. Man is also prone to take flight under the pressure of fear for his life. Unlike the horse, he controls his actions by reason, more or less. But to fly from danger is, in most circumstances, allowable to the civilian, under the law of self-preservation. He can run away without any hurt to his self-esteem, or any risk of being called a coward.

It is a crime for a soldier on the field to turn his back on danger. Of course there is nothing despicable in a retirement under orders when faced with overwhelming odds. We can see Wellington at Salamanca, caught in the *mêlée* of a British flight before a dashing charge of French cavalry—as Maxwell saw him, "With his straight sword drawn, riding at full speed, and smiling." He fled that he might live, and win the battle. But the soldier must stand firm when the shells are bursting terrifically around him and the bullets whistle their death tune in his ears, or advance undauntedly towards the hidden enemy, who thus menace him with death and mutilation, until a command or a bullet stops him.

Yet even in the soldier to shrink from pain, danger and death is a natural impulse, for it is one of the instincts of which no amount of training and discipline can entirely divest humanity. President Abraham Lincoln was very reluctant to sanction the execution of soldiers for cowardice during the American Civil War. He used to say it was impossible for a man always to control his legs. "How do I know," he would ask, "that I should not run away myself?" Happily there are things which help to sustain and embolden the soldier in that terrible trial. Some of these enheartening influences are external to the soldier himself. His country's cause and the reputation of his regiment help to brace him for the ordeal. The companionship of his comrades in a common danger and the fury and tumult of battle are also very animating. But in the last resort the soldier must rely upon his own innate qualities, both mental and physical. For bravery lies in the blood, and courage in the mind, and valour is the combination of the often thoughtless fire and dash of the one, and the calculated enterprise and determination of the other.

Bearing these considerations always in mind, let us never cast the contumelious stone, or say a bitter word, against any regiment, or party of men, who in war are overborne by the black terror of apprehension suddenly arising; but rather let us ever give the greater honour and glory to those rare beings, those supermen, who without a thought of self, dash into the fiery blast to save a stricken comrade, or who strike a ringing blow for their cause under the jaws of horrid death, whose hands are stretched out to clutch them.

In the light of these general reflections on human nature let us consider first the achievement of Drummer William Kenny, who, though serving in the 2nd Battalion of the Gordon Highlanders, is a Drogheda man. Near Ypres, on October 23rd, 1914, he exposed himself to heavy fire on five separate occasions, in order to rescue wounded men. Twice previously he saved machine-guns by carrying them out of action. "Also on numerous occasions," says the official record, "Drummer Kenny conveyed urgent messages in very dangerous circumstances over fire-swept ground." What makes Kenny's heroism very remarkable is that it was not displayed in a single instance, by one act; but was, as we see, repeated over and over again, and in a variety of ways.

He is a very modest as well as fearless man. I saw him at the Mansion House, London, one day in March, 1915, when he was presented with a gold watch by the Lord Mayor, on behalf of the Musicians' Company. The first thing that caught my attention in his appearance was the mingled kindliness and resolution expressed in his face. It was obvious, from his shy manner, that he was greatly embarrassed, if not made quite miserable, indeed, by being so much noticed, and would have rather remained in the background. "Thank you all," was his simple acknowledgment of the Company's expressions of admiration and regard. He is also a reticent man. Not a word did he say to anyone about his exploits until the announcement that he had been awarded the Victoria Cross appeared in the newspapers.

Even then, he declined to be regarded as a hero. "It was just what anyone would do in the circumstances," he said. "There are many others out there who have done the same thing, only nobody knows it. You see some of your pals lying out in the open under fire. You know it is they or you; so you just go out and fetch them in." It was the same in regard to his single-handed action in saving the machine-guns. "The Maxims had to be fetched," he said; "and I did it. That's all." As a case of unobtrusive and, indeed, unconscious heroism that of Drummer Kenny would be hard to beat.

His native town of Drogheda has reason to be proud of Kenny, and it showed its esteem in a splendid way. On St. Patrick's Day, 1915, the Mayor and Corporation went to High Mass with Kenny, who was accompanied by his mother and father; and afterwards, at a public meeting in the square, attended by an enormous crowd, the noble fellow was presented with a cheque for £120, and the freedom of the borough. When he wrote his name on the roll of Drogheda's freemen, Kenny found among the preceding signatures those of such famous historical personages as the Duke of Ormond (1704); Henry Grattan (1782); Sir Arthur Wellesley (1807); Isaac Butt (1877); Charles Stewart Parnell (1881), and Sir Garnet Wolseley (1882).

The deeds of three other Irishmen who have won the Victoria Cross were, like those of Kenny, deeds of mercy—the rescue of wounded comrades. For a full appreciation of them it is necessary to understand the awful plight of the soldiers who are stricken down on the unsheltered open ground between the opposing trenches. When the engagement in which the men fell is over this space is swept, on the slightest movement, by volleys from rifles and machine-guns. It is often impossible, therefore, to bring timely help to the wounded. At night only, in the sheltering darkness, some of the least disabled wounded may be able to crawl back to their trenches. Otherwise they have to lie out there in the open while life ebbs away to the most bitter torments.

That is, unless there are at hand men moved by the unselfish and tender emotion of pity, men susceptible to suffering, men of refined and imaginative minds; and therefore able to project themselves by the power of thought into the cruel situation of their tortured and helpless mates, and feel to the full all the horror of it; and men, too, whose high ideal of duty and right conduct impel them irresistibly to go out to succour, even at the risk of meeting the same terrible fate themselves. Of such noble men are Drummer Kenny, and also Lance-Corporal Joseph Toombs, 1st Battalion King's Liverpool Regiment, who comes from Warrenpoint, Co. Down; Private Robert Morrow, 1st Royal Irish Fusiliers, a native of Co. Tyrone, and Private John Caffrey, 2nd York and Lancaster Regiment, who was born at Birr, King's County, and has his home in Nottingham.

The official account of the achievements for which Toombs was awarded the Victoria Cross is as follows:—

> For most conspicuous gallantry near Rue du Bois on June 16th, 1915. On his own initiative he crawled out repeatedly under a very heavy shell and machine gun fire to bring in wounded men who were lying about one hundred yards in front of our trenches. He rescued four men, one of whom he dragged back

by means of a rifle sling placed round his own neck and the man's body. This man was so severely wounded that unless he had been immediately attended to he must have died.

Morrow got the V.C.—

> .... for most conspicuous bravery near Messines, on April 12th, 1915, when he rescued and carried successfully to places of comparative safety several men who had been buried under the debris of trenches wrecked by shell fire. Private Morrow carried out this gallant work on his own initiative and under very heavy fire from the enemy.

I am able to supplement this official record by a statement made by one of the men who was saved by Morrow:

> The enemy opened fire unexpectedly. A shell fell in the trench, burying over a dozen men, of whom I was one, in the wreckage. Those who were able ran to shelter, for that shell was followed by many more; and the trench having been laid bare, the enemy opened a hot rifle and machine-gun fire upon it. At the same time the enemy was making an attack in force. Accordingly it was a risky thing to be there. Morrow didn't mind. He came up to where we were pinned under the remains of the parapet and a dugout. He dragged me out and carried me on his back to a place of safety. Then he went back to look for others. He made the journey six times, bringing all the men that were alive. It was slow, laborious work, and all the time Morrow was under heavy fire from the Germans.

On the same day that the notice of Private Morrow's distinction was published, his death was announced in the list of casualties. He was killed on April 25th, 1915, at St. Julien, while in the act of again succouring the wounded. His widowed mother, at Newmills, Dungannon, received the Victoria Cross that was awarded to her gallant boy with an autograph letter of sympathy from the King.

Private John Caffrey got the Victoria Cross for a gallant display of bravery and humanity near La Brique on November 16th, 1915. A man of the West Yorkshire Regiment had been badly wounded, and was lying in the open, unable to move, in full view of, and about 300 to 400 yards from, the enemy's trenches. Corporal Stirk, Royal Army Medical Corps, and Caffrey at once started out to rescue him, but at the first attempt they were driven back by shrapnel fire. Soon afterwards they started again, under close sniping and machine-gun fire, and succeeded in reaching and bandaging the wounded man, but, just as Corporal Stirk had lifted him on Private Caffrey's back, he himself was shot in the head. Caffrey put down the wounded man, bandaged Corporal Stirk, and helped him back into safety. He then returned and brought in the man of the West Yorkshire Regiment. "He had made three journeys across the open, under close and accurate fire," says the official record, "and had risked his own life to save others with the utmost coolness and bravery."

No more moving story of the devotion of a private to an officer, to whom he was regimentally attached, is to be found than that enshrined in the record of the deed for which the Victoria Cross was given to Private Thomas Kenny, 13th (Service) Battalion Durham Light Infantry, part of "Kitchener's Army." Kenny, aged thirty-three, was living with his wife and seven children, and following the occupation of a quarry-man, at Hart Bushes, a hamlet two miles outside Wingate, County Durham, when on the outbreak of war he joined the Army. His battalion was sent to the front on August 25th, 1915. On the night of November 4th, 1915, Kenny won the Victoria Cross near La Houssoie, for conspicuous bravery and devotion to Lieutenant Brown of his battalion. The deed is finely described in a letter written by Major C.E. Walker, of the 13th Durham Light Infantry:—

> I just want to write to you to tell you how proud we all are of your husband, Pte. T. Kenny, for the magnificent pluck and endurance he showed under very heavy fire when Lieut. P.A. Brown was wounded. Your husband was what we call 'observer' to Lieut. Brown—that is to say, he acted as a sort of shadow to his officer, who never moved anywhere without him. The Lieutenant went out in front of our trenches in a thick fog to superintend a party of our men mending our barbed wire, Kenny, as usual, accompanying him. They over-ran our wire and lost their bearings in the fog.
> Finding that they were on unfamiliar ground they sat down to listen for sounds to guide them. After a while they decided to go back. As soon as they rose a rifle was fired from a listening post about 15 yards away. (They were only about 30 yards from the enemy trenches, and a listening post runs out from their front line.) Lieut. Brown fell, shot through both thighs. Kenny at once went to his assistance, and although Lieut. Brown was a good-sized man, got him slung on to his back and started off with him.

The Germans in the listening post—there are generally four to six there—opened rapid fire at him. He therefore dropped to his hands and knees and began crawling, with the officer still on his back. Lieut. Brown was hit about 9.45. Kenny carried him in this manner, under heavy fire from the enemy every time they heard him, for over an hour in spite of the wet, clinging nature of the ground.

At last he came to a ditch he recognised, and being utterly exhausted, he made the Lieutenant as comfortable as he could and then started off for our lines for help. He found an officer and a few men of his battalion at a listening post, and having guided them back to where he had left his officer, Lieutenant Brown was brought in still living, but died at the dressing station. His last words were, 'Kenny—you're a hero!' The General is delighted with the pluck, endurance, and devotion shown by your husband, and has recommended him for the Victoria Cross. Kenny is a splendid fellow, and you may well be proud of him.

Lieutenant Brown's mother wrote from Beckenham, Kent, to Kenny, expressing her deep gratitude for his services to her son:

I am thankful to feel that he died among friends and that he was able to thank you," she says. "I know you will value his last words. He had often mentioned you to me in his letters home, and talked of 'my observer Kenny, a very nice Irishman from Co. Durham, who goes with me everywhere.' His life had been a very different one before this dreadful war, but he gave up everything for pure patriotism.

These are rare, fine, and noble actions. They are not necessarily actions which only a true soldier could accomplish. They are the outcome of fortitude, that spirit which supports a man to go through with a tremendous task, involving pain of body and trouble of mind, but a task from which his sense of duty will not permit him to turn aside; and fortitude is a quality found not uncommonly in the ordinary daily round of civil life as well as on the battlefield. The other awards of the Victoria Cross to Irishmen were made for deeds of quite a different character; real soldierly deeds, bold, dashing, and intrepid; deeds, if not of reckless bravery, certainly of bravery reckless of life for the attainment of the purpose in view. In a word, they are deeds more representative of the traditional fiery fearlessness of Celtic valour.

There is the case of Private Edward Dwyer, of the East Surrey Regiment, who was born at Fulham, London, of Irish parents, his father being a Galway man and his mother a native of Omeath. I saw him one sunny day in July, 1915, coming down the Strand at the head of a recruiting procession, and his appearance gave me at first a shock of surprise. I do not know why it should be so, but it is the fact that we usually associate intrepidity and resolution with men of powerful physique and demeanour that suggests fearlessness. Perhaps the illusion has taken its rise from misty recollections of the heroes of the fiction-reading of our youth. That illusion has been dispelled, for me, at least, by those V.C.-men of the war whom I have seen, and I have seen several of them. In all of them, without exception, I should say it was the mind that told and not so much the body.

Dwyer looked quite a boy, and one of small stature, too, as he walked that day between two burly sergeants, to whose shoulders his head just about reached. But I could see the Victoria Cross of dark bronze and its red ribbon on the left breast of his khaki tunic. His hearty laughter and smiles told of his pride and joy in the demonstration, of which he was the central figure—silk-hatted men baring their heads to him; women, young and old, pressing forward to kiss him; and the air filled with shoutings and the blare of brass instruments. Then, from the plinth of the Nelson Monument in Trafalgar Square, standing between two of Landseer's great lions, he made a sprightly recruiting speech.

"I promise you this," said he, "a drink and a cigar for the first ten recruits to come up here. Age is nothing. I was only sixteen when I joined. I think the recruiting-sergeant must have been a little short-sighted on purpose, because he enlisted me without any trouble. Out at the Front there are men who are grey-headed. Doesn't it shame you?" he cried, turning sharply to the young men in the crowd.

What was it that was done by this youngest of the V.C.'s this stripling of eighteen who, before he enlisted, was a messenger-boy to a greengrocer? He displayed "most conspicuous bravery and devotion to duty" at Hill 60 on April 20th, 1915; and he did so in a very singular way. "When his trench was heavily attacked by German grenade throwers," says the official record, "he climbed on to the parapet, and although subjected to a hail of bombs at close quarters, succeeded in dispersing the enemy by the effective use of his hand grenades." Those vague, general terms do not enable us to see the episode. It discloses itself vividly in the terse sentences of Dwyer himself:—

All our chaps were either killed or wounded. I was the only unwounded man left in the trench. The Germans were in a trench only fifteen yards away, so close that I could hear them talking in their lingo. I knew that if they took the trench I was in it would be a bad job for our trenches behind. So I collected all the hand grenades left in our trench until I had about a hundred in all. There were three steps leading up to the parapet of the trench. For a while I sat crouched on the middle step. Then I found myself on the parapet hurling grenades at the Germans. Shells and hand bombs were bursting all over and around me, but nothing touched me at all. I kept on throwing until help came and the trench was safe. I was pretty well done up when I jumped down into the trench, mad with joy and without a scratch. The relieving party chaffed me a lot, and called me 'The King of the Hand Grenades.'"

Dwyer gives an interesting account of his sensations in battle. As a rule, introspection in such circumstances is almost impossible, for the mind, when concentrated solely on the existing situation and strained with excitement almost to the cracking point, cannot well observe itself; but Dwyer is made of uncommon stuff mentally as well as physically.

"Fear is a funny thing," he says. "It gets at you in all kinds of curious ways. When we've been skirmishing in open order under heavy fire I've felt myself go numb. Then the blood has rushed into my face—head and ears become as hot as fire, and the tip of my tongue swollen into a blob of blood. It isn't nice, I can tell you; but the feeling passes and one's nerves become steadier."

He added what showed his real mettle: "I've never expected to get out of any fight I've ever been in. And so I just try to do my bit, and leave it at that." Dwyer made a most successful recruiter for the Irish regiments, in which, on account of his nationality, he specially interested himself.

Turning now for a while from the Irish privates to the Irish regimental officers who have won the V.C., we find the same pluck, endurance, and devotion to duty displayed. Second Lieutenant George Arthur Boyd-Rochfort, of the 1st Battalion Scots Guards, is a type of the Irish gentry who have contributed to the British Army so remarkably large a number of gallant regimental officers and distinguished commanders, from the Duke of Wellington to Viscount French of Ypres. He had done no soldiering before the present war. The eldest son of the late Major R.H. Boyd-Rochfort, of the 15th Hussars, he succeeded to the family property at Middleton Park, Westmeath.

Aged thirty-five, and the head of his family, all his interests centred in the work of the estate. Yet when the war broke out Mr. Boyd-Rochfort felt it his duty to join the Army, so that he might serve his country along with his younger brothers—Captain H. Boyd-Rochfort, of the 21st Lancers (now Brigade-Major of the 21st Cavalry Brigade), and Lieutenant Cecil Boyd-Rochfort, of the Scots Guards. To qualify himself physically for a commission in the Scots Guards he had to undergo two operations, which confined him to hospital for close on five months. He got his commission in April, 1915, went to the Front in June, and won the Victoria Cross on August 3rd, in the trenches between Cambria and La Bassée.

Lieutenant Boyd-Rochfort was afterwards wounded in a single-handed fight with two Germans—he knocked one down with the butt-end of his empty revolver and the other with his fist—and was invalided home, when the whole countryside turned out to do him honour. He gave the following account of his exploit:—

> It was at break of day, just before we were ordered to 'stand to,' we were working in the first line of trenches, and a trench that was nothing more than a graveyard. The first German trench was no more than fifty yards away, and their mortars and rifle grenades were simply spilling into us. Our trench was getting badly knocked about by the flying missiles. You must distinguish between these mortars and shells, because the mortars have a time fuse which explodes them without striking. I was just raising my head over the front of the trench, and, hearing the whiz, I said to my men, 'Look out.' Down they went. The bomb landed, and started to roll down from the top of the trench. I dashed forward and seized it, and threw it over the top of trench. Scarcely had it left my hand and reached the outside of the trench than it exploded with a terrific report. We were all buried under falling earth, but fortunately no one was hurt, although my cap was blown to pieces. My men were very appreciative of my action, and cheered and thanked me. Afterwards they wrote and signed a statement of what I had done, which they handed to the colonel.

Another gallant Meath man was the late Lieutenant Maurice James Dease, 4th Batt. Royal Fusiliers (City of London Regiment), who fell during the retreat from Mons, and was the first officer to gain the Victoria Cross in the great war. He was the only son of Mr. Edmund F. Dease, Culmullen, Drumree, Meath, and heir-presumptive to his uncle, Major Gerald Dease, of Turbotston, Westmeath. He was born September 28th, 1889, and was educated at Stonyhurst and at the Army Class, Wimbledon College. He entered the Royal Military College, Sandhurst, and was gazetted Second Lieutenant in the Royal Fusiliers in February, 1910, becoming Lieutenant in 1912. In the same year he was appointed machine-gun officer to his regiment, and it was whilst in command of this section at Nimy, near Mons, on August 23rd, 1914, that Lieutenant Dease was killed and awarded the Victoria Cross. The official record is as follows:—

> During the action the machine-guns were protecting the crossing over a canal bridge, and Lieutenant Dease was several times severely wounded, but refused to leave the guns. He remained at his post until all the men of his detachment were either killed or wounded and the guns put out of action by the enemy's fire.

From the South of Ireland came the late Captain Gerald Robert O'Sullivan, 1st Royal Inniskilling Fusiliers, who won the V.C. in Gallipoli. A son of the late Lieutenant-Colonel George Ledwill O'Sullivan, 91st Argyll and Sutherland Highlanders, and of Mrs. O'Sullivan, of Rowan House, Dorchester, he was born at Frankfield, near Douglas, county Cork, and spent most of his boyhood in Dublin. He passed into Sandhurst in 1907, and was gazetted to the Inniskillings on May 15th, 1909. Captain O'Sullivan was awarded the V.C. for conspicuous gallantry on two occasions, the official record of his deeds being as follows:—

> For most conspicuous bravery during the operations southwest of Krithia, on the Gallipoli Peninsula. On the night July 1st-2nd, 1915, when it was essential that portion of a trench which had been lost should be regained. Captain O'Sullivan, although not belonging to the troops at this point, volunteered to lead a party of bomb-throwers to effect the recapture. He advanced in the open under very heavy fire, and in order to throw his bombs with greater effect got up on the parapet, where he was completely exposed to the fire of the enemy occupying the trench. He was finally wounded, but not before his inspiring example had led on his party to make further efforts,

which resulted in the capture of the trench. On the night of June 18th-19th, 1915, Captain O'Sullivan saved a critical situation in the same locality by his great personal gallantry and good leading.

This gallant officer is believed to have been killed during the attack on Hill 70, or Burnt Hill, at Suvla Bay, on August 21st, 1915. He advanced at the head of his men to the second line of Turkish trenches, where he fell. The body was not recovered.

From the North of Ireland came the late Captain Anketell Moutray-Read, of the 1st Northamptonshire Regiment, who was killed on the night of September 24-25th, 1915, at the Battle of Loos, and was posthumously awarded the Victoria Cross. He was the youngest son of the late Colonel John Moutray-Read, of Aghnacloy, County Tyrone, and one of his ancestors was High Sheriff of the county as far back as 1721. Owing to casualties in the Northamptons Captain Moutray-Read was in temporary command of the battalion when he fell. The official record of the award of the Victoria Cross is as follows:—

For most conspicuous bravery during the first attack near Hulluch on the morning of September 25th, 1915. Although partially gassed, Captain Read went out several times in order to rally parties of different units which were disorganised and retiring. He led them back into the firing line, and, utterly regardless of danger, moved freely about encouraging them under a withering fire. He was mortally wounded while carrying out this gallant work. Captain Read had previously shown conspicuous bravery during digging operations on August 29th, 30th, and 31st, 1915, and on the night of July 29th-30th he carried out of action an officer, who was mortally wounded, under a hot fire from rifles and grenades.

In all the theatres of war representatives of that famous fighting stock, the Irish gentry, are to be found defending the British Empire by maintaining the martial reputation of their race. At Shariba, Mesopotamia, the late Major George Godfrey Massy Wheeler, 7th Hariana Lancers, Indian Army, won the Victoria Cross for "most conspicuous bravery." He was a descendant of General Sir Hugh Massy Wheeler, whose son, John George Wheeler, was married to a Miss Massy, of Kingswell House, Tipperary. "On April 12th, 1915," says the official record, "Major Wheeler asked permission to take out his squadron and attempt to capture a flag which was the centre point of a group of the enemy who were firing on one of our pickets. He advanced and attacked the enemy's infantry with the lance, doing considerable execution amongst them. He then retired while the enemy swarmed out of hidden ground and formed an excellent target to our Royal Horse Artillery guns. On April 13th, 1915, Major Wheeler led his squadron to the attack of the 'North Mound.' He was seen far ahead of his men, riding single-handed straight for the enemy's standards. This gallant officer was killed on the mound."

In another far-distant and remote field of operations, the German protectorate of the Cameroons, West Africa, a scion of the same stock of Irish gentry likewise achieves glory, leading blacks against blacks led by Germans. There the hero is Captain John Fitzharding Paul Butler, of the famous Butlers of Ormond, Tipperary, attached to the Pioneer Company, Gold Coast Regiment, West African Frontier Force. "On November 17th, 1914," says the record, "with a party of thirteen men, he went into the thick brush and attacked the enemy, in strength about one hundred, including several Europeans, defeated them and captured their machine-guns, and many loads of ammunition.

On December 27th, 1914, when on patrol duty with a few men, he swam the Ekan River, which was held by the enemy, completed his reconnaissance on the further bank, and returned in safety. Two of his men were wounded while he was actually in the water." Bald as the story is, thus officially told, it kindles the imagination, and we can picture the wild and hazardous life led by this adventurous Irishman in that mysterious land of mountain and forest.

The Brookes of Colebrooke have been settled in Fermanagh since the time of Queen Elizabeth. If you look through Burke's "Peerage and Baronetage" you will see that in every generation the family have given sons to the Army and Navy. Lieutenant J.A.O. Brooke (grandson of the late Sir Arthur Brinsley Brooke of Colebrooke, baronet), 2nd Gordon Highlanders, has crowned the martial reputation of the family by winning the Victoria Cross. Near Gheluvelt, on October 29th, 1914, he led two attacks on the German trenches under heavy rifle and machine-gun fire, and regained a lost trench at a very critical time. He was killed at the moment of success. "By his marked coolness and promptitude on this occasion," says the official record, "Lieutenant Brooke prevented the enemy from breaking through our line at a time when a general counter-attack could not have been organised." Two Victoria Crosses have thus been won for the Gordon Highlanders by Irishmen—Drummer Kenny and Lieutenant Brooke.

Chapter 12
"For Valour"

In order to be able rightly to appreciate the honour and glory of the Victoria Cross, it is necessary to know the conditions regulating its bestowal. A tradition has been established in the Services, though there is nothing in the institution of the Victoria Cross really to warrant it, that the decoration is to be given only for a deed not done under orders. The deed must be a signal one in every respect—exceptionally daring, and difficult, of the highest military value, particularly in the saving of life, and, with all this, absolutely voluntary.

Nevertheless, it will be noticed that in none of the deeds of all these bold, brave, and intrepid Irishmen is there the slightest suggestion of seeking fame and glory at the cannon's mouth. "I almost gasped," said Private Dwyer, "when I was told I was awarded the V.C." Each of the others appears to have been likewise unconscious of his heroism. He did not go and do what he did, thinking of being mentioned in despatches or decorated. He was concerned only about doing what at the moment he felt to be his duty. Fame and glory were probably never farther from his thoughts than at the very time he was winning them forever. For the roll of the Victoria Cross, on which his name and deed are commemorated, is imperishable; and his glorious memory will shine as long as Great Britain and Ireland endure.

For sheer daring, contempt of risks, resourcefulness, and extraordinary physical powers, a high place must be given to the action by which Corporal William Cosgrave, 1st Royal Munster Fusiliers, won the Victoria Cross in Gallipoli. It took place on April 26th, 1915, the day after the famous landing of the Dublins and Munsters at "Beach V," when the survivors of these battalions were advancing to the attack on the Turkish positions on the heights of Sedd-el-Bahr. The first defensive obstacles encountered were barbed wire entanglements of exceptional strength and intricacy, behind which was a trench of enemy riflemen and machine-guns. "Those entanglements," says Sir Ian Hamilton, "were made of heavier metal and longer barbs than I have ever seen elsewhere." A party of the Munsters were sent forward to cut them down, but the men's pliers had not strength and sharpness enough to snip the wires. Then it was that Cosgrave, a giant in stature and vigour—6 ft. 5 in. in height and only twenty-three years of age—"pulled down the posts of the enemy's high wire entanglements single-handed, notwithstanding a terrific fire from both front and flanks thereby greatly contributing to the successful clearing of the heights," to quote the official record. The deed has a distinction peculiarly its own, for it is the only thing of the kind to be found in the long roll of the Victoria Cross.

Cosgrave was wounded in the bayonet charge which subsequently carried the trench. A bullet struck him in the side, and passing clear through him splintered his backbone. He was invalided home to Aghada, a little fishing hamlet in County Cork, where he was born and reared and worked as a farm boy until he enlisted in 1910. Seen there, he told the story of his exploit, as one of the party of fifty Munsters ordered to rush forward and remove the entanglements:—

> Sergeant-Major Bennett led us, but just as we made a dash a storm of lead was concentrated on us; Sergeant-Major Bennett was killed with a bullet through his brain. I then took charge and shouted to the boys to come on. The dash was quite one hundred yards, and I don't know whether I ran or prayed the faster. I wanted to succeed in my work, and I also wanted to have the benefit of dying with a prayer in my mind. Some of us having got up to the wires we started to cut them with the pliers, but you might as well try to cut the round tower at Cloyne with a pair of lady's scissors. The wire was of great strength, strained like fiddle strings, and so full of spikes that you could not get the pliers between. Heavens! I thought we were done; I threw the pliers from me. 'Pull them up!' I roared to the fellows; and I dashed at one of the upright posts, put my arms round it, and heaved and strained at it until it came up in my arms, the same as you would lift a child.
>
> I believe there was great cheering when they saw what I was at, but I only heard the scream of bullets and saw dust rising all round me. Where they hit I do not know, or how many posts I pulled up. I did my best, and the boys that were with me did

every bit as good as myself.

When the wire was down the rest of the lads came through like devils and reached the trenches. We won about 200 yards' length by twenty yards deep and 700 yards from the shore. We met a brave, honourable foe in the Turks, and I am sorry that such decent fighting men were brought into the row by such dirty tricksters as the Germans.

In Sir Ian Hamilton's despatch describing the storming of "Beach W"—close to "Beach V"—by the Lancashire Fusiliers, there are some striking passages relating to men of the battalion who rushed forward to cut passages through the entanglements.

> Again the heroic wire-cutters came out. Through glasses they could be seen quietly snipping away under a hellish fire, as if they were pruning a vineyard.

For his gallantry in this undertaking Private William Keneally, one of the many Irishmen in the Lancashires, got the Victoria Cross. The distinction is greatly enhanced by the fact that Keneally was selected by his comrades in the ranks as the one among them best entitled to it. The official record says:—

> On April 25th, 1915, three companies and the Headquarters of the 1st Battalion Lancashire Fusiliers, in effecting a landing on the Gallipoli Peninsula to the west of Cape Helles, were met by a very deadly fire from hidden machine-guns which caused a great number of casualties. The survivors, however, rushed up to and cut the wire entanglements, notwithstanding the terrific fire from the enemy, and, after overcoming supreme difficulties, the cliffs were gained and the position maintained. Amongst the many very gallant officers and men engaged in this most hazardous undertaking, Captain Willis, Sergeant Richards, and Private Keneally have been selected by their comrades as having performed the most signal arts of bravery and devotion to duty.

Precedents for the choice of a comrade by his fellows to wear the V.C. on their behalf are to be found in the records of the Indian Mutiny, and it is an interesting fact that in each case the man chosen was an Irishman serving in an English or Scottish regiment. In September, 1857, the Cross was awarded to Private John Divane, of the 60th King's Royal Rifles, for successfully heading a charge against the trenches at Delhi. Divane was elected by the privates of his regiment for the distinction. In November of the same year Lance-Corporal J. Dunley, 93rd Highlanders, the first man of the regiment to enter the Secundra Bagh with Captain Burroughs, whom he supported against heavy odds, was similarly chosen by his comrades for the V.C., and likewise Lieutenant A.K. French, 53rd Regiment, who showed distinguished gallantry on the same occasion, was elected by his brother officers to wear the decoration.

Keneally was born in Parnell Street, Wexford, in 1886. His father, Colour-Sergeant John Stephen Keneally, served for twenty-four years in the Royal Irish Regiment. In 1890 Keneally's parents removed to Wigan. The father got work as a miner in the Wigan coalfield, and the son, at the age of thirteen, started in the same life as a pit-boy. William afterwards joined the Army, served for six years, and on returning to civil life worked again in the pits. On the outbreak of war he rejoined his old regiment, the Lancashire Fusiliers, and was then one of five brothers serving with the Colours.

The brave fellow did not survive to enjoy the honour of having the V.C. pinned to his breast by the King. He was wounded on July 29th, 1915, in the course of an attack on a Turkish position, which was repulsed, and was never seen afterwards. "It is a matter of sincere regret to me," says the King in a kindly letter to the hero's father, "that the death of Private Keneally deprived me of the pride of personally conferring on him the Victoria Cross—the greatest of all military distinctions."

For quite a different achievement the Victoria Cross was awarded to Sergeant John Hogan, 2nd Battalion Manchester Regiment, an Irish lad who was brought up at Oldham, Lancashire. On October 29th, 1914, Hogan and Second Lieutenant Leach (who also got the V.C.) recaptured unassisted a trench that had been lost by the regiment. Two attempts to retake the trench in force having been repulsed, Leach and Hogan voluntarily set out one morning to try to recover it themselves. The trench was about sixty yards' distance from the nearest German trench. It did not run in a straight line, but took a zig-zag course, consisting of a number of traverses in this form:—

Though it was held by the Germans, its connection with the other

British trenches was not cut off. Starting at one end of the trench, Leach and Hogan drove the Germans out of each traverse, one after the other, by putting their right hands round each corner and firing their revolvers, while they kept their bodies concealed. It happened that the Germans were armed only with rifles, and those weapons they could not use without exposing themselves to the revolver fire of their attackers. Thus favoured, Leach and Hogan advanced by crawling on their stomachs, capturing corner after corner, and section after section, until they got near to the other end of the trench, when they heard a voice exclaiming in English, "Don't shoot; the Germans want to surrender."

The speaker was one of their own men, who had been taken prisoner by the Germans when they captured the trench. Altogether Leach and Hogan killed eight Germans, wounded twenty, and took sixteen prisoners. It was a peculiar exploit, cleverly planned, and daringly executed. The story of how Private John Lynn, 2nd Lancashire Fusiliers, a County Tyrone man, won the V.C., is inspiring for its bravery and endurance. Near Ypres on May 2nd, 1915, as the Germans were advancing behind their wave of asphyxiating gas, Private Lynn, although almost overcome by the deadly fumes, handled his machine-gun with very great effect against the enemy, and when he could not see them he moved his gun higher up on the parapet, which enabled him to bring even more effective fire to bear, and eventually checked any further advance. The great courage displayed by this soldier had a fine effect on his comrades in the very trying circumstances. He died the following day from the effects of gas poisoning.

"It's a long, long way to Tipperary," says the soldier's favourite song. But, long as it is, Sergeant Somers, 1st Royal Inniskilling Fusiliers, brought there the Victoria Cross from Gallipoli, when he came home invalided to stay with his parents at Cloughjordan, in September, 1915. Naturally, the Tipperary village was decorated, and the hero was received by Tipperary crowds, with bands and banners; and, better still, War Loan stock to the value of £240, subscribed for by as many as 1,500 of the local Tipperary community, was presented to him at a public meeting by Major-General Friend, Commander of the Forces in Ireland.

At the meeting Mr. B. Trench, secretary to the reception committee, made the remarkable statement that out of a total of eighty Victoria Crosses then awarded for services in the war eighteen had been won by Irishmen. "If the people of Great Britain had done as well," said Mr. Trench, "they ought, according to their population, to have received 220 Victoria Crosses."

Sergeant Somers is a well-built, good-looking young fellow of twenty-one, full of high spirits, and was boyishly delighted with all the attention paid to him in Ireland. His father was for several years sexton in the parish church, Belturbet, county Cavan; and he himself was a footman in Bantry House, county Cork, before he joined the Inniskilling Fusiliers in 1912. Like Dwyer, of the East Surreys, he got the V.C. for a daring bombing exploit. The official record of the award is as follows:—

> For most conspicuous bravery. On the night of July 1st-2nd, 1915, in the southern zone of the Gallipoli Peninsula, where, owing to hostile bombing, some of our troops had retired from a sap, Sergeant Somers remained alone on the spot until a party brought up bombs. He then climbed over into the Turkish trench, and bombed the Turks with great effect. Later he advanced into the open, under heavy fire, and held back the enemy by throwing bombs into their flank until a barricade had been established. During this period he frequently ran to and from our trenches to obtain fresh supplies of bombs. By his gallantry and coolness Sergeant Somers was largely instrumental in effecting the recapture of portion of our trench which had been lost.

Recounting his experiences, Sergeant Somers said that the Turks advanced to the trenches and compelled the Gurkhas and the Inniskillings to retire. He alone stopped in the trench, refusing to leave. He shot many Turks with his revolver, killed about fifty with bombs, and forced them to retire. The enemy, however, rushed into a sap trench, and he commenced to bombard them out of it, but twice he failed. Just before dawn he stole away for the purpose of getting men up to the trench to occupy it. Some of the officers said it was impossible to put the Turks out; but Somers returned to the position, taking with him a supply of grenades, under rifle and Maxim-gun fire, and eventually succeeded in bombing the Turks out of the sap trench. He had one narrow escape on the morning of July 2nd—a splinter struck him across the spine, but he rained in the bombs until he fell from loss of blood and fatigue in the afternoon.

By that time, however, the trench had been recaptured. The Turks retreated crying, "*Allah! Allah!*" and "We gave them La La," said Somers with great glee. Somers tells all about it with great enthusiasm, and constantly recurring in his stories is the phrase, "I did my duty," or "General Sir Ian Hamilton told me when he made me King's Sergeant on the field that I did my duty"; and again, "I want to get back to duty." That was the main idea in this young Irishman's mind.

"For helping to bring the guns into action under heavy fire at Nery, near Compiègne, on September 1st, 1914, and, while severely wounded, remaining with them until all ammunition was exhausted, although he had been ordered to retire to cover."

This is the brief and cold official account of the thrilling deed for which the Victoria Cross was given to Sergeant David Nelson, L Battery, Royal Horse Artillery, a native of Derraghlands, Stranooden, county Monaghan. In all retreats the artillery is seriously handicapped, and it was so with the British artillery in the retreat from Mons. Still, they made many a gallant fight. One which stands out most conspicuously is that of L Battery, which fought for hours with one gun, and although outnumbered eight to one, succeeded in silencing the German artillery.

The battery of six guns had camped for the night by a farmhouse. At dawn, as they were watering their horses before continuing the retirement, they were shelled by a German battery of eight guns posted on a height overlooking the farm, not 700 yards away. This hill had been evacuated during the night by French cavalry without having given notice to the British. So fierce and destructive was the fire of the Germans that four guns of the L Battery were disabled, and many of the men and officers were stricken down within a few minutes. The survivors rushed to the two other guns and brought them into action. The fifth gun was quickly silenced by the killing of its entire detachment.

It was the sixth gun, served by Nelson and three other men—Sergeant-Major Dornell, Gunner Derbyshire, and Driver Osborne—that, despite all the painful and distracting incidents happening in the farmyard, was worked with such speed and cool and deadly accuracy that the Germans were compelled to depart. The British gun was crippled and almost completely shattered, but it was saved. All the heroic gunners were badly wounded, and all were decorated. Nelson had one of his ribs so crushed in that it pressed upon his right lung. On his recovery he was promoted to a second lieutenancy.

The official record of the services of the 1st Canadian Division in Flanders shows that the late Company Sergeant-Major William Hall,

8th Canadian Infantry, who won the Victoria Cross near Ypres, was a native of Belfast. Hall was awarded the coveted distinction in the following circumstances:

> On April 24th, 1915, in the neighbourhood of Ypres, when a wounded man who was lying some fifteen yards from the trench called for help, Company Sergeant-Major Hall endeavoured to reach him in the face of a very heavy enfilade fire which was being poured in by the enemy. The first attempt failed, and a non-commissioned officer and a private soldier who were attempting to give assistance were both wounded. Company Sergeant-Major Hall then made a second most gallant attempt, and was in the act of lifting up the wounded man to bring him in when he fell mortally wounded in the head.

Sir Max Aitken, M.P., who has written the official record, states that Hall was originally from Belfast, but his Canadian home was in Winnipeg. He joined the 8th Battalion at Valcartier, Quebec, in August, 1914, as a private.

Finally we come to the epic of Michael O'Leary, of the Irish Guards, which remains the finest and most amazing feat of the war. I remember well that afternoon of Friday, February 19th, 1915, when the announcement of the award of the Victoria Cross to O'Leary was given to the public. It was sent out in the afternoon, so that it first appeared in the evening newspapers. The record was one of a dozen, each of which told a tale of thrilling adventure. Yet all the London evening papers with one accord seized upon the exploit of O'Leary's capture, single-handed, of two enemy barricades—thus saving his comrades from being mowed down by a machine-gun—and killing eight Germans in the process, as the "splash" line for their contents bills. "How Michael O'Leary Won the V.C." "How Michael O'Leary, V.C., Kills Eight Germans and Takes Two Barricades." "The Wonderful Story of Michael O'Leary, V.C."

Thus the streets of London flashed and resounded with the name of Michael O'Leary—that name which sounds so musically, and so irresistibly suggests the romance and dare-devildom of the Irish race, and under its spell people rushed to read the story of his deed. What appealed to the imagination was the touch of strangeness and fantasy in the exploit. How curious it all is, when one comes to think of it! As one is walking along a London street a name suddenly emerges out of the unknown, and lo! it is fixed in the memory with a halo for ever.

It was in the brickfields at Cuinchy, on February 1st, 1915, that Michael O'Leary won his enduring fame. Taken by surprise, the Coldstream Guards had lost a trench and failed to recapture it. The Irish Guards, who were in reserve, were told to have a try. No. 1 Company, in which O'Leary was Lance-Corporal, formed the storming party. They were only too glad of any excuse to get out of the mud and slush of their trenches. Before the main body advanced across the open ground—a brickfield, with here and there a stack of bricks—O'Leary, who, in fact, was off duty, and need not have joined in the attack at all, slipped away to the left towards a railway cutting.

He had set out spontaneously on his own initiative to give the enemy a bit of a surprise. What would be the nature of the surprise, O'Leary himself did not quite know at the moment. It would all depend upon the development of the situation and the actual circumstances when the time came for him to decide. But for days before as he lay in the trenches he had brought his powers of observation into play, and having grasped all the essential details of the geographical situation and the military position, he reasoned out a plan with himself.

According to that plan, the first thing he had to do was to get into the railway cutting on his left. This he did with all speed, and very soon afterwards he re-ascended to the top of the embankment and found himself almost in a direct line with the first German barricade, one of the brick stacks, about twenty or thirty yards square, and about twenty feet high and solid. With five shots he killed as many of the German defenders. Then seeing the headlong and irresistible dash of his comrades across the field he came to the conclusion that the remaining Germans had no chance of escape.

So he quickly disappeared down the railway cutting once more, and again came up to the top on the right front of the second German barricade. Here there was a machine-gun. In fact the officer in command had just slewed round the gun on the Irish Guards still busy at the first barricade, and had his finger on the button to let go the hail of lead upon them when he was dropped by a bullet from O'Leary's rifle. Michael also shot two other Germans, and the remaining five surrendered by putting up their hands to the deadly, unerring marksman on the embankment.

Thus it happened that when the No. 1 Company of the Irish Guards got to the second barricade without a single casualty, instead of, as they had expected, serious loss of life, their surprise was turned into amazement on seeing O'Leary there before them in sole and complete possession of the place, with a German machine-gun and five prisoners as spoil. "How the divil did you get here, Mike!" Such was the exclamation of O'Leary's intimate comrades. Mike only realised that he had done something of importance and value, as well as of splendid gallantry, when officers and men crowded round him to shake his hand. The commanding officer, Major the Hon. J.F. Trefusis, promoted him full sergeant on the field.

There must always be an element of chance or luck in such an abnormal achievement. But it is the man that is the thing. All the good fortune in the world would be without avail if the man were not of an exceptional type, possessed of perfect courage, marvellous self-confidence, and supreme resolution. Not less wonderful than what O'Leary did was the deliberate and efficient way in which he accomplished it. He knew that death might come at any moment. But he put the fear immediately aside lest it might in the least unnerve him in the pursuit of his purpose. Everything showed that he was in full possession of all his faculties.

What the United Kingdom thought of the deed was expressed by London in the tumultuous welcome which it gave to Sergeant Michael O'Leary, when, in his war-stained uniform, he drove through the streets with Mr. T.P. O'Connor, to speak in Hyde Park on Saturday afternoon, July 10th, 1915. There was terrific crushing and rushing on the part of hundreds of thousands of people eager to catch a glimpse of the hero—a slim youth of twenty-five, in khaki, with fair hair, and a pleasant smile lighting up his blue eyes and freckled face. No wonder, indeed. As Conan Doyle, the novelist, remarked:

> No writer of fiction would dare to fasten such an achievement on any of his characters.

And only a few years before Michael was helping to mind his father's stock on a little farm at Inchigeela, County Cork. So they made him an officer, Lieutenant O'Leary, of one of the Tyneside Irish battalions of the Northumberland Fusiliers. And rightly so, for he proved himself to be possessed of all the qualities of a leader—observation and reasoning, quick to receive impressions, and quick to act upon them—resource, daring, and yet discretion, coolness and self-mastery in an enterprise of difficulty and danger. The two most damnable drawbacks on the field of battle are unpreparedness and slowness in officers, and stolidness and lack of initiative in men.

Well, Michael himself was never able fully to appreciate the gallantry of his action. What could be more modest than his letter to his father and mother on the subject:—

"Dear Parents—I know you will be glad to hear that I am awarded the Victoria Cross for conspicuous gallantry in the field. Hoping all are well, as I myself am in the best of health. From your fond son.—Michael."

There is the same simplicity, with a touch of humour, in the remark he made when being seen off at Victoria Station after all his glorification in London:—"It's glad I am to be going back to the trenches for a bit of a rest."

And the only man in the whole wide world to show any desire to disparage Michael's exploit was Michael's father himself. The old man was asked if he was surprised at his son's bravery. "Surprised, is it!" he exclaimed.

> What I am surprised at is that he didn't do more. Sure often myself I laid out ten Irishmen with a stick coming from Macroom Fair when I was a gossoon like Mick—Irishmen, mind you, an' stout hearty lads at that same. An' it was rather a bad fist Mick made of it that he could kill only eight Germans, and he having a rifle and bayonet.

How is that for the old Irish spirit?

The Irish at the Somme

Michael MacDonagh

Contents

Introduction	145
Preface	151
In the Trenches With the Connaught Rangers	153
Exploits of the Ulster Division	162
Ulsters' Attack on the Slopes of Thiepval	169
Four Victoria Crosses to the Ulster Division	180
Combativeness of the Irish Soldier	187
With the Tyneside Irish	195
The Wearing of Religious Emblems at the Front	208
The Irish Soldier's Humour and Seriousness	223
The Irish Brigade	234
Irish Replies to German Wiles and Poison Gas	241
Storming of Guillamont by the Irish Brigade	249
The Brigade's Pounce on Guinchy	255
Honours and Distinctions for the Irish Brigade	260
The Wooden Cross	266
More Irish Heroes of the Victoria Cross	272
Relations Between Enemy Trenches	286

To the Memory
of
Major William Redmond,
M.P. Royal Irish Regiment (Irish Brigade)
Who Died of Wounds
Received in Action June 7, 1917
Leading His Men
in the Attack on
Wytschaete Wood

Introduction

The Response of the Irish Race

This war is a war of liberation, and its battle-cry is the rights and liberties of humanity. From the very beginning of the conflict my colleagues of the Irish Party, and I myself, have availed of every opportunity in Parliament, on the platform, and in the Press, to present this view of it to the Irish race at home and abroad; and despite the tragic mistakes made in regard to Ireland by the successive Governments which have held office since war broke out, we are still unshaken in our opinion that Ireland's highest interests lie in the speedy and overwhelming victory of England and the Allies.

The response of the Irish race the world over to our appeal to rise in defence of civilisation and freedom has been really wonderful. The example was set by Ireland herself.

At the outbreak of the war I asked the Irish people, and especially the young men of Ireland, to mark the profound change which has been brought about in the relations of Ireland to the Empire by wholeheartedly supporting the Allies in the field. I pointed out that at long last, after centuries of misunderstanding, the democracy of Great Britain had finally and irrevocably decided to trust Ireland with self-government; and I called upon Ireland to prove that this concession of liberty would have the same effect in our country as it has had in every other portion of the Empire, and that henceforth Ireland would be a strength instead of a weakness. I further pointed out that the war was provoked by the intolerable military despotism of Germany, that it was a war in defence of small nationalities, and that Ireland would be false to her own history and traditions, as well as to honour, good faith and self-interest, if she did not respond to my appeal.

The answer to that appeal is one of the most astonishing facts in history. At the moment, fraught with the most terrible consequences to the whole Empire, this Kingdom found for the first time in the history of the relations between Great Britain and Ireland that the Irish Nationalist members, representing the overwhelming mass of the people of Ireland, were enabled to declare themselves upon the side of England. They did that with their eyes open. They knew the difficulties in the way. They knew—none so well—the distrust and suspicion of British good faith which had been, in the past, universal almost in Ireland. They recognised that the boon of self-government had not been finally granted to their country. They knew the traditional hostility which existed in many parts of Ireland to recruiting for the British Army.

Facing all these things, and all the risks that they entailed, they told Ireland and her sons abroad that it was their duty to rally to the support of the Allies in a war which was in defence of the principles of freedom and civilisation. We succeeded far better than we had anticipated, or hoped at the commencement. This is a notorious fact. There is genuine enthusiasm in Ireland on the side of the Allies. Addressing great popular gatherings in every province in Ireland in support of the Allies, I called for a distinctively Irish army, composed of Irishmen, led by Irishmen and trained at home in Ireland. With profound gratitude I acknowledge the magnificent response the country has made. For the first time in the history of the Wars of England there is a huge Irish army in the field.

The achievements of that Irish army have covered Ireland with glory before the world, and have thrilled our hearts with pride. North and South have vied with each other in springing to arms, and, please God, the sacrifices they have made side by side on the field of battle will form the surest bond of a united Irish nation in the future.

From Ireland, according to the latest official figures, 173,772 Irishmen are serving in the Navy and Army, representing all classes and creeds amongst our people. Careful inquiries made through the churches in the north of England and Scotland and from other sources, show that, in addition, at least 150,000 sons of the Irish race, most of them born in Ireland, have joined the Colours in Great Britain . It is a pathetic circumstance that these Irishmen in non-Irish regiments are almost forgotten, except when their names appear in the casualty lists. Some of the Irish papers have, for a considerable time past, been publishing special lists of killed and wounded under the heading, "Irish Casualties in British Regiments."

One of these daily lists, taken quite haphazard, and published on November 1, 1916, contains 225 names, all distinctively Irish—O'Briens, O'Hanlons, Donovans, etc. These men were scattered amongst the following non-Irish regiments—

Grenadier Guards.
Coldstream Guards.
Scots Guards.
Welsh Guards.
Royal Field Artillery.
Royal Engineers.
Royal Scots Fusiliers.
The Black Watch.
Northumberland Fusiliers.
Yorkshire Regiment.
East Yorks. Regiment.
Dorsetshire Regiment.
Cheshire Regiment.
York and Lancaster Regiment.
Lancashire Fusiliers.
King's Royal Rifles.
London Regiment.
Manchester Regiment.
King's Liverpool Regiment.
Loyal North Lancashire Regiment.
Royal Warwickshire Regiment.
Highland Light Infantry.
Leicestershire Regiment.
Worcestershire Regiment.
Sherwood Foresters.
King's Own Yorks. Light Infantry.
Border Regiment.
Durham Light Infantry.
Notts. & Derby Regiment.
Machine Gun Corps.
Army Service Corps.
Army Cyclist Corps.

As showing the extent to which Scottish regiments at the Front are made up of Irishmen, one newspaper quotes four hundred names from the casualty lists issued on four successive days one week. All the names are Irish, all the addresses are Scotch, and in only about twenty cases were the men enrolled in Irish regiments, all the others being attached to Scottish regiments. These sad records show the many thousands of Irishmen serving in non-Irish regiments who are never taken into account to the credit of Ireland, in estimating the part she is playing in this war, until they come to light in the casualty lists.

In addition to these voluntary contributions of Ireland and her sons in Great Britain to the British Army, I am informed on the highest authority that from twenty to twenty-five *per cent*, of all the troops from the oversea Dominions are men of Irish blood. General Botha sent me this cablegram from South Africa:

> "I entirely endorse your view that this victory"—he is referring to his great defeat of the Germans in their colonies "is the fruit of the policy of liberty and the recognition of national rights in this part of the Empire."

General Botha had enormous difficulties to face, serious racial animosity, and bitter national memories. Does any fair-minded man think that General Botha could have overcome those difficulties as he did if the war had broken out just after the recognition of those national rights to which he referred and before they had come into operation? The national rights of Ireland are recognised, but they have not yet come into operation. Yet it is true to say that the overwhelming sentiment of the Irish people is with the Empire for the first time. That fact is of incalculable value. Its influence has spread to every corner of the Empire. If the sentiment of the Irish people at home had not been with England in this war, the depressing and benumbing effect would have been felt everywhere in the self-governing Dominions.

Ireland herself has made a splendid response, and the result has been that a wave of enthusiasm has stirred the hearts of men of Irish blood throughout the Empire. I received a New Year's card from the commanding officer and the other officers of a regiment raised in Vancouver, commanded by Irishmen and composed of Irishmen. They call themselves "The Vancouver Irish Fusiliers." Then, not long since, in Cape Town, green flags were presented by General Botha's wife—a member of the historic Emmet family—to an Irish regiment raised there. These facts constitute a striking result of the action we felt it our duty to take to bring feeling in Ireland in regard to the war into line with that of the rest of the Empire.

Then there is that remarkable Irish battalion of the Canadian Expeditionary Force, the Irish Canadian Rangers, which is composed of

Irish Catholics and Irish Protestants in equal numbers, commanded by officers more than half of whom are Catholics and having a Catholic chaplain and a Protestant chaplain. This battalion, unique among the fighting units raised at home or abroad during the war, and a magnificent body of men, made a tour through the ancient motherland of their race in January 1917 (on their way to the Front), and received in Dublin, Belfast, Cork and Limerick the most enthusiastic popular welcomes.

Ireland is very proud of these sons of the Irish race who, in every part of the Empire, have followed the lead which she herself has given in rallying to the cause with which she has always sympathised and has always supported—the cause of right against might. The Irish race is represented in this war by at least half a million of men who have voluntarily joined the Colours. How gallantly they have fought this book, in part, relates. In his first series of *The Irish at the Front* Mr. MacDonagh deals with the achievements of the Irish Guards and the Regular Irish regiments of the Line in Flanders and France in the earlier years of the war; the landing of the Munsters and Dublins of the immortal 29th Division at Beach V, Gallipoli; and the fighting of the 10th (Irish) Division of the New Armies at Suvla Bay. The story of these glorious deeds sent a wave of emotion through the land. The King, addressing a battalion of the Irish Guards on St. Patrick's Day, 1916, said—

> On St. Patrick's Day, when Irishmen the world over unite to celebrate the memory of their Patron Saint, it gives me great pleasure to inspect the reserve battalion of my Irish Guards, and to testify my appreciation of the services rendered by the regiment in this war.... I gratefully remember the heroic endurance of the 1st Battalion in the arduous retreat from Mons, again at Ypres on the critical November 1st, when, as Lord Cavan, your Brigadier, wrote, those who were left showed the enemy that Irish Guards must be reckoned with, however hard hit. After twenty-eight days of incessant fighting against heavy odds, the battalion came out of the line less than a company strong, with only four officers—a glorious tribute to Irish loyalty and endurance.... In conferring the Victoria Cross on Lance-Corporal, now Lieutenant, Michael O'Leary, the first Irish Guardsman to win this coveted distinction, I was proud to honour a deed that, in its fearless contempt of death, illustrates the spirit of my Irish Guards. At Loos the 2nd Battalion received its baptism of

fire and con- firmed the high reputation already won by the 1st Battalion.

The Daily Telegraph (London), writing on March 18, 1916, said—

There is one key to the soul of Ireland—the word 'freedom.' It was realised instantly that this was no dynastic war on the part of the Allies, no struggle for material ends, but a life and death conflict for liberty of thought and action. Once the issue was exposed, Irishmen, with all the white heat which injustice inspires in their breasts, threw themselves into the battle. The enemy has since felt Irish steel and fallen under Irish bullets. Whatever the future may have in store, the British people will never forget the generous blood of the sister nation, which has been shed on so many hard-fought battlefields since the world-war began.

In this, the second series of *The Irish at the Front*, the thrilling story is continued. The Irish troops dealt with are all of the New Armies-the Ulster Division, the Irish Division and the Tyneside Irish Brigade. I am as proud of the Ulster regiments as I am of the Nationalist regiments. I do not want to boast of their valour. We Irishmen are inclined to take it as a matter of course. These Irish regiments, Unionist and Nationalist, merely keep up the tradition of our race. But I say that Lord Kitchener's words remain true—the words that he wrote to the Viceregal Recruiting Conference in Dublin in 1915, when he said that in the matter of recruiting, "Ireland's performance has been magnificent." Let me ask any fair-minded man this question: If five years ago any one had predicted that in a great war in which the Empire was engaged 173,772 men would have been raised from Ireland, and that there would be more than half a million Irishmen with the Colours, would he not have been looked upon as a lunatic? It is the free offering of Ireland. Surely it must be regarded as a proud and astonishing record!

J. E. Redmond.

Preface

This narrative is concerned chiefly with the three distinctively Irish units of the New Armies engaged on the Western Front—the Ulster Division, the Irish Division (representative of the south and west), and the "Tyneside Irish," in which Irishmen living in the north of England enlisted. It also deals incidentally with the Irish Regular regiments of the Line, and with that numerous body of Irishmen serving in English, Scottish and Welsh battalions and in the Anzacs and Canadians.

The first series of *The Irish at the Front* covers, first, the fighting of the Irish regiments of the Regular Army in France, Flanders and the Dardanelles during the early stages of the war; and, secondly, the operations of the 10th (Irish) Division—composed entirely of "Kitchener's men"—against the Turks at Gallipoli. The latter, an exceptionally fine body of young Irishmen, gallantly fought and fell—as the story discloses—in that expedition, so ill-fated and, yet so romantic, though they had never handled a rifle or done a day's drill before the war. In this series we see Irishmen of the same type matched against the Germans in France. As we know, Germany confidently expected that such levies, hastily raised and insufficiently trained, would break in pieces at the first encounter with her seasoned troops. But it was the formidable German lines that were broken, and they were broken by these very raw levies at the bayonet's point.

For the telling of the Irish part in the story of the Somme I am much indebted to the assistance given by officers and men of the Irish battalions engaged in that mighty battle. But the Irish soldiers are not only "splendid fighting material"—a rather non- human phrase now much in vogue, as if the only thing that matters in warfare is the physical capacity of man—they have souls and minds and hearts, as well as strong right hands, and of these also some- thing is said in this book.

Michael MacDonagh.

CHAPTER 1

In the Trenches With the Connaught Rangers

"The men are as anxious for the road, sir, as if 'twere to Galway races they were going, no less, or to Ballinasloe Fair," said the company sergeant-major to the captain. Those referred to belonged to a battalion of the Connaught Rangers ordered to the firing-trenches for the first time. "The real thing at last;" "The genuine McCoy, and no mistake," they said to one another as, in preparation for the march, they hurriedly packed their things in the barns and cowsheds that served as billets, and, to provide further vent for their jubilation, danced Irish jigs and reels and sang national songs.

These Irishmen had read a lot about the fighting, and had heard a great deal more, but they felt that print and talk, however graphic and copious, left many strange things to be disclosed by the actual experience. Some of them would "get the beck"—the call from Death—but what matter? Were not soldiers who died in action to be envied, rather than pitied, by those who found themselves alive when the war was over, and had not been to the mysterious Front at all? So they thought and said, and now that they were on the road there was a look of proud elation on their faces, as though they had been singled out by special favour for a grand adventure.

They did not regard themselves in the least as heroes, these entirely unsophisticated men, without a trace of self-consciousness. They had volunteered for service in the belief that Ireland would be false to her historical self if she did not take part in this war for freedom, democracy and humanity. But now there was nothing in their minds about revenging the wrongs of Belgium, or driving the invader from the soil of France, or even of saving the British Empire. It was the fight that was the thing. It was the chance of having a smack at "the Gerrys"- as the enemy is called by the Irish soldiers—that they prized. More exalted feelings would come again when the battle was over and won. Then, and not till then, as they return with many gaps in their ranks, do Irish troops see themselves as an army of redemption and deliverance; and the only land they think of having saved is Ireland. To them Ireland personifies all the great causes of the war, and a blow struck for these causes, no matter where, is a blow struck for her.

By the light of many stars sparkling in the sky that dark October night the men could see signs that battles had been fought in the country they were traversing. It was a devastated bare expanse, stretching for miles and miles, very muddy and broken up with shell holes. Roads had been made across it, and along one of these the battalion went in the wake of the guides with swinging lanterns. The men were fully loaded. In addition to his fighting equipment, almost every one carried something extra, such as a pick or shovel, a bag of rations, or a bundle of firewood. The company officers also had heavy packs strapped on their shoulders.

Great good-humour prevailed. Whenever, at awkward turns of the road, or at very dark points, progress was interrupted, those in front would shout some preposterous explanation of the delay to their comrades behind. "Begonnies, boys, we're taking tickets here for Galway. Word has come down that the war is over," cried one joker. Deep groans of pretended dismay and disappointment rose from the rear ranks. "And poor me, without a German helmet, or even a black eye, to show that I was in it," was one of the responses.

When the open plain was quitted the battalion disappeared into a trench like a narrow country lane winding between high banks. It was much darker in these deeps than it had been outside. The gloom was broken occasionally by the light of lanterns carried by sentinels, or electric torches at junctions" where several trenches crossed. Soon the trench became narrower and more tortuous. It also became more soaked with rain. Pools of water were frequently encountered. The battalion was now a floundering, staggering, overloaded and perspiring closely packed mass of men, walking in couples or in single file and treading on each other's heels.

The mishaps arising from this crowded scramble in the dark through mud and mire, between banks of unsupported crumbling earth, did not exhaust the Irish cheerfulness of the battalion. There was laughter when a man got a crack on the skull from a rifle which a comrade carried swung across his shoulder. There was louder laughter still when another, stooping to pick up something he had dropped, was bumped into from behind and sent sprawling. So sucking and tenacious was the mud that frequently each dragging footstep called for quite a physical effort, and a man was thankful that he did not have to leave a boot behind. "Ah, sure this is nothin' to the bog away in Connemara, where I often sunk up to me neck when crossing it to cut turf," was the comfort imparted in a soft brogue. "True for you, Tim," remarked another. "It's an ould sayin' and a true one that *there's nothin' so bad but it could be worse.*"

The trench certainly proved the truth of the saying. Bad as it had been, it sank to a still lower degree of slush. There were deep holes filled with water into which the men went with an abrupt plunge and passed through with much splashing. Just ahead of one of these particularly treacherous points singing was heard. The chorus was taken up by many voices, and its last line was rapped out with hearty boisterousness—

Out and make way for the bould Fenian Men.

This joyous noise heralded the appearance of a party of the Dublin Fusiliers, belonging to the same division, who were coming down the trench. By the light of lanterns and lamps it was seen that they had taken off their trousers and socks and, holding up their shirts, were wading in their boots blithely through the pools, like girls in bare legs and lifted petticoats paddling at the seaside.

The Connaught men laughed hilariously. "Sure the Dublin jackeens have never been beaten yet for cuteness," they cried. "They stripped to their pelts so as they wouldn't get the 'fluensy by means of their wet clothes. And, faix, 'twould be the greatest pity in the world anything would ail stout and hearty boys like them." As they spoke, the men of the west lay close against the embankments to let the men of the east go by. But weren't the Dublins in the divil of a hurry back to billets? the Rangers went on to remark. And why not? answered the Dublins. Sure if they'd only sniff with their noses they would smell the roast beef and the steaming punch that were being got ready for them by special orders of Field-Marshal Haig for the great things they did away up in the firing-line.

"Lucky boys!" shouted the Rangers, responding to the joke. "And tell us now, have ye left us a Gerry at all alive to get a pelt at, and we new at the game?"

A Dublin man gave the reply as he went past. "To tell ye the truth, except there's a raid, there isn't much divarshion in the way of fighting; but every man of ye will have his full and plenty of mud and water before he's much oulder."

"Well, there's nothing in that to yowl about."

"Maybe not, if you can swim."

The trench resounded with laughter at the exchange of banter. But for fear any of the Rangers might take some of the talk as half a joke and whole earnest, a kind-hearted sergeant of the Dublins, wishful to say the cheery word, called out, "Don't mind them playboys; there's no more water and mud in it than is natural in such wet weather as we're getting."

The Rangers reached their destination just as the day was dawning in a cold drizzle from a grey, lowering sky. They were all plastered with yellowish mud. Mud was on their hands, on their faces, in their hair, down their backs; and the barrels of their rifles were choked with mud. For the next four days and nights of duty in the trenches they were to be lapped about with mud. War was to be for them a mixture of mud and high explosives. Of the two mud was the ugliest and most hateful. Soon they would come to think that there was hardly anything left in the world but mud; and from that they would advance to a state of mind in which they doubted whether there ever had been a time in their existence when they were free from mud. But through it all this battalion, like the others in the division, preserved their good-humour. They are known, in fact, as "The Light-Hearted Brigade." Every difficulty was met with a will to overcome it, tempered with a joke and a laugh. No matter how encrusted with filth their bodies might be, their souls were always above contamination.

Men off duty at night slept in shelter pits dug deep into the soil by the side of the trenches. It was overcrowded in stark violation of all the sanitary by-laws relating to ventilation in civil life. No time was wasted in undressing. The men lay down fully clad in their mud-crusted clothes, even to their boots, wrapped round in blankets. During the night they were awakened by a loud explosion. "All right, boys; don't stir," cried the sergeant. "It's only one of those chape German alarum clocks going off at the wrong time. Get off to sleep again, me heroes."

In the morning more time was saved by getting up fully dressed, and not having to wash or to shave, so as to spare the water. A private, looking round the dugout and noticing the absence of windows, remarked, "Faix, those of us who are glaziers and window-cleaners will find it hard to make a living in this country."

As the battalion was new to the trenches, another Irish battalion of more experience shared with them the holding of this particular line. To a group of lads gathered about a brazier of glowing coke in a sheltered traverse an old sergeant that had seen service in the Regular Army was giving what, no doubt, he thought was sound and valuable advice, but which was at times of a quality calculated more to disturb, perhaps, than to reassure.

"Bullets are nothin' at all," said he. "I wouldn't give you a snap of me fingers for them. Listen to them now, flyin' about and whinin' and whimperin' as if they wor lost, stolen or strayed, and wor lookin' for a billet to rest in. They differ greatly, do these bullets; but sure in time you'll larn them all by sound and be able to tell the humour each one of them is in. There's only one kind of bullet, boys, that you'll never hear; and that is the one which gives you such a pelt as to send you home to Ireland or to kingdom come. But," he continued, "what'll put the fear of God into your sowls, if it isn't there already, is the heavy metal which the Gerrys pitch across to us in exchange for ours.

"The first time I was up here I was beside a man whose teeth went chatterin' in a way that put me in fear of me life. Sure, didn't I think for a minute it was a Gerry machine-gun—may the divil cripple them!—startin' its bloody work at me ear. Now, there must be none of that in this trench. If you're afraid, don't show it; remimber always that the Gerrys are in just as great a fright, if not more so. Show your spunk. Stand fast or sit tight, and hope for the best. Above all, clinch your teeth."

The bombardment of a trench by shells from guns in the rear of the enemy's lines, or by bombs thrown from mortars close at hand, is probably the greatest test of endurance that has ever been set to humanity. The devastating effect is terrific. At each explosion men may be blown to pieces or buried alive. Even the concussion often kills. A man might escape being hit by the flying projectiles and yet be blinded or made deaf or deprived of his speech by the shock. All reel as if their insides had collapsed. The suspense of waiting for the next shell or bomb, the uncertainty as to where it is going to fall, followed by the shake which the detonation gives the nervous system, are enough to wear out the most stout-hearted of soldiers. It is then that companionship and discipline tell. The men catch from one another the won't-appear-frightened determination, and the spirit of won't-give-in.

Crash! A fierce gust of wind sweeps through the trench. Men are lifted from their feet and flung violently to the ground amid showers of earth and stones. There is a brief pause; and then is heard the most unexpected of sounds not the moaning of pain, but a burst of laughter! Four men of the battalion were playing "Forty-five," a card game beloved of Hibernians, seated under a piece of tarpaulin propped up on poles, as much at their ease as if they lay under a hedge on a Sunday evening in summer at home in Ireland, with only the priest to fear, and he known to be on a sick call at the other side of the parish. The bomb came at the most inopportune moment, just as the fall of the trick was about to be decided. When the card party recovered their senses, the man who held the winning card was found to be wounded. "'Twas the Gerrys—sweet bad luck to them!—that jinked the game that time, boys," he exclaimed. His companions, standing round him, burst into laughter at the remark.

Merriment is not uncommon as the shells are bursting. The spectacle of four or five men hurriedly tumbling for shelter into the same "funk hole," a wild whirl of arms and legs, has its absurd side and never fails to excite amusement. The way in which men disentangle themselves from the ruins caused by the explosion is often also grotesque. Racy oddities of character are revealed. One man was buried in the loose earth. His comrades hastened to rescue him, and to cheer him up told him he would be got out next to no time, for Tim Maloney, the biggest as well as the fastest digger in the company was engaged on the job. "I feel that right well," cried the victim, as he spluttered the mud from his mouth. "But I've enough on top of me without him! Pull me out of this from under his feet." There was an explosion close to a man at work repairing the trench. The man was overheard saying to himself, as he turned his back disdainfully to the shell, "Oh, go to blazes, with yez."

But it is not all comedy and farce. How could it be with stern, black-visaged Death always watching with wolfish eyes to see men die? Fate plays unimaginable tricks with its victims. A bullet stops many a casual conversation forever. "Look at this!" cries a man, holding up his cap for a comrade to see the bullet-hole that had just been made through it. "A close shave," he adds; "but what matter? Isn't a miss as good as a mile?" And, as he was putting the cap on again, he fell a corpse to a surer bullet.

There he lay, just a bundle of muddy khaki; and a dozing comrade, upon whom he dropped, elbowed him aside, saying impatiently, "Get out of that, with yer andrew-martins" (jokes and tricks); "can't you let a poor divil get a wink of sleep?"

Tragedy takes on, at times, queer, fantastic shapes. A man has his right arm blown off close to the shoulder. He picks the limb up with his left hand, shouting, "My arm! my arm! Oh, holy mother of God, where's my arm?" In raging agony he rushes shrieking down the trench carrying the limb with him until he encounters his company officer. "Oh, captain, darlin'," he cries. "Look what the Gerrys have done to me! May God's curse light upon them and theirs forever! An' now I'll never shoulder a rifle for poor ould Ireland anymore."

The night, and only the night, has terrors for the Irish soldiers, especially those from the misty mountains and remote seaboard of the west and south. In the daylight they are merry and prolific of jest. Strongly gregarious by instinct, they delight in companionship. They are sustained and upheld by the excitement of battle's uproar. They will face any danger in the broad daylight. But they hate to be alone in the dark anywhere, and are afraid to pass at night even a graveyard in which their own beloved kith and kin lie peacefully at rest for ever. They feel "lonesome and queer" as they would say themselves.

So it is that when by himself at a listening post in a shell hole in No Man's Land, lapped about with intense blackness, peering and hearkening, the superstitious soul of the Irish soldier seems to conjure up all the departed spectral bogies and terrors of the Dark Ages. He is ready to cry out like Ajax, the Greek warrior, in *Homer*, "Give *us but light, O Jove; and in the light, if thou seest fit, destroy us.*"

Even a Cockney soldier, lacking as he is in any subtle sympathy with the emotional and immaterial sides of life, confesses that it gives him the creeps proper to be out there in the open jaws of darkness, away from his mates and almost right under the nose of old *Boche*. An Irish soldier will admit that on this duty he does have a genuine feeling of terror. Crouching in the soft, yielding earth, he imagines he is in the grave, watching and waiting he knows not for what. Everything is indefinite and uncertain. There is a vague presentiment that some unknown but awful evil is impending. Perhaps a thousand hostile German eyes are staring at him through the darkness along rifle barrels; or, more horrible still, perhaps a thousand invisible devils are on the prowl to drag his soul to hell. The supernatural powers are the only forces the Irish soldier fears.

The senses of the sentry are so abnormally alert that if grass were growing near him he had only to put his ear to the ground to hear the stirring of the sap. But though he listens intently, not a sound comes out of the blackness. He regards the profound stillness as confirmation of his worst fears. All is silence in the trench behind him, where his comrades ought to be. He would welcome the relief of voices and the sound of feet in the enemy's lines. But the Gerrys give no sign of life. Is he alone in the whole wide world, the solitary survivor of this terrible war? What would he not part with to be able to get up and run! But he is fixed to his post by a sense of duty, just as strong as if he were chained there by iron bands. To cry out would afford immense relief to his overwrought feelings. But his tongue seems paralysed in his mouth.

Then he bethinks him of his prayers. From his inside tunic pocket he takes out his beads—which his mother gave him at parting and made him promise faithfully always to carry about his person—and, making the sign of the cross, he is soon absorbed in the saying of the Rosary. Resignation and fortitude came to his aid. The invisible evil agencies by which he had really been encompassed—loneliness, anxiety, melancholy—are dispelled.

Scouting is the night work that appeals most to the Irish soldiers. There is in it the excitement of movement, the element of adventure and the support of companionship, too, for four, five or six go out together. Oh, the fearful joy of crawling on one's stomach across the intervening ground, seeking for a passage through the enemy's wire entanglements or wriggling under it, taking a peep over their parapets, dropping down into a sparsely occupied part of the trench, braining the sentry and returning with rifle and cap as trophies! This is one of the most perilous forms of the harassing tactics of war, and for its success uncommon pluck and resource are required.

Yet, like everything else at the Front, it often has an absurd side. A Connaught Ranger, back from such an expedition, related that, hearing the Gerrys talking, he called out, "How many of ye are there?" To his surprise he got an answer in English: "Four." Then, throwing in a bomb, he said, "Divide that between ye, an' be damned to ye." "Faix, 'twas the bomb that divided them," he added, "for didn't they come out of the trench after me in smithereens."

Another party returned from a raid with tears streaming down their cheeks. "Is it bad news ye bring, crying in that way?" they were asked. No! they hadn't bad news; nor were they crying. If it was crying they were, wouldn't they be roaring and bawling? and there wasn't a sound out of them for anyone to hear. Only asses could say such a thing as that. 'Twas they that looked like silly asses, they were told, with the tears pouring out of their eyes like the Powerscourt waterfall. What the mischief was the matter with them, anyway? Well, then, if any one cared to know, was the reply, 'twas the Gerrys that treated them to a whiff of lachrymose gas!

The fatigue, the disgust, and the danger of life in the trenches are, at times, stronger than any other impulse, whether of the flesh or of the soul. "'Tis enough to drive one to the drink: a grand complaint when there's plenty of porter about," said a private; "but a terrible fate when there's only the water we're wading in, and that same full up-the Lord save us!—of creeping and wriggling things."

"True for you; it's the quare life, and no mistake," remarked another. "You do things and get praise for them, such as smashing a fellow's skull, or putting a bullet through him, which if you were to do at home you'd be soon on the run, with a hue and cry and all the police of the country at your heels."

Back in billets again, for a wash and a shave and a brush up, and lying in their straw beds in the barns, the Rangers would thus philosophise on their life. The bestial side of it—the terrible overcrowding of the men, the muck, the vermin, the gobbling of food with filthy hands, the stench of corrupting bodies lying in the open, or insufficiently buried, and, along with all that, its terror, agony and tragedy are, indeed, utterly repellent to human nature. Still, there was general agreement that they had never spent a week of such strange and exquisite experiences. Fear there was at times, but it seemed rather to keep up a state of pleasurable emotion than to generate anguish and distress.

Certainly most Connaught Rangers will swear that life in the trenches has at least three thrilling and exalting moments. One is when the tot of rum is served round. Another is the first faint appearance of light in the sky behind the enemy's lines, proclaiming that the night is far spent and the day is at hand. The third is the call to "stand to," telling that a visit from the Gerrys is expected, when the men cease to be navvies and become soldiers again—throwing aside the hateful pick and shovel and taking up the beloved rifle and bayonet.

CHAPTER 2

Exploits of the Ulster Division

BELFAST'S TRIBUTE TO THE DEAD

"I am not an Ulsterman, but as I followed the amazing attack of the Ulster Division on July 1, I felt that I would rather be an Ulsterman than anything else in the world. With shouts of 'Remember the Boyne' and 'No Surrender, boys,' they threw themselves at the Germans, and before they could be restrained had penetrated to the enemy fifth line. The attack was one of the greatest revelations of human courage and endurance known in history." A British officer on the exploits of the Ulster Division, July 1, 1916.

One of the most striking and impressive tributes ever paid to the heroic dead was that of Belfast on the 12th of July, 1916, in memory of the men of the Ulster Division who fell on the opening day of that month in the great British offensive on the Somme. For five minutes following the hour of noon all work and movement, business and household, were entirely suspended. In the flax mills, the linen factories, the ship yards, the munition workshops, men and women paused in their labours. All machinery was stopped, and the huge hammers became silent. In shop and office business ceased; at home the housewife interrupted her round of duties; in the streets traffic was brought to a halt, on the local railways the running trains pulled up.

The whole population stood still, and in deep silence, with bowed heads but with uplifted hearts, turned their thoughts to the valleys and slopes of Picardy, where on July 1 the young men of Ulster, the pride and flower of the province, gave their lives for the preservation of the British Empire, the existence of separate and independent States, and the rule of law and justice in their international relations.

"The Twelfth" is the great festival of Belfast. On that day is celebrated the Williamite victories of the Boyne, July 1, and Aughrim, July 12, 1690, in which the cause of the Stuarts went down forever. It is kept as a general holiday of rejoicing and merry-making. The members of the Orange lodges turn out with their dazzling banners and their no less gorgeous yellow, crimson and blue regalia; and the streets resound with the lilt of fifes, the piercing notes of cornets, the boom and rattle of many drums, the tramp of marching feet and the cheers of innumerable spectators. There was no such demonstration on July 12, 1916.

For the first time in the history of the Orange Institution the observance of the anniversary was voluntarily abandoned, so that there might be no stoppage of war work in the ship yards and munition factories. But at the happy suggestion of the Lord Mayor (Sir Crawford McCullagh), five minutes of the day were given reverently to lofty sorrow for the dead, who, by adding "The Ancre," "Beaumont Hamel" and "Thiepval Wood" to "Deny," "Enniskillen," "The Boyne" and "Aughrim" on the banners of Ulster, have given a new meaning and glory to the celebration of "The Twelfth" in which all Ireland can share. Major-General O. S. W. Nugent, D.S.O., commanding the Ulster Division, in a special Order of the Day, issued after the advance, wrote—

Nothing finer has been done in the War.

The Division has been highly tried and has emerged from the ordeal with unstained honour, having fulfilled in every part the great expectations formed of it.

None but troops of the best quality could have faced the fire which was brought to bear on them, and the losses suffered during the advance.

A magnificent example of sublime courage and discipline."

This glory was gained at a heavy cost. There was cause for bitter grief as well as the thrill of pride in Ulster. Nothing has brought home more poignantly to the inhabitants of a small area of the kingdom the grim sacrifices and the unutterable pathos of the war than the many pages of names and addresses of the dead and wounded—relatives, friends and acquaintances—which appeared in the Belfast newspapers for days before "The Twelfth" and after. So blinds were drawn in business and private houses; flags were flown at half-mast; and bells were mournfully tolling for Ulster's irremediable losses when, at the stroke of twelve o'clock, traffic came instantaneously to a standstill, and for five minutes the citizens solemnly stood with bared heads in the teeming rain thinking of the gallant dead, the darkened homes and the inconsolable mothers and wives.

The Ulster Division possesses an individuality all its own. It has no like or equal among the units of the British Army on account of its family character; the close and intimate blood relationship of its members; its singleness of purpose; the common appeal of racial, political and religious ideals that binds it together by stronger links than steel. The United Kingdom, as a whole, may be said to have been totally unready when war broke out. But it happened that one small section of this industrial and peace-loving community was prepared, to some extent, for the mighty emergency. That was Ulster.

It was immersed in business at the time, just as much as Manchester or Sheffield, and in making money out of its flourishing prosperity. But, unlike those English industrial centres, Ulster had in its history and traditions an influence which bred a combative disposition, and ever kept burning a martial flame, even in its marts and workshops. The community was convinced that in defence of all they hold dearest in religious beliefs and political principles they might have some day, not, as in England when opinions are at stake, to flock to the polling stations at a General Election, but take to the field and fight. The very pick of the manhood of the province joined the Ulster Volunteer Force, and armed and trained themselves as soldiers.

So it was that in the years immediately preceding the war it seemed almost certain they would have to follow the example of their forefathers centuries before and raise the Orange flag at Enniskillen and Derry. Then came the challenge of Germany to British ideals. The aim and purpose of the Ulster Volunteer Force remained the same, as the members conceived it, but it was turned into a wholly unexpected channel. By an astounding transformation of events they were to bleed and give their lives for all they revere and cherish, not in Ulster but on the hills and in the woods of Picardy.

The Ulster Division is entirely Protestant and Unionist; or was, until it was decimated on the Somme. It was formed out of the men who had previously bound themselves together by a solemn covenant, signed on "Ulster Day," Saturday, September 28, 1912, to stand by one another in defending, for themselves and their children, their cherished civil and religious heritage, should Home Rule be established. Thus the Division is unparalleled for its kind since Cromwell's "Ironsides" in enlisting stern religious fervour and political enthusiasm in a fighting phalanx. It consists of twelve battalions forming three brigades. It is wholly Irish.

Nine of the battalions have the regimental title of Royal Irish Rifles. The other battalions have the titles of the Royal Inniskilling Fusiliers and the Royal Irish Fusiliers, the two other regiments of the Line associated with Ulster. The battalions have also territorial classifications denoting their origin from the Ulster Volunteer Force, such as "North Belfast Volunteers"; "East Belfast Volunteers"; "Young Citizen Volunteers"; "South Belfast Volunteers"; "West Belfast Volunteers"; "South Antrim Volunteers"; "Down Volunteers"; "County Armagh Volunteers"; "Central Antrim Volunteers"; "Tyrone Volunteers"; "Donegal and Fermanagh Volunteers"; "Derry Volunteers." It has its own Engineers, Army Service Corps, Army Medical Corps and a complete Ambulance equipment.

There are also reserve battalions. In the pleasant surroundings of the Botanic Gardens, Belfast, a splendid hospital was established for the care of the wounded, and the provision of artificial limbs to those who might need them; and as evidence of the characteristic thoroughness with which everything was attended to, a fund has been raised to assist members of the division who may be left maimed and broken in health, and to support the dependents of the fallen, outside any aid that may be derived from the State. The commander, Major-General Nugent, is a county Cavan man, a deputy lieutenant for the county, and a kinsman of the Earl of Westmeath. He served in the King's Royal Rifles for seventeen years, and was wounded in both the Chitral and South African campaigns.

The division completed its training at Seaford, in Sussex. On visiting the district I was amused to find that the advent of "the wild Irish" had been anticipated by the inhabitants with much misgiving. They were apprehensive of their ancient peace being disturbed by the hilarity and commotion that spring from high and undisciplined spirits. What did happen agreeably surprised the Sussex folk. The Ulstermen quickly earned the esteem of every one for their affable qualities and good-humour. What was particularly remarkable was that they were found to be most pliant and tractable—qualities which, by common tradition, are supposed not to be looked for in any body of Irishmen; and as for their moral behaviour, what was more astonishing still was that the church or the chapel was to them infinitely more attractive than the inn.

So the division prepared themselves for taking the field against the enemy. They were reviewed by the King shortly before leaving for the

Front.

"Your prompt patriotic answer to the nation's call to arms will never be forgotten," said his Majesty. "The keen exertions of all ranks during the period of training have brought you to a state of efficiency not unworthy of any Regular Army. I am confident that in the field you will nobly uphold the traditions of the fine regiments whose names you bear. Ever since your enrolment I have closely watched the growth and steady progress of all units. I shall continue to follow with interest the fortunes of your division. In bidding you farewell I pray God may bless you in all your undertakings."

In the autumn of 1915 they went to France, determined to uphold the highest traditions of the fighting qualities of the Irish race, and burning for a chance of distinction.

During the winter months of 1915-16 the division took its turns in the firing-line. Every battalion experienced the hardships and dangers of the front trenches, when the weather was at its worst for chills, bronchitis, pneumonia and frost-bite, and when the Germans were most active at sniping and bombarding. Names of men in the division began to appear in the lists of casualties within ten days of the landing in France. The battalions passed through these preliminary stages with courage, endurance and splendid determination. They quickly earned a fine reputation among the highest military commanders for such soldierly qualities as willingness and cheerfulness in doing any sort of work, however unpleasant, that fell to them in the trenches, and their coolness and alertness on such dangerous missions as going out at night to the listening posts in No Man's Land and repairing the wire entanglements.

Eager to snatch their share of peril and glory, they were also among the foremost in volunteering for such wild adventures as bombing raids on the German trenches under cover of darkness. One such daring exploit by the Tyrone Volunteers was the subject of a special order of the day issued by Major-General Nugent, commanding the division. It was as follows—

A raid on the German trenches was carried out at midnight on —— by the Royal Inniskilling Fusiliers. The raiding party consisted of Major W. J. Peacocke, Captain J. Weir, Lieutenant W. S. Furness, Second-Lieutenant L. W. H. Stevenson, Second-Lieutenant R. W. M'Kinley, Second-Lieutenant J. Taylor, and eighty- four other ranks. The raid was completely successful, and was carried out exactly as planned. Six German dugouts, in which it is certain there were a considerable number of men, were thoroughly bombed, and a machine-gun was blown up, while a lively bombing fight took place between the blocking detachments of the raiding party and the Germans.

Having accomplished the purpose of the raid, the party was withdrawn, with the loss of one man killed and two wounded. The raid was ably organised by Major Peacocke, and was carried out by the officers and men of the party exactly in accordance with the plan, and the discipline and determination of the party was all that could be desired. The Divisional Commander desires that his congratulations should be extended to all who took part in it.

Brigadier-General Hickman, in a special brigade order, says the arrangements and plans reflect the greatest credit on Colonel A. St. Q. Ricardo, D.S.O., commanding the battalion, Major Peacocke, and the other officers concerned. The whole scheme was executed with great dash and determination, cool judgment and nerve.

Such was the fame of the raid and its success that the commander-in-chief, Sir Douglas Haig, visited the battalion and personally congratulated them.

Dr. Crozier, Archbishop of Armagh and Primate of all Ireland, visited the division in January 1916; and after a week spent with the battalions, brought home a deep impression of their spirit and devotion. "A more capable, energetic and cheerful body of men I have never come across," he writes.

> I have seen them at rifle practice, bomb-throwing, route marching, road-mending, and in the trenches, and everywhere my experience was the same officers and men working in splendid harmony, and taking the keenest interest in any and every job they were given to do. One night I met a couple of hundred men coming back from eight days' weary work in water-logged trenches, and they were singing so lustily that I really thought at first they were coming from a concert. And yet the war is to them a terrible reality, and they have already experienced some of its horror.
>
> I could not help noticing that this has produced a deep sense of responsibility, and has intensified their belief in the reality of duty; and whether at Sunday services or at weekday informal

addresses, there were no restless or inattentive men, but they seemed to welcome every word that spoke of God's presence and guidance in all life's difficulties and dangers.

CHAPTER 3

Ulsters' Attack on the Slopes of Thiepval

Not a Man Turned to Come Back, Not One

The division was put to the great test on July 1, 1916, the memorable day of the opening of the Battle of the Somme and the British attack in force to break through the German trenches in Picardy. It was a formidable task. The strength of the enemy positions was that they stood on high ground. That, also, was the reason of their importance. The tableland must be taken and held to permit of an advance in the stretch of open country spreading on the other side to the north. It was to be uphill work. So the battle became the greatest the world has ever known, so far, for its dimensions, the numbers engaged and the duration.

The Ulstermen were in the left wing of the British lines, and the scene of their operations was, roughly, three miles of broken country, dips and swells, on each side of the River Ancre, between the village of Beaumont Hamel, nestling in a nook of the hill above the river, eastwards to the slopes of Thiepval, perched on a height about 500 feet, below the river, all within the German lines. The main body of the Division assembled in the shelter of a Thiepval wood. "Porcupine Wood" it was called by the men. The trees were so stripped of foliage and lopped into distorted shapes by enemy gunfire that their bare limbs stood up like quills of the fretful porcupine.

At half-past seven in the morning the advance commenced. For ten days the British batteries had been continuously bombarding the whole German front. There was no sudden hush of the cannonade at the moment of the attack. For a minute there was a dramatic pause while the guns were being lifted a point higher so that they might drop their shells behind the enemy's first lines. Then the British infantry emerged from their trenches and advanced behind this furious and devastating curtain of fire and projectiles.

The morning was glorious and the prospect fine. The sun shone brightly in the most beautiful of skies, clear blue flecked with pure white clouds; and as the Ulstermen came out of the wood and ranged up in lines for the push forward, they saw, in the distant view, a sweet and pleasant upland country, the capture of which was the object of the attack. In the hollows the meadows were lush with grass, thick and glossy. There was tillage even, green crops of beetroot growing close to the ground, and tall yellowing corn, far behind the main German trenches. It was like a haunt of husbandry and peace. The only sound one would expect to hear from those harvest fields was that of the soothing reaping-machine garnering the wheat to make bread for the family board of a mother and a brood of young children.

But no tiller of the soil was to be seen, near or far. The countryside to the horizon ridge was tenantless, until these tens of thousands of British soldiers suddenly came up out of the ground. Even in the Franco-Prussian War of 1870 the agriculturists of northern France–then, as now, the zone of conflict remained in the homes and pursued their avocations. During the battle of Sedan, which sealed the fate of France, an extraordinary incident occurred—a peasant was observed in one of the valleys within the area of the fight calmly guiding the plough drawn by a big white horse.

"Why should the man lose a day?" says Zola in *The Downfall*. "Corn would not cease growing, the human race would not cease living, because a few thousand men happened to be fighting."

But war is waged differently now. It is spread along fronts hundreds of miles in extent and depth. Millions of men are engaged. They burrow underground and are armed with terrific engines of destruction. So it was that behind that green and pleasant land, bathed in sunshine, ferocity and death are skulking underground. Those elaborately interlacing white chalky lines over the face of the landscape mark the run of the German trenches.

Each dip is a death-trap. The copses are barricaded with fallen timber and wired; the villages are citadels, the farmsteads are forts, the ridges of the two plateaux are each one succession of batteries. Swallows were darting to and fro hawking for flies for their young, and in the clear air soaring larks were singing to their mates brooding on their eggs in the grass, showing that Nature was still carrying on her eternal processes, but the husbandman had fled the deceiving scene, and the after-crops from his old sowings of corn and mustard were mixed with weeds in No Man's Land.

Things befell the Ulstermen, when they appeared in the open, which were things indeed. The fortunes of war varied along the British advance. A group of war correspondents on a height near the town of Albert, about midway in the line, noticed that while some of the British battalions were comparatively unmolested, the resistance of the enemy to the left or west was of the fiercest and most desperate character. The Germans seem to have expected the main assault at this part of the field of operations. Their guns and men were here most heavily massed. On the left of the valley made by a curve of the River Ancre is a crest, in a crease of which lay on that July morning the village of Beaumont Hamel, or rather its site, for it had been blown almost out of existence by the British artillery fire.

Under the village—as shown by explorations made after it fell—were a vast system of passages and cellars, in which whole battalions of Germans found shelter from the bombardment. On the right of the valley is the plateau of Thiepval. It was as strong a position as the consummate skill of German engineers and gunners could make it. On the sky line at the top of a ridge of the plateau were the ruins of the village of Thiepval—heaps of bricks and slates and timber that once were walls and roofs of houses—encircled by blackened stumps of trees that once in the spring were all pink and white of the apple blossom.

The ground sloping down to the valley, and the valley itself was a network of German trenches—mostly turned into a maze of upheaved earth-mounds by shell-fire—studded with many machine-gun posts. The main part of the Ulster Division advanced across the valley that rose gently, with many undulations upwards, to the slopes on the western or left side of Thiepval. They had to take what were called the A, B and C lines of trenches. As will be seen, they pushed far beyond their objective.

Clouds of smoke had been liberated from the British lines to form a screen for the attackers. Into it the men disappeared as they marched, line after line, in extended order, over the intervening stretch of ground. But almost immediately they were all scourged—especially the Ulster battalions on the extreme left moving towards Beaumont Hamel—with machine-gun fire poured at them from various points, to the continuous accompaniment of short, sharp, annihilating knocks.

The bullets literally came like water from an immense hose with a perforated top. The streams of lead crossed and re-crossed, sweeping the ranks about the ankles, at the waist; breast high, around their heads. Comrades were to be seen falling on all sides, right, left, front and rear. So searching was the fire that it was useless to seek cover, and advance in short rushes in between. So the lines kept undauntedly on their way, apparently not minding the bullets any more than if they were a driving and splashing shower of hail.

"Let her rip, ye divils!" shouted some of the Ulstermen in jocular defiance at the enemy and his machine-gun; "and," said an officer relating the story, "the *Bosche* let her rip all right."

One of the wounded rank and file told me that in the advance he lost entire perception of the roar of the British guns which was so impressive as he lay with his comrades in the wood, though they still continued their thundering. Their terrible diapason of sound seemed to be lulled into absolute silence, so far as he was concerned, by the hollow, crepitating "tap-t-t-tap" of the German machine-guns; and the swish, swish, swish of the bullets, of all the noises of battle the most unnerving to soldiers assailing a position. But the Ulstermen were in a mood of the highest exaltation, a mood in which troops may be destroyed but will not easily be subjugated. The day had thrilling historic memories for them.

July the First on the banks of the Boyne,
There was a famous battle.

The opening lines of their song, "The Boyne Water," recounting the deeds of their forefathers, came inevitably to their minds. "Just as we were about to attack," writes Rifleman Edward Taylor of the West Belfast Volunteers, "Captain Gaffikin took out an orange handkerchief and, waving it around his head, shouted, 'Come on, boys, this is the first of July!'"

"No surrender!" roared the men. It was the answer given by the gallant defenders of Derry from their walls to King James and the besieging Jacobites. On the fields of Picardy new and noble meanings were put into these old, out-worn Irish battle-cries. One sergeant of the Inniskillings went into the fray with his Orange sash on him. Some of the men provided themselves with orange lilies before they went up to the assembly trenches, and these they now wore in their breasts. But, indeed, their colours were growing in profusion at their feet when they came out of the trenches—yellow charlock, crimson poppies and blue cornflowers, and many put bunches of these wild flowers in their tunics. So the Ulstermen were keen to prove their metal. They divided their forces and advanced to German positions on the right and left. Through it all their battle-shout was "No surrender." But there was one surrender which they were prepared to make, and did make—the surrender, for the cause, of their young lives and all the bright hopes of youth.

When the battalions on the right reached the first German line they found shapeless mounds and cavities of soil and stones and timber, shattered strands and coils of barbed wire, where the trenches had been, and the dead bodies of the men who were in occupation of them at the bombardment. The Ulstermen then pushed on to the second line, which still held living men of courage and tenacity who had to be disposed of by bayonet and bomb. On to the third line the Ulstermen went at a steady pace. They were still being whipped by machine-gun fire. Their ranks were getting woefully thinner. In their tracks they left dead and wounded. At the sight of a familiar face among the curiously awkward attitudes and shapes of those instantaneously killed there was many a cold tug at the heart-strings of the advancing men, and many a groan of sorrow was suppressed on their lips.

The moaning of the wounded was also terrible to hear, but their spirit was magnificent. "Lying on the ground there under fire, they had no thought of their own danger, but only of the comrades who were going forward, and they kept shouting words of encouragement after the attacking column until it was well out of sight," said an Inniskilling fusilier. "One company, recruited mainly from the notorious Shankill road district of Belfast, was going forward, when a wounded man recognised some of his chums in it. 'Give them it hot for the Shankill road,' he cried, and his comrades answered with a cheer."

The same man, giving a general account of the fiercely contested attack on the enemy positions, said, "It was a case of playing leapfrog with death, but all obstacles were overcome, and the fusiliers carried the enemy trenches with a magnificent rush. The Huns turned on them like baffled tigers and tried to hurl the Irishmen out again, but they might as well have tried to batter down the walls of Derry with toothpicks. The Inniskillings held their ground, and gradually forced the enemy still further back."

The German trenches, with their first, second, third, fourth and fifth lines, formed a system of defences of considerable depth, into which the Ulstermen had now penetrated for distances varying from two to three miles in depth. It was a land of horrible desolation. The ground at this point was almost bare of vegetation. It was torn and lacerated with shell holes. The few trees that remained standing were reduced to splintered and jagged stumps. All was smoke, flashes, uproar and nauseating smells. In this stricken battle area the defence was as stubborn and desperate as the attack.

It seemed impossible for men with a nervous system and imagination to retain their reason and resolution in the terrific, intensive and searching preliminary bombardment. Nevertheless, the Germans did it. The British guns had, indeed, wrought widespread havoc. Not only lines of trenches were pounded to bits, but spots outside, affording concealment for guns and troops, were discovered and blown to atoms. There were, however, deep dugouts going as many as thirty feet below ground, and in some cases, even at that depth, there were trapdoors and stairs leading to still lower chambers, and up from these underground fortifications the Germans came when the cannonade lifted. There were also hidden machine-gun shelters in the hollows and on the slopes which the British artillery failed to find.

The resistance offered to the advance of the Ulstermen was accordingly of the most obstinate and persistent nature. The hand-to-hand fight with bayonet and bomb at the third line of trenches was described by a man of the Irish Rifles as "a Belfast riot on the top of Mount Vesuvius." No more need be said. The phrase conveys a picture of men madly struggling and yelling amid fire and smoke and the abominable stench of battle. Yet the enemy's fourth line fell before these men who would not be stopped. There remained the fifth line, and the Ulstermen were preparing to move forward to it when the order came to fall back. The state of affairs at this time of the evening is well explained by one of the men—

> We had been so eager that we had pressed too far forward, and were well in advance of our supporting troops, thus laying ourselves open to flank attacks. The position became more serious as the day advanced, and the supporting troops were unable to make further progress, while the Huns kept hurrying up fresh men. We kept shouting the watchword of 'No Surrender,' with which our fathers had cheered themselves in the siege of Derry, and every time the Huns attacked we sent them reeling back with something to remind them that they were fighting Irishmen. We couldn't help taunting them a lot. 'Would you like

some Irish rebellion?' we called out to them, and they didn't like it. They kept throwing in fresh reinforcements all day, and gradually the pressure became almost unbearable. Still we held our ground, and would have continued to hold it if necessary.

"Retirement," he adds, "is never a pleasant task, especially after you have fought your corner as we fought ours. We felt that the ground won was part of ourselves, but orders had to be obeyed, and so we went back."

The retirement was to the third line of trenches, at the point known as "the Crucifix," just north-west of Thiepval. It was carried out at nightfall, after fourteen hours' continuous fighting. This section of the division, in the words of Major-General Nugent, "captured nearly 600 prisoners, and carried its advance triumphantly to the limits of the objective laid down."

The battalions, two in number, operating on the left at Beaumont Hamel, were not so fortunate. They were broken to pieces by the devastating machine-gun fire. The remnants, by a magnificent effort, succeeded in getting into the German trenches. They were held up there by an utterly impassable curtain of shells and bullets. It was not their fault that they could not advance any further. They had to face a more terrific ordeal than any body of men have had to encounter in battle before. "They did all that men could do," says Major Nugent, "and, in common with every battalion in the Division, showed the most conspicuous courage and devotion."

Lieut.-Colonel Ambrose Ricardo, D.S.O., of Lion House, Strahane, commander of the Tyrone battalion of the Royal Inniskilling Fusiliers, gives an account of the experience of the Ulster Division which is of the greatest value for the reasons it supplies why the division lost so heavily and thus were unable to hold the advanced positions they had taken. He first describes how his men set out for their plunge into the terrible unknown. "Every gun on both sides fired as fast as it could, and during the din our dear boys just walked out of the wood and up rumps we had cut through our parapet and out through lanes in our wire," he says. "I shall never forget for one minute the extraordinary sight. The Derrys on our left were so eager they started a few minutes before the ordered time, and the Tyrones were not going to be left behind, and they got going without delay.

"No fuss, no shouting, no running; everything orderly, solid and thorough, just like the men themselves. Here and there a boy would wave his hand to me as I shouted good luck to them through my megaphone, and all had a happy face. Most were carrying loads. Fancy advancing against heavy fire carrying a heavy roll of barbed wire on your shoulder!"

Then dealing with the division generally, Colonel Ricardo states that the leading battalions suffered comparatively little until they almost reached the German front line, when they came under appalling machine-gun fire which obliterated whole platoons. "And, alas for us," he cries, "the division on our right could not get on, and the same happened to the division on our left, so we came in for the concentrated fire of what would have been spread over three divisions. But every man who remained standing pressed on, and, without officers or non-commissioned officers, they carried on, faithful to their job. Not a man turned to come back, not one."

Eventually small parties of all the battalions of the division—except the two operating towards Beaumont Hamel—gathered together in the section of the German third line, which was their part in the general British advance. They had captured, in fact, a portion of the famous Schwabon Redoubt on the summit of the ridge facing them, and set to work to consolidate it. "The situation after the first two hours was indeed a cruel one for the Ulster Division," continues Colonel Ricardo. "There they were, a wedge driven into the German lines, only a few hundred yards wide, and for fourteen hours they bore the brunt of the German machine-gun fire and shell-fire from three sides, and even from behind they were not safe. The parties told off to deal with the German first and second lines had in many cases been wiped out, and the Germans sent parties from the flanks in behind our boys. Yet the division took 800 prisoners, and could have taken hundreds more, had they been able to handle them."

Major John Peacocke, "a most gallant and dashing officer" (as Colonel Ricardo describes him), was sent forward to see how matters stood. He crossed "No Man's Land" at a time when the fire sweeping it was most intense. Taking charge of the defence of the captured position, he gave to each unit a certain task to do in furtherance of the common aim. Then he sent runners back with messages asking for reinforcements, for water and for bombs.

"But," says Colonel Ricardo, "no one had any men in reserve, and no men were left to send across. We were told reinforcements were at hand, and to hold on, but it was difficult, I suppose, to get fresh troops up in time. At any rate the help did not come. In the end, at 10.30 p.m. (they had got to the third line at 8.30 a.m.), the glorious band in front had to come back. They fought to the last and threw their last bomb, and were so exhausted that most of them could not speak. Shortly after they came back help came, and the line they had taken and held was reoccupied without opposition, the Germans, I suppose, being as exhausted as we were. Our side eventually lost the wedge-like bit after some days. It was valueless, and could only be held at very heavy cost. We were withdrawn late on Sunday evening, very tired and weary."

A private in one of the battalions sent to his parents in Ulster a very vivid account of the advance. As he was crossing "No Man's Land" two aspects of it, in striking contrast, arose in his mind. "How often had I, while on sentry duty in our own trenches, looked out over that same piece of ground," he says. "How calm and peaceful it looked then; how fresh, green, and invitingly cool looked that long, blowing-grass! Now, what a ghastly change! Not a level or green spot remained. Great, jagged, gaping craters covered the blackish, smoking ground, furrowed and ploughed by every description of projectile and explosive. In the blue sky above white, puffy clouds of shrapnel burst, bespattering the earth below with a rain of bullets and jagged shrapnel missiles."

Tripping and stumbling went the men over the broken and ragged ground. "Fellows in front, beside, and behind me would fall; some, with a lurch forward, wounded; others, with a sudden, abrupt halt, a sickly wheel, would drop, give one eerie twist, and lie still—dead!" They find the first line in the possession of comrades; and moving on to the second, came to blows there with the enemy. "An Inniskilling, scarcely more than a boy, standing on the parapet, yells madly 'No surrender,' and fires several shots into the German mob. From every part of the trench we closed forward, bayonet poised, on the crowd of grey figures. A short scuffle; then we swayed back again, leaving a heap of blood-stained greyishness on the ground. 'Come on, boys!' yells the lieutenant, springing up on to the parapet. 'Come on, the Ulsters.' Up we scramble after him and rush ahead towards the far-off third line. Vaguely I recollect that mad charge. A few swirlings here and there of grey-clad figures with upraised hands yelling '*Kamerad*.' Heaps of wounded and dead. Showers of dust and earth and lead. Deafening explosions and blinding smoke. But what concerned me most and what I saw clearest were the few jagged stumps of the remnants of the wire entanglements and the ragged parapet of the third line—our goal!"

From this enemy trench the Ulsterman looked back over the ground he had covered, and this is what he saw:

"Through the dense smoke pour hundreds and hundreds of Tommies, with flashing bayonets and distorted visages, apparently cheering and yelling. You couldn't hear them for the noise of the guns and the exploding shells. Everywhere among those fearless Ulstermen burst high-explosive shells, hurling dozens of them up in the air, while above them and among them shrapnel bursts with sharp, ear-splitting explosions. But worst of all these was the silent swish, swish, swishing of the machine-gun bullets, claiming their victims by the score, cutting down living sheaves, and leaving bunches of writhing, tortured flesh on the ground."

He, too, noticed that their co-operating divisions had failed, for some reason, to advance. "Look there, something *must* be wrong!" he called out to his comrades. "Why, they're not advancing on *that* side at all," pointing towards the left flank. "Not a sign of life could be seen," he says. "The Ulster Division were out to the Huns' first, second, third, fourth, and even fifth lines, with all the German guns pelting us from every side and at every angle."

Many a brave and self-sacrificing deed was done in these affrighting scenes. Here are a few instances taken haphazard from the records of one battalion alone, the 9th Royal Inniskilling Fusiliers. They were repeated a hundredfold throughout the division.

Corporal Thomas M'Clay, Laghey, County Donegal, assisted Second-Lieutenant Lawrence to take twenty prisoners. He conveyed them single-handed over "No Man's Land," and then returned to the German third line, all the time having been under very heavy fire. When he got back he had been fighting hard for ten hours. Private Thomas Gibson, of Coalisland, saw three Germans working a machine-gun. He attacked them alone, and killed them all with his clubbed rifle. Corporal John Conn, Caledon, came across two of our machine-guns out of action. He repaired them under fire, and with them destroyed a German flanking party. He carried both guns himself part of the way back, but had to abandon one, he was so utterly exhausted.

Lance-Corporal Daniel Lyttle, Leckpatrick, Strabane, was trying to save two machine-guns from the enemy when he found himself cut off. He fired one gun until the ammunition was spent, then destroyed both guns and bombed his way back to the rest of his party at the Crucifix line. Sergeant Samuel Kelly, Belfast, volunteered to take a patrol from the Crucifix line to ascertain how things were going on our right. Corporal Daniel Griffiths, Dublin; Lance-Corporal Lewis Pratt, Cavan; and Private William Abraham, Ballinamallard, went with him. The latter was killed, but the remainder got back with valuable information. Sergeant Kelly did great work to the last in organising and encouraging is men when all the officers of his company had fallen. Corporal Daniel Griffith, Lance-Corporal Lewis Pratt, with Private Fred Carter, Kingstown, bombed and shot nine Germans who were trying to mount a machine-gun.

Private Samuel Turner, Dundrun, and Private Clarence Rooney, Clogher, forced a barricaded dugout, captured fifteen Germans and destroyed an elaborate signalling apparatus, thereby preventing information getting back. Lance-Corporal William Neely, Clogher; Private Samuel Spence, Randalstown; Private James Sproule, Castlederg; and Private William R. Reid, Aughnacloy, were members of a party blocking the return of Germans along a captured trench. Their officer and more than half their comrades were killed, but they held on and covered the retirement of the main party, eventually getting back in good order themselves and fighting every inch of the way.

Private Fred Gibson, Caledon, pushed forward alone with his machine-gun, and fought until all his ammunition was used. Private James Mahaffy, Caledon, was badly wounded in the leg early in the day, and was ordered back. He refused to go, and continued to carry ammunition for his machine-gun. Lance-Corporal John Hunter, Coleraine, succeeded in picking off several German gunners. His cool and accurate shooting at such a time was remarkable. Private Robert Monteith, Lislap, Omagh, had his leg taken off above the knee. He used his rifle and bayonet as a crutch, and continued to advance. Private Wallie Scott, Belfast, met five Germans. He captured them single-handed, and marched them back to the enemy second line, where a sergeant had a larger party of prisoners gathered.

CHAPTER 4

Four Victoria Crosses to the Ulster Division

The most signal proof of the exceptional gallantry of the Ulstermen is afforded by the awarding of four Victoria Crosses to two officers and two privates of the division. There is many a division that has not won a single V.C. They must not be belittled on that score; their ill-fortune and not their service is to blame. But the rarity of the distinction, and the exceptional deed of bravery and self-sacrifice needed to win it, reflects all the more glory on the achievements of the Ulstermen. By the winning of four Victoria Crosses the Ulster Division have made a name which will shine gloriously for all time in the imperishable record of British gallantry on the battlefield.

Private William Frederick McFadzean of the Royal Irish Rifles was posthumously awarded the Victoria Cross for sacrificing himself deliberately to save his comrades. The men of the battalion were packed together in a concentration trench on the morning of July 1. Just prior to the advance bombs were being distributed for use when the German lines were reached. One of the boxes of these missiles slipped down the trench and emptied its contents on the floor. Two of the safety pins fell out. Shouts of alarm were raised. Men who would face the German bombs undaunted shrank with a purely physical reaction from the peril which thus accidentally threatened them. They knew that in a moment these bombs would explode with a terrific detonation and scatter death and mutilation among them.

In that instant McFadzean flung himself bodily on the top of the bombs. He was a bomber himself, and he well knew the danger, but he did not hesitate. The bombs exploded. All their tremendous powers of destruction were concentrated upon the body which enveloped them in an embrace. McFadzean was blown literally to bits. One only of his comrades was injured.

McFadzean was only twenty-one years of age. He was born at Lurgan, County Armagh, and was a Presbyterian. A member of the Ulster Volunteer Force, he joined the Young Citizens' Battalion (Belfast) of the Royal Irish Rifles in September 1914.

The other private who won the Victoria Cross is Robert Quigg, also of the Royal Irish Rifles. On the morning after the advance he went out seven times, alone and in the face of danger, to try to find his wounded officer, Sir Harry

Macnaghten of Dundaraye, Antrim, and returned on each occasion with a disabled man. Private Quigg is thirty-one, the son of Robert Quigg, a guide and boatman at the Giant's Causeway, Antrim. He was a member of the Ulster Volunteer Force, and enlisted in the Royal Irish Rifles (Central Antrim Volunteers) in September, 1914. He is an Episcopalian, an Orangeman and a member of the flute band of his lodge.

The official account of Private Quigg's exploit is as follows—

For most conspicuous bravery. He advanced to the assault with his platoon three times. Early next morning, hearing a rumour that his platoon officer was lying out wounded, he went out seven times to look for him under heavy shell and machine-gun fire, each time bringing back a wounded man. The last man he dragged in on a waterproof sheet from within a few yards of the enemy's wire. He was seven hours engaged in this most gallant work, and finally was so exhausted that he had to give it up.

It was also "for most conspicuous bravery" in searching for wounded men under continuous and heavy fire that Lieutenant Geoffrey Shillington Cather of the Royal Irish Fusiliers got the Victoria Cross. He lost his life in thus trying to succour others on the night and morning after the advance of the Ulster Division. "From 7 p.m. till midnight he searched 'No Man's Land,' and brought in three wounded men," says the official account. "Next morning, at 8 a.m., he continued his search, brought in another wounded man, and gave water to others, arranging for their rescue later. Finally, at 10.30 a.m., he took out water to another man, and was proceeding further on when he was himself killed. All this was carried out in full view of the enemy, and under direct machine-gun fire, and intermittent artillery fire. He set a splendid example of courage and self-sacrifice."

Lieutenant Cather was twenty-five years of age, a son of Mrs. Cather, Priory Road, West Hampstead, London. His father, who was dead, had been a tea merchant in the City. On his mother's side, Lieutenant Cather was a grandson of the late Mr. Thomas Shillington, of Tavanagh House, Portadown; and on his father's side, of the late Rev. Robert Cather, a distinguished minister of the Irish Methodist Church. He was a nephew of Captain D. Graham Shillington, of Ardeevin, Portadown, who, with his son, Lieutenant T. G. Shillington, was serving in the same battalion of the Royal Irish Fusiliers. Lieutenant Gather was educated at Rugby. He first joined the Public Schools' Battalion of the Royal Fusiliers (City of London Regiment), and obtained his commission in the County Armagh Volunteers in May, 1915.

The second officer of the Ulster Division to win the Victoria Cross was Captain Eric N. F. Bell of the Royal Inniskilling Fusiliers, whose gallantry on July 1 also cost him his life. He was about twenty-two years old, one of three soldier sons of Captain E. H. Bell, formerly of the Inniskillings (serving in Egypt in a garrison battalion of the Royal Irish Regiment), and Mrs. Bell, an Enniskillen lady living in Bootle. The two brothers of the late Captain Bell hold commissions in the Ulster Division. The deeds for which he was awarded the Victoria Cross are thus set out in the official account—

> For most conspicuous bravery. He was in command of a trench mortar battery, and advanced with the infantry in the attack. When our front line was hung up by enfilading machine-gun fire Captain Bell crept forward and shot the machine gunner. Later, on no less than three occasions, when our bombing parties, which were clearing the enemy's trenches, were unable to advance, he went forward and threw trench mortar bombs among the enemy. When he had no more bombs available he stood on the parapet, under intense fire, and used a rifle with great coolness and effect on the enemy advancing to counter-attack. Finally he was killed rallying and reorganising infantry parties which had lost their officers. All this was outside the scope of his normal duties with his battery. He gave his life in his supreme devotion to duty.

Colonel Ricardo, in a very fine and sympathetic letter to the bereaved mother, gives additional particulars of Captain Bell's gallantry—

The General, hearing that his parents were old friends of mine, has asked me to write on his behalf, sending his sympathy and telling of the gallantry of Eric, which was outstanding on a day when supreme courage and gallantry was the order of the day. Eric was in command on July 1 of his trench mortar battery, which had very important duties to perform, and which very materially helped the advance. We know from his servant, Private Stevenson, a great deal of Eric's share in the day's work. He went forward with the advance, and, coming under heavy machine-gun fire, and seeing where it came from, he took a rifle and crawled towards the machine-gun and then shot the gunner in charge, thus enabling a party on his flank to capture the gun. This gallant action saved many lives.

When in the German lines Eric worked splendidly, collecting scattered units and helping to organise the defence. He was most energetic, and never ceased to encourage the men and set all a very fine example. Having exhausted all his mortar ammunition, he organised a carrying party and started back to fetch up more shells; it was whilst crossing back to our own line that Eric was hit. He was shot through the body, and died in a few moments without suffering. His servant stayed with him to the end and arrived back quite exhausted, and has now been admitted into hospital. Nothing could have exceeded the courage and resource displayed by Eric. The Brigade are proud that he belonged to it. It is only what I should have expected from him. It must be a solace to his father and mother that he died such a gallant death. He was a born soldier and a credit to his regiment. May I add my heartfelt sympathy to my dear old friends.

Among the many other distinctions gained by the division were Military Crosses to two of the chaplains: Captain Rev. J. Jackson Wright and Captain Rev. Joseph Henry McKew. Captain Wright was the Presbyterian minister of Ballyshannon, County Donegal. He gave up that position temporarily to accept an Army chaplaincy, and was posted to the Ulster Division in November, 1914, being attached to the Inniskilling Brigade. He was ordained in 1893. Captain McKew was curate of the parish of Clones prior to being appointed Church of Ireland chaplain to the troops in August, 1915. He is a Trinity man, and during his university career won a moderatorship in history. Ordained in 1914, he has spent his entire ministry under Canon Ruddell in Clones. Before going to the Front he was a chaplain at the Curragh.

The company officers led their men with conspicuous gallantry and steadfastness. "Come on, Ulsters;" "Remember July the First," they cried. They were severely thinned out before the day was far advanced. It was the same with the non-commissioned ranks. At the end several parties of men desperately fighting had not an officer or a non-commissioned officer left. Among the officers lost were two brothers, Lieutenant Holt Montgomery Hewitt, Machine-gun Corps (Ulster Division), and Second-Lieutenant William Arthur Hewitt, Royal Inniskilling Fusiliers (Tyrone Volunteers). They were the sons of Mr. J. H. Hewitt, manager of the workshops for the blind, Royal Avenue, Belfast. A third son, Lieutenant Ernest Henry Hewitt, Royal Lancaster Regiment, was killed in action on June 15, 1915.

The three brothers were members of the Ulster Volunteer Force before the War. They were prominent athletes, and played Rugby football for the North of Ireland club. In that respect they were typical of the officers of the Ulster Division. They were also typical of them for high-mindedness and cheerful devotion to duty. "Poor Holt, the most genial and lovable of souls!" exclaims Lieutenant E. W. Crawford, the adjutant of his battalion of the Inniskillings. "Willie led his platoon fearlessly over the top." The commanding officer of the battalion, Colonel Ricardo, in a letter to Mr. Hewitt, pays a remarkable tribute to Second-Lieutenant William Holt. He says:—

> It was a sad day for us, and I feel quite stunned and heart- broken. Your Willie was one of the nicest-minded boys I ever knew. My wife saw a letter he wrote to the widow of a man in his company, and she told me it was the most beautiful letter of sympathy she had ever read. No one but a spiritually-minded boy could have written such a letter. I made him my assistant-adjutant, and of all my young lads I could spare him the least. No words can express the sympathy we all feel for yourself and Mrs. Hewitt and your family in this grievous double blow.

Captain C. C. Craig, Royal Irish Rifles (South Antrim Volunteers), M.P. for South Antrim and brother of Colonel James Craig, M.P. for East Down, was taken prisoner. When last seen he was lying wounded in a shell hole at the most advanced point of the narrow and dangerous salient carved by the Ulstermen in the enemy lines, shouting encourage- ment to his company. In a letter to his wife, written from a hospital at Gutersloh, Westphalia, Germany, and dated July 13, Captain Craig states it was while he was directing his men to convert the C line of trenches into defences against the Germans by making them face the opposite way, that he was hit by a piece of shrapnel in the back of the leg below the knee. "This put me out of action," he says. "I was bandaged up, and, as I could not get about, I sent a message to R. Neill to take command, and I crawled to a shell-hole, where I lay for six hours. This was at about 10 a.m. on the 1st July. During this six hours the shelling and machine-gun fire was very heavy, but my shell-hole protected me so well that I was not hit again, except for a very small piece" of shrapnel on the arm, which only made a small cut."

At about four o'clock in the afternoon the enemy made a counter attack, during which Captain Craig was found and taken prisoner. Describing his treatment as a prisoner, Captain Craig says—

> I had to hobble into a trench close at hand, where I stayed till ten o'clock, till two Germans took me to another line of trenches about 400 or 500 yards further back. This was the worst experience I had, as my leg was stiff and painful. The space between the lines was being heavily shelled by our guns, and my two supporters were naturally anxious to get over the ground as quickly as possible, and did not give me much rest, so I was very glad when, after what seemed an age, though it was not more than fifteen minutes or so, we got to the trench. I was put in a deep dugout, where there were a lot of officers and men, and they were all very kind to me, and gave me food and water, and here I spent the night. My leg was by now much swollen, but not painful except when I tried to walk.
> There were no stretchers, so in the morning I had to hobble as best I could out of the trenches till we came to a wood. Soon after I passed a dugout where some artillery officers lived, and the captain seeing my condition refused to allow me to go any further on foot, and took me in and gave me food and wine, and set his men to make a kind of sling to carry me in. This proved a failure; as I was so heavy, I nearly broke the men's shoulders. He then got, a wheelbarrow, and in this I was wheeled a mile or more to 'a dressing station, where my wound was dressed, and I was inoculated for tetanus. That night I was taken to a village, and had a comfortable bed and a good sleep.

Another officer of the division who was "pipped," as he calls it, tells in an interesting-story how he worked himself along the ground towards the British lines, and his experiences on the way. "By and by," he says, "a *Boche* corporal came crawling along after me. He shouted some gibberish, and I waved him on towards our lines with my revolver. He wasn't wounded, but he was devilish anxious to make sure of being a prisoner—begad, you don't get our chaps paying them the same compliment. They'll take any risks sooner than let the *Boche* get them as prisoners. So this chap lay down close beside me. I told him to be off out o' that, but he lay close, and I'd no breath to spare. That crawling is tiresome work.

"Presently I saw a man of ours coming along, poking round with his rifle and bayonet. He'd been detailed to shepherd in prisoners. He was surprised to see me. Then he saw my *Boche*. 'Hell to yer sowl!' says he; 'what the divil are ye doin' there beside my officer? Get up,' says he, 'an' be off with ye out a' that!' And he poked at him with his bayonet; so the fellow squealed and plucked up enough courage to get up on his feet and run for our lines. Our own man wanted to help me back—a good fellow, you know—but I'd time enough before me, so told him to carry on. I wriggled all the way back to our line, and a stretcher-bearer got me there, so I was all right."

When they were relieved, the survivors of the division came back very tired and bedraggled, their faces black with battle smoke and their uniforms white from the chalky soil. But they were in a joyous mood; and well they might be, for they had battered in one of the doors of the supposed impregnable German trenches and left it ajar. Their exploits add a brilliant chapter to the record of Irish valour and romance. Grief for the dead will soon subside into a sad memory, but the glory of what they accomplished will endure forever. Because of it, the First of July is certain to be as great a day for Ulster in the future as the Twelfth has been in the past.

CHAPTER 5

Combativeness of the Irish Soldier

There is a story of Wellington and his army in the Peninsular campaign which embodies, in a humorous fashion, the still popular idea of the chief national characteristics of the races within the United Kingdom.

It says that if Wellington wanted a body of troops to get to a particular place quickly by forced marches he gave an assurance that on their arrival Scottish regiments would be given their arrears of pay; English regiments would have a good dinner of roast beef, and the bait held out to Irish regiments to give speed to their feet, however weary, was an all-round tot of grog. The Welsh, it will be noticed, are not in the story. This cannot be explained by saying they had yet to achieve separate national distinction on the field of battle.

The 23rd Regiment of Foot (Royal Welsh Fusiliers) served under Wellington and contributed more than their fair share to the martial renown of the British Army. It is solely due, I think, to the fact that they had not yet emerged from their absorption in the English generally. But, to round off the story, what motive of a material kind would impel the Welsh Regiments to greater military exertions? Shall we say any one of the three inducements mentioned—pay, grub or grog, or, better still, all of them together?

The present war has provided the most searching tests of the qualities of the races involved in it. They have all been profoundly moved to the uttermost deeps of their being, both in the mass and as individuals. The superficial trappings of society and even of civilisation have fallen from them, and they appear as they really are—brave or cowardly, noble or base, unselfish or egotistical. We see our own soldiers, English, Scottish, Welsh and Irish, not perhaps quite as each came from the hands of Nature, but certainly as the original minting of each has been modified only by the influence of racial environment.

All the races within the United Kingdom are alike in this, that each is a medley of many kinds of dissimilar individuals with very varied faculties and attributes. But there are certain broad, main characteristics which distinguish in the mass each racial aggregate of dissimilar units; and it is these instincts, ideas, habits, customs, held in common, that fundamentally separate each nationality from the other. That is what I mean by racial environment.

The soldiers of the United Kingdom possess in general certain fine qualities of character and conduct which may be ascribed to the traditions and training of the British Army. But when we come to consider them racially we find that their points of difference are more striking even than their points of similarity. Each nationality evolves its own type of soldier, and every type has its distinctly marked attributes. As troops, taken in the mass, are the counterpart of the nations from which they spring, and, indeed, cannot be anything else, so they must, for one thing, reveal in fighting the particular sort of martial spirit possessed by their race.

Though I am an Irishman, I would not be so boastful as to say that the Irish soldiers have a superior kind of courage to which neither the English, the Scottish nor the Welsh can lay claim. They are all equally brave, but the manifestation of their bravery is undoubtedly different—that is, different not so much in degree as in kind. In a word, courage, like humour, is not racial or geographical, but, like humour also, it takes on a racial or geographical flavour.

General Sir Ian Hamilton has written:

> When, once upon a time, a Queen of Spain saw the Grenadier Guards she remarked they were strapping fellows; as the 92nd Highlanders went by she said, 'The battalion marches well'; but, at the aspect of the Royal Irish, the words 'Bloody War!' were wrung from her reluctant lips.

After a good deal of reading on the subject, and some thought, I venture to suggest the following generalisations as to the qualities which distinguish the English, Scottish, Welsh and Irish, in valour, one from another.

English—the courage of an exalted sense of honour and devotion to duty, and of the national standard of conduct which requires them to show, at all costs, that they are better men than their opponents, whoever they may be.

Scottish—the courage of mental as well as physical tenacity, coolly set upon achieving the purpose in view.

Welsh—the courage of perfervid emotion, religious in its intensity.

Irish—the courage of dare-devilry, and the rapture of battle.

All these varieties of courage are to be found, to some extent, in each distinct national unit, and thus they cross and recross the racial boundary lines within our Army. Still, I think they represent broadly the dominant distinguishing characteristics of the English, Scottish, Welsh and Irish as fighting men. The qualities lacking in one race are supplied by the others; and the harmonious whole into which all are fused provide that fire and dash, cool discipline, doggedness and high spirits for which our troops have always been noted.

The commander-in-chief, Sir Douglas Haig, is said to have made a most interesting estimate of the qualities of the soldiers of the three home races under his command. The Irish are best for brilliant and rapid attack, and the English are best for holding a position against heavy onslaughts. The Scottish, he thinks, are not quite so fiery and dashing in assault as the Irish, but they are more so than the English, and not quite so tenacious in holding on under tremendous fire as the English, but they are more so than the Irish.

It is this combination of attributes which enables the British Army, more perhaps than any other army, to get out of a desperate situation with superb serenity and honour. There is an old saying that *it never knows when it is beaten.* Soult, Marshal of France, whose brilliant tactics in the Peninsular War so often countered the consummate strategy of Wellington and the furious dash of the Irish infantry, bore testimony in a novel and vivid way to this trait of the British. "They could not be persuaded they were beaten," he said. "I always thought them bad soldiers," he also said. "I turned their right, pierced their centre, they were everywhere broken; the day was mine; and yet they did not know it and would not run."

Any other troops, in a hopeless pass, would retreat or surrender, and would do so without disgrace. There are numberless instances in British military history where our troops, faced with fearful odds, stood, magnificently stubborn, with their backs to the wall, as it were, willing to be fired at and annihilated rather than give in. Mr. John Redmond tells a story of a reply given by an English general when asked his opinion of the Irish troops. "Oh," he said, "they are magnificent fighters, but rotten soldiers. When they receive an order to retire their answer is, 'Be damned if we will.'"

I may add, in confirmation of this story, that one of the incidents of the retreat from Mons, which was the subject afterwards of an inquiry by the military authorities, was the refusal of a few hundred men of a famous Irish regiment to retire from what appeared to be an untenable position, much less to surrender, one or other of which courses was suggested by their superior officer. The answer of the men was as stunning as a blow of a shillelagh, or as sharp as a bayonet thrust. "If we had thrown down our arms," one of them said to me, "we could never have shown our faces in Ireland again."

Racial distinctions are to be seen on the weak side as well as on the strong side of character. Each nationality, regarded as fighters, has therefore its own particular failing. The Irish are disposed to be foolhardy, or heedless of consequences. It is the fault of their special kind of courage. "The British soldier's indifference to danger, while it is one of his finest qualities, is often the despair of his officers," says Mr. Valentine Williams, one of the most brilliant and experienced of war correspondents, in his book, *With our Army in Flanders,* and he adds, "The Irish regiments are the worst. Their recklessness is proverbial." They are either insensible to the perils they run, or, what is more likely, contemptuous of them.

I have been given several examples of the ways they will needlessly expose themselves. Though they can get to the rear through the safe, if wayward, windings of the communication trenches, it is a common thing for them to climb the parapets and go straight across the open fields under fire so as to save half an hour. To go by the trenches, they will argue, doubles the time taken in getting back without halving the risk.

In like manner, they prefer to go down a road swept by the enemy's artillery, which leads direct to their destination, rather than waste time by following a secure but circuitous way round. There is an Irish proverb against foolhardy risks which says it is better to be late for five minutes than dead all your lifetime, but evidently it is disregarded by Irish soldiers at the Front.

An English officer in the Royal Irish Regiment writes: "Really the courage and cheerfulness of our grand Irish boys are wonderful. They make light of their wounds, and, owing to their stamina, make rapid recoveries. The worst of them is they get very careless of the German bullets after a while and go wandering about as if they were at home."

Another English officer begins an amusing story of an Irish orderly in an English regiment with the comment: "I shall never now believe that there is on this earth any man to beat the Irish for coolness and pluck." The officer was in his dugout, and first noticed the Irishman chopping wood to make a fire for cooking purposes on a road which was made dangerous during the day by German snipers. He remarked to another officer, "By Jove! that man will get shot if he isn't careful."

"No sooner had I said the word," he writes, "when a bullet splattered near his head. Then another between his legs. I saw the mud fly where the bullet struck. The man, who is the captain's servant, turned round in the direction of the sniper and roared, 'Good shot, *Kaiser*. Only you might have hit me, though, for then I could have gone home.' After this the orderly proceeded to roast a fowl, singing quite unconcernedly, '*I often sigh for the silvery moon.*'

"Another bullet came and hit him in the arm. He roared with delight; and, as he basted the fowl, exclaimed, 'Oh, I'm not going to lave you, me poor bird.' The officer shouted to him to come into the dugout. He did so, but when he had licked the wound in his arm and bound it up, he said he must get the fowl, or it would be overdone; and before the officer could utter a word of protest, he ran across the road to the fire, started singing again, though the bullets, once more, came whistling past his ear. When he returned to the dugout with the fowl nicely roasted he remarked cheerily, 'People may say what they like, but them Germans are some marksmen, after all.'"

The whimsical side of Irish daring is further illustrated by a story of some men of the Royal Munster Fusiliers. To while away the time in the trenches one night they made bets on doing this or that. One fellow wagered a day's pay that he would go over to the German lines and come back with a maxim gun, which was known to be stationed at a particular point. In the darkness he wriggled across the intervening space on his stomach, and, coming stealthily upon the guard, stabbed him with a dagger. Then slinging the maxim across his shoulder, he crawled safely back to the trenches. "Double pay today!" he cried to the comrade he made the bet with.

"But you haven't won," said the other. "Where's the machine's belt and ammunition?"

The next night he sallied forth on his belly again, and returned with the complete outfit. The spirit of the anecdote is true to the Irish temperament, though the episode it records may be fanciful. There is no doubt that things of the kind are done very frequently by Irish soldiers. They call it "gallivanting"; and the mood takes on an air of, say, recklessness which, at times, seems very incongruous against the frightful background of the war.

The very root of courage is forgetfulness of self. Self-consciousness is, in no great degree, an Irish failing, or virtue, either, if it is to be regarded as such. Especially when he is absorbed in a martial adventure, the Irishman has no room in his mind left for a thought of being afraid, or even nervous. He likes the thrill of movement, the fierce excitement of advancing under fire for a frontal attack on the enemy, the ferocity of a contest at close grips. This is the temperament that responds blithely to the whistle—"Over the parapets!" His blood is stirred when the actual fighting begins, and as it progresses he is carried more and more out of himself.

The part of warfare repugnant to him, most trying to his temper, is that of long watching and waiting. For the work of lining the trenches a different kind of courage is required. The slush, the miseries, the herding together, the cramped movements, are enough to drive all the heat out of the blood. The qualities needed for the severe and incessant strain of this duty are an immovable calm, a tireless patience, an endurance which no hardships can break down. Here the English and the Scottish shine, for by nature they are more disciplined, more submissive to authority, and they hold on to the end with an admirable blend of good-humour and doggedness.

On the other hand, I am told, on the authority of an officer of the Welsh Guards, that when the Irish Guards are in the trenches they find the long dreary vigil and the boredom of inaction so insupportable that it is a common thing for parties of them to go to the officer in command and say, "Please, sir, may we go out and bomb the Germans?"

As Lord Wolseley had "the Irish drop in him," perhaps it is not to be wondered at that he discounts the old proverb that *the better part of valour is discretion.*

"There are a great many men," he writes, "who pride themselves upon simply doing their duty and restricting themselves exclusively to its simple performance. If such a spirit took possession of an army no great deeds can ever be expected from it."

What more can one do, it may be asked, than one's duty? Evidently Lord Wolseley would have duty on the battlefield spiced or gingered with audacity. The way the Irish look at it is well illustrated, I think, in a letter which I have seen from a private in a Devon regiment. He states that while he and some comrades were at an observation post in a trench near the enemy's line six Germans advanced close to them, and though they kept firing at them they could not drive them back.

"Two fellows of the Royal Irish Rifles came up," continues the Devon man, "and asked us what was on. We told them. Then one turned round to the other and said, 'Come on, Jim, sure we'll shift them.' Then the two of them fixed their bayonets and rushed at the Germans. You would have laughed to see the six Germans running away from the two Irishmen."

We have here an exhibition of the spirit of the born fighter who does not stop to count the odds or risks too cautiously. The incident recalls, in a sense, the scene depicted by Shakespeare in *King Henry V* at the camp before Harfleur, France, when Fluellen the Welshman—all shilly-shallying and dilly-dallying in enterprise—wants to argue with Captain Macmorris, the Irishman, concerning the disciplines of war. But the Irishman wants not words but work. Away with procrastination! So he bursts out, in Shakespeare's most uncouth imitation of the brogue—

> It is no time to discourse, so Chrish save me: the day is hot, and the weather, and the wars and the King, and the dukes: it is no time to discourse. The town is beseeched, and the trumpet call us to the breach, and we talk, and, be Chrish, do nothing; 'tis shame for us all: so God sa' me 'tis shame to stand still; it is shame by my hand; and there is throats to be cut, and works to be done; and there isn't nothing done, so Chrish sa' me, la!

Lord Wolseley also lays greater store on the spontaneous courage of the blood, the intuitive or unconscious form of courage, which is peculiarly Irish, than on moral courage, the courage of the mind, the courage of the man who by sheer will-power masters his nervous system and the shrinking from danger which it usually excites. In Lord Wolseley's opinion the man who is physically brave—the man of whom it may often be said that he has no sense of fear because he has no perception of danger—is the true military leader who draws his men after him to the achievement of deeds at which the world wonders.

That is the kind of courage which of old led the mailed knight, bent on a deed of derring-do, to cleave his way with sword or battle-axe to the very heart of the enemy's phalanx for the purpose of bringing their banner to the ground, or dealing them a more vital blow by slaying their commander. There may be little opportunity in trench warfare and in duels between heavy guns, both sides concealed behind the veils of distance, for such a show of spectacular bravery. War is no longer an adventure, a game or a sport. It is a state of existence, and what is needed most for its successful prosecution, so far as the individual fighter is concerned, is a devotion to duty which, however undramatic, never quails before any task to which it is set.

But the Irish soldier still longs for the struggle to the death between man and man, or, better still, of one man against a host of men. At dawn one day a young Irish soldier, inexperienced and of a romantic disposition, took his first turn in the trenches. He had come up filled with an uplifting resolve to do great things. The Germans immediately began a bombardment. The lad at first was filled with vague wonderments. He was puzzled especially by the emptiness of the battlefield. He had in mind the opposing armies moving in sight of each other, as he had seen them in manoeuvres. Where was the enemy? Whence came these shells? Then the invisibility of the foe, and this mechanical, impersonal form of fighting appalled him. One of his comrades was blown to pieces by his side. A dozen others disappeared from view in an upheaval of the ground. This was a dastardly massacre and not manly warfare, thought the youth.

He could stand the ordeal no longer. He ran, bewildered, up the trench, shouting "Police! Police"

"Hello, there; what are you up to?" said an officer, barring the way.

"Oh, sir," cried the young soldier, "there's bloody murder going on down there below, and I am looking for the police to put an end to it."

CHAPTER 6

With the Tyneside Irish

The men of the Tyneside Irish battalions stood to arms in the assembly trenches by the Somme on the morning of July 1, 1916. Suddenly the face of the country was altered, in their sight, as if by a frightful convulsion of Nature. Their ears were stunned by shattering explosions, and looking ahead, they saw the earth in two places upheaving, hundreds of feet high, in black masses of smoke. The ground rumbled under their feet, so that many feared it would break apart and bring the parapets down on top of them. Two mines had been sprung beneath the first line of the German trenches to the south-west and north-east of the heap of masonry and timber that once had been the pretty little hamlet of La Boiselle. It was the signal to the division, which included the Tyneside Irish, that the hour of battle had come.

The part in the general British advance allotted to the division was first to seize the heights on which La Boiselle stood. This was a few miles beyond the town of Albert, held by the Allies, on the main road to the town of Bapaume, in the possession of the Germans. Thence they were to move forward to Bailiff's Wood, to the north-west of Contalmaison, and to a position on the cross-roads to the north-east of that village. Contalmaison lay about four miles distant, almost in ruins amid its devastated orchards, and with the broken towers of its *chateau* standing out conspicuously at the back.

One brigade had to take the first line of German trenches, other battalions of the division had to take the second and third lines, after which the Tyneside Irish were to push on over all these lines to the farthest point of the Brigade's objective, the second ridge on which Contalmaison stood, where they were to dig themselves in and remain.

The Tyneside Irish had already had their baptism of fire, and had proved themselves not unworthy of the race from which they have sprung. Captain Davey—formerly editor of the *Ulster Guardian* (a Radical and Home Rule journal)—records a stirring incident of St. Patrick's Day, 1916. On the night of March 15-16 a German patrol planted a German flag in front of the Tyneside Irish, half-way across "No Man's Land." It was determined to wipe out the insult.

During the day snipers were allowed to amuse themselves firing at the flag, and it was not long before a lucky shot smashed the staff in two, and left the German ensign trailing in the dust. But the real work was reserved for the night. There were abundance of volunteers, but Captain Davey, with pride in his own province, selected an Ulsterman for the adventure. The man chosen was Second-Lieutenant C. J. Ervine, of Belfast. Mr. Ervine, supported by two Tyneside Irishmen, set out on the eve of St. Patrick's Day, and entered the gloomy depths of "No Man's Land." An hour passed and they returned but without the flag. The enemy was too keenly on the alert. But in the early hours of St. Patrick's Day Lieutenant Ervine set off again this time by himself. What happened is thus described by Captain Davey—

> For an hour and a half we waited for his return, expecting each minute to hear the confounded patrol and machine-gun making the familiar declaration that 'We will not have it.' So keen were the sentries that even when relieved they would not leave their posts. After an hour had passed, Mr. Ervine's sergeant, getting impatient, went over the parapet and crawled to our wire so as to see better. Punctually at a quarter to three a German star-light went up, and by it we could see a dark form making in our direction.
>
> In five minutes it reached our wire, and in ten it was over the parapet. The Germans had been caught napping. In less than half an hour, while the spoiler of the Huns stood by in the crude garb of a Highlander in trench boots for he had fallen into a ditch full of water on the way and we bring no change of clothing to the trenches—another officer and myself had erected a flagstaff in a firing-bay and nailed to it was the German ensign, while ABOVE it floated a green flag with the harp which had been presented to our company before we left home. And so we ushered in St. Patrick's Day!

Captain Davey proceeds—

> Proudly the green banner floated out, while, of course, we flat-

tered ourselves that the black, white and red of Prussia hung its head in shame below. It was not long before the Germans showed that they were wide awake at last, and the bullets began to sing about our newly-erected monument to Ireland and Ireland's patron saint. But it was a stout flagstaff, and though dozens of bullets struck it, nothing short of a shell could have shifted it.

And there it stood all day with the Green above the Black, White and Red. It was no longer a case of 'Deutschland' but of '*Ireland Uber Alles.*' I don't know if any similar sight has been seen in a British trench. I know the green flag has led Irish troops to victory in this war, but I think this is the first time the spectacle has been seen of the Irish ensign hoisted above a captured German flag. At any rate the spectacle was sufficiently novel to cause us to have admiring visitors all day long from other parts of the line.

Unfortunately there is a sad pendant to this story of St. Patrick's Day at the Front. Lieutenant Ervine, the gallant hero of the exploit, died from wounds.

The country which faced the Tyneside Irish on July 1, 1916, had been an agricultural country, inhabited by peasant cultivators before the war. The ravages of war had turned it into a barren waste. The productive soil was completely swept away. Nothing remained but the raw, elemental chalk. It was bare of vegetation, save where, in isolated spots, the hemlock, the thistle, and other gross weeds, proclaimed the rankness of the ground, and also that the processes of Nature ever go on unchecked, even in a world convulsed by human hate. Not only were the villages pounded into rubbish by gunfire, but the woods-also numerous in these parts—appeared, as seen from a distance, to be but mere clusters of gaunt and splintered tree stumps devoid of foliage. Not a human being was to be seen.

Yet that apparently empty waste was infested with men—men turned into burrowing animals like the badger, or, still more, like the weasel, so noted for its ferocious and bloodthirsty disposition. In every shattered wood, in every battered hamlet, in all the slopes and dips by which the face of the country was diversified, they lie concealed, tens of thousands of them, in an elaborately and cunningly contrived system of underground defences, armed with rifles, bombs, machine-guns, trench-mortars, and ready to spring out, with all their claws and teeth displayed, on the approach of their prey, the man in khaki. But, as things turned out, the man in khaki pared the nails of Fritz, and broke his jawbone.

"Before starting, and when our guns were at their heaviest, there was a good deal of movement, up and down, and talking in the trenches. A running fire of chaff was kept up, and there was many a smart reply, for Irish wit will out even in the face of death," said Lieutenant James Hately, who was wounded in that battle. "Some of the fellows were very quiet, but none the less determined. Most of us were laughing. At the same time I felt sorry, for the thought would obtrude itself on my mind that many of the poor chaps I saw around me would never see home again. As for myself, curiously enough, it never occurred to me that I would even be hit. Perhaps that was because I am of a sanguine or optimistic disposition. I started off, like many another officer, with a cigarette well alight. Many of the men were puffing at their pipes. Officers and men exchanged 'good-lucks,' 'cheer-ohs' and other expressions of comradeship and encouragement."

Many were, naturally, in a serious mood. They felt too near to death for the chaff of the billets or trenches to be seemly. They thought of home, of dear ones, of life in the workshops and offices of Newcastle and Sunderland, and the gay companions of favourite sports and amusements, and, more poignant still, some recalled the last sight of the cabin in Donegal, before turning down the lane to the valley and the distant station, on their way to try their fortune in England. Thus there was some restlessness and anxiety, but the company officers in closest touch with the men agree that the general mood was eagerness to get into grips with the enemy, and relish for the adventure, without any great concern as to its results to themselves individually.

When the command was given, "up and over," the brigade, in fact, was like a huge electric battery fresh from a generating station, for its immense driving force and not less for the lively agitation of its varied emotions. Up and over the battalions went, and moved forward in successive waves, the men in single file abreast, the lines about fifty yards apart. For about two hundred yards or so nothing of moment happened. Then they came under heavy fire. Shells burst about them, shrapnel fell from above, bullets from rifle and machine-gun tore through the air, or caused hundreds of little spurts of earth to leap and dance about their feet. One of the men told me that the shrieking and hissing of these deadly missiles reminded him of banshees and serpents, a confused and grotesque association appropriate to a battlefield as to a nightmare.

It must not be supposed that everything was carried with a rush and a shout, at point of the bayonet. An impetuous advance is what the men would have liked best. It would be most in tune with the ardour of their feelings, and less a strain on their nerves. But there were many reasons why that was impossible. The country, in its natural formation, was upward sloping, and all dips and swells. It was broken up into enormous shell-holes and mine-craters, seamed with zigzag lines of white chalky rubble marking the German trenches, and strewn with the wire of demolished entanglements, fallen trees and the wreckage of houses.

The men were heavily equipped in what is called righting order. They carried haversacks, water-bottles, gas-helmets, *bandoliers* filled with cartridges, as well as rifles and bayonets. Some were additionally burdened with bombs and hand grenades. Behind them came the working parties with entrenching tools, such as picks and shovels. Accordingly, the physical labour of the advance alone was tremendous. It would have been stiff and toilsome work for the strongest and most active, even if there had been no storm of shot and shell to face besides. There was, furthermore, the danger in a too hasty progress of plunging headlong into the curtain of high explosives which the artillery, firing from miles behind, hung along the front of the infantry, lifting it and moving it forward as the lines were seen to advance.

Nevertheless the men went on steadily, undaunted by the fire and tumult; and the shuddering earth; undaunted even by the spectacle of the dead and dying of the battalions which preceded them in the attack; shaken only by one horror—a horror unspeakable—that of seeing fond comrades of their own falling bereft of life, as in a flash, by a bullet through the brain or heart; or, worse still, just as suddenly disappearing into bloody fragments amid the roar and smoke of a bursting shell. Now and then men stopped awhile, trembling at the sight and aghast; and, under the sway of impulses that were irresistible, put their right hands over their faces as a protection to their eyes—an appeal, expressed in action rather than in words, that they might be mercifully spared their sight—or else made a sweeping gesture of the arm, as if to brush aside the bullets which buzzed about them like venomous insects.

The pace, therefore, was necessarily slow. It was rather a succession of short rushes, a few yards at a time, with intervening pauses behind such shelter as was available in order to recover breath. The right soldierly quality is not to be over rash, but to adapt oneself to the nature of the righting and its scene; the circumstances of the moment, the ever-varying requirements of the action. Such an advance, whatever precautions be taken, entails great sacrifices. Every life that is lost should be made to go as far as possible in the gaining of the victory. Foolhardy movements, due to unreflecting bravery, were accordingly discouraged. Advantage was to be taken of any cover afforded by the natural features of the country or the state into which it had been transformed by the pounding of high explosives.

The influence of the officers, so cool and alert were they, so suggestive of capability in direction, was most reassuring and stimulating to the men. On the other hand, the officers were relieved by the intelligence, the amenable character of the men and their fine discipline, from the worry and annoyance which company commanders have so often to endure in the course of an action by the casual doings, and the lack of initiative on the part of those under their charge. Simple, biddable, gallant and faithful unto death, it was the wish of the Tyneside Irish that, if they were to fall, their bodies might be found, not in the line of the advance, but at the German positions to the north-west of Contalmaison, out of both of which they had helped to drive the enemy.

But now the lines or waves of men which had left the trenches in extended formation were broken up into separate little bodies, all independently engaged in various grim tasks. They had mounted La Boiselle hill, and moved down into the valley which still intervened between them and Bailiff's Wood and Contalmaison. Thus they were in the very centre of the labyrinth of the enemy's system of defences. An air of intolerable mystery and sinister hidden danger hung over it. Was it not possible that those brutes, those dirty fighters, the inventors of poisonous gas, liquid fire and flame jets, who had established themselves in the very vitals of the place, might not have other devilish inventions prepared for the wholesale massacre of their adversaries? The thought arose in the minds of many, and caused a vague sense of apprehension.

The Germans, however, had no further hellish surprises. Even so, the place was baneful and noxious enough. The Germans had suffered terrible losses and were morally shaken by the artillery bombardment—gigantic, devastating, thunderous—which preceded the British advance. It is the fact, nevertheless, that most of the survivors had enough courage and tenacity left doggedly to contest every inch of the way. They lay concealed in all sorts of cunning traps and contrivances, apart from their demolished trenches.

Machinery on the side of the British—in the form of big guns—had done its part. The time had come for the play of human qualities, the pluck, the endurance and the stout arm of the British infantry man. Snipers had to be dislodged from their burrows; hidden machine-gun posts had likewise to be found out and silenced. So the men of the Tyneside Irish were rushing about in small parties, shooting, bayoneting, clubbing, bombing; and the triumphant yells which arose here and there proclaimed the discovery of yet another lair of the foe.

Many a stirring story of personal adventure could be told. Sergeant Knapp of Sunderland, who won his stripes in the advance, gives this account of his experiences—

> I had just taken the machine-gun off my mate to give him a rest when 'Fritz' opened fire on us from the left with a machine-gun, which played havoc with the Irish. Then I heard my mate shout, 'Bill, I've been hit,' and when I looked round I saw I was by myself; he, poor chap, had fallen like the rest. Now I had to do the best I could, so I picked up a bag of ammunition for the gun and started across 'No Man's Land.' Once I had to drop into a shell-hole to take cover from machine-gun fire.
>
> After a short rest I pushed on again and got into the German second line. By this time I was exhausted, for I was carrying a machine-gun and 300 rounds of ammunition, besides a rifle and 120 rounds in my pouches, equipment, haversack and waterproof cape, so I had a fair load. I stopped there for a few minutes picking off stray *Boches* that were kicking about. Then along came a chap, whom I asked to give me a help with the gun, which he did. We had scarcely gone ten yards when a shell burst on top of us. I stood still. I don't think I could have moved had I wanted to. Then I looked around for my chum, but alas! man and gun were missing. Where he went to I don't know, for I have not seen him or my precious weapon since.

Who that has talked with many wounded soldiers has not found that often they are unable to give any coherent account of their own actions and feelings during a battle. In some cases it is due to an unwillingness to revive haunting memories, a wish to banish out of mind forever the morbid, terrible and grotesque, the ugly aspects in which many experiences in battle present themselves, surpassing the nightmares of any opium eater. In other cases there is an obvious distaste for posing.

All one gallant Irish Tynesider would say to me was, "Sure I only went on because I had to. Didn't the officers tell us before we left the trenches that there was to be no going back?" He brushed aside everything he had done that terrible day which got him the Distinguished Conduct Medal, with the jocose assumption that he was but the most unheroic of mortals, that he went to a place where he would not have gone if he had had any choice in the matter. The incommunicativeness of the soldier is also due to the fact that he cannot recall his sensations. During an engagement his mind is in a whirl. He has no disposition to note his thoughts and feelings in the midst of the fighting.

In fact, few men can analyse the processes of their emotions in such a situation, either at the time or afterwards. As a rule, an overmastering passion possesses the soldier to stab, hack and annihilate the foe who want to take that life which he so greatly desires to preserve. All else is confused and blurred—a vague sense of desperate happenings shrouded in fire and smoke, out of which there emerges, now and then, with sharp distinctness, some specially horrible incident, such as the shattering of a comrade into bits.

But I have met with cases still more strange, where the mind was a blank during the advance through the showering bullets and shrapnel and the exploding shells. Even the simplest process of the brain-memory, or self-consciousness—was dormant. The soldiers in this mental condition appear to have been like the somnambulist who does things mechanically as he walks in his sleep, and when aroused has an impression of having passed through some unusual experience, but what he cannot tell, so vague and formless is it all. Suddenly all the senses of these hypnotised soldiers became wide awake and alert. This happened when they caught sight of figures in skirted grey tunics and flat grey caps with narrow red bands, emerging from cavernous depths into the light of day, or unexpectedly came upon them crouching in holes or behind mounds of earth away from the trenches.

Germans! Face to face with the *Bosche* at last! The effect was like that of a sudden and peremptory blast of a bugle in a deep stillness. Each Irish Tynesider braced up his nerves for bloody deeds. "My life, or theirs," was the thought that sprang to his mind. Thus it was a scene of appalling violence. It resounded with the clash of bayonets; the crackle of musketry; the explosion of bombs; the rattle of machine-guns; and in that confusion of hideous mechanical noises were also heard the shriek of human anguish and the cry of victory.

It was in a wood not far off Contalmaison that the fighting was most desperate and sanguinary of all. The place was full of Germans. The paths and glades were blocked or barricaded with fallen trees. Beneath the splintered and blackened trunks that were still standing, the undergrowth, freed from the attentions of the woodman in the two years of the war, was dense and tangled. Right through the wood were trenches with barbed wire obstructions. At its upper end were peculiarly strong outposts, which poured machine-gun fire through the trees and bushes. It was commanded by batteries on two sides—from Contalmaison on the right and Oviliers on the left.

The attackers had to penetrate this dreadful wood, scrambling, tearing, jumping, creeping in the sultry and stifling heat of the day. There were ferocious personal encounters. The form of fighting was one of the most terrible to which this most hideous of wars has given rise. Probably there has been nothing like it since early man fought those horrid and extinct mammoth animals, the skeletons of which are now to be seen in museums, what time they were alive and savage and ruthless in their haunts in the primeval forest.

The battle was marked by ever-varying vicissitudes of advance and repulse. "*The German Guardsmen fought like tigers to hold it,*" is a phrase in one letter of an Irish Tynesider. Our own official despatches relating to the Somme battle also show that this part of the German front—Oviliers, La Boiselle, Bailiff's Wood, Contalmaison, Mametz Wood—was held by battalions of the Guards, composed of the flower of the youth of Prussia, and standing highest in the mightiest army in the world. These were not the kind of men to put up their hands and cry "*Kamerad*, mercy!" at the sight even of that pitiless and unnerving thing—a bayonet at the end of a rifle in the hands of a brawny Irishman, with the fury of battle flaming in his eyes. They held on tenaciously, and gave blow for blow.

A long bombardment, night and day, by modern heavy guns, is a frightful ordeal. Its ejects are, first, to kill wholesale; and, next, to paralyse the survivors with the fear of death, so that they could but offer only a feeble resistance to the advancing troops. Shaken and despairing men were, therefore, encountered—filthy, unshaven, vile-looking, and so mentally dazed as to act and talk like idiots. But they were not all like that. So well-designed and powerful were their subterranean defences that large numbers were unaffected by the visitations of the high explosives, and through it preserved their courage and their rage.

Conspicuous among these were the Prussian Guards. They made furious efforts to stop the advancing lines of the Tyneside Irish, and that they were overpowered is a splendid testimony to the martial qualities of our men. Think of it! Two years ago, or so, these young lads of various industrial callings—farmhands, railway porters, clerks, drapers' assistants, policemen, carters, messenger boys, miners—would have regarded as preposterous the idea that at any time of what seemed to them to be their predestined humdrum existence, or in any period even of a conceivably mad and topsy-turvy world, they would not only be soldiers but would encounter the Germans on the fields of France; and—most incredible phantasy of all—defeat the renowned Prussian Guards—men whose hearts from their earliest years throbbed high at the thought that they were to be soldiers; men highly disciplined and trained, belonging to the proudest regiments in the German Army, and always ready and eager for the call of battle.

Bailiff's Wood and Contalmaison appear to have been the furthest points reached on the first day of the Battle of the Somme. If they did not then fall, the superb action of the Tyneside Irish made breaches in these strongholds which, when widened and deepened by subsequent assaults, led to their complete capture on July 10. As Captain Downey, an officer of the Tyneside Irish says: "Our men paved the way for various other British regiments who swept through some days later." A few companies of one of these battalions which got into Contalmaison on July 7, and were driven out, brought back some Tyneside Irish and Scottish that were imprisoned in a German dugout in the village. They also found outside the village the bodies of several Tyneside Irish, gallant fellows who died in the attempt to push on to the point they had orders to reach.

The effectiveness of the attack by the Brigade on July 1 depended a good deal upon the progress made by troops of other divisions who were co-operating on both sides. "On our left flank the parallel division was held up; on our right the division moved slowly," says an officer of the Irish Brigade. The difficulties of the advance would probably have held up indefinitely any other troops in the world. But there is never any danger of the momentum of an attack by Irish troops being weakened through excessive caution against what is called "over running."

Indeed, it is a fault of their courage that they are sometimes prone to act with too much precipitation, and, in fact, on this occasion it was not so much that the divisions to the right and left were behind time as that the Irish Brigade were somewhat ahead of it. The result, however, was that the Irish Tynesiders were exposed on their right to a deadly enfilading fire that swept across from Oviliers, which was not yet in British possession. Nevertheless, they did not stop. "No matter who cannot get on, we must." That was the order of the officers in command, and so dauntless was the response to it that by one o'clock the men got to a point in front of Contalmaison. Here what remained of the brigade held on for some days and nights, until the reserves came to their relief on July 4.

The casualties among all ranks were heavy. The officers, sharing every hardship and being foremost in every danger, suffered most grievously. "Our Brigadier, our colonels, our company commanders, were badly wounded. Every officer, with the exception of two subalterns, was hit. Some were hit in no less than three places. Yet they carried on. Those too weak to walk crawled until they eventually gave up through loss of blood. The losses among the N.C.O.s were just as large." This is the testimony of Captain Downey. Lieut.-Colonel L. Meredith Howard of the Tyneside Irish was severely wounded, and died two days afterwards.

Among the officers of the Brigade who fell in action was Second-Lieutenant Gerald FitzGerald. A brother officer says, "He died shouting to his men: 'Come on.'" His father was Lord Mayor of Newcastle the year in which the brigade was raised. Other officers killed were Captain Kenneth Mackenzie of Kinsale, Co. Cork, whose father was formerly an Irish Land Commissioner; Lieutenant Louis Francis Byrne of Newcastle, who was serving his articles as a solicitor when war broke out; and Lieutenant J. R. C. Burlureaux, a journalist.

The disappearance of so many of the officers was enough to have dispirited and confused any body of men. Would it be possible for them to extricate themselves from the fearful labyrinth in which they were involved? Would there be any of them left for the final dash at their objective? The non-commissioned officers rose splendidly to the emergency. One battalion had not far advanced when all the officers were shot down.

Quartermaster-Sergeant Joseph Coleman took command and continued onward. Soon he found himself with only three men left. Everything seemed lost in his part of that scene of tumult and death but for his coolness and gallantry. He went back, gathered up the remnants of other scattered companies, and led a willing and eager band to the capture of the position put down to the battalion in the scheme of operations. For this Coleman got the Distinguished Conduct Medal, and had it pinned on his breast by General Munro, the Brigadier.

When the Brigade was relieved, their return to the haven behind the lines was attended with almost as much danger as their advance to the hell beyond the ridge had been. As the men ascended the slope of La Boiselle, down which they had charged a few days before, the German machine-guns were still rattling from the opposite hill, and snipers were picking off the stragglers.

The hideousness of the field of action had also increased. The devastated ground, with its shell-holes, its great gaping craters and its trenches, was now strewn with the unsavoury litter of the wake of battle — discarded rifles, helmets, packs, burst and unburst shells; boots, rags, meat-tins, bottles and newspapers. Such of the wounded as could walk at all limped along on the arms of comrades. Everyone was inconceivably dirty. Down their blackened faces were white furrows made by their sweat. Thus they came back, the Irish Tynesiders, with bloody but unbowed heads.

"I saw our battalions file out from their bivouac under cover of night, and, though each man knew of the deadly work before him, the ready jest and witty retort were as abundant as ever," writes Lieutenant F. Treanor, quartermaster of one of the battalions of the Tyneside Irish, and a native of Monaghan. "In the dressing-stations afterwards I saw many of them, and there were still the same heroic fortitude and the exchange of comments, many grimly humorous, as that of one poor fellow who remarked, when asked if he had any souvenirs. 'Be danged, 'twas no place for picking up jewellery.'"

The brigade received the highest praises from the commander of the Army Corps and the commander of the division, as well as from their own general. The corps commander wrote: "The gallantry, steadiness and resource of the Brigade were such as to uphold the very highest and best traditions of the British Army." Major-General Ingouville-Williams, who commanded the division, wrote to the Tyneside committee —

> It is with the greatest pride and deepest regret that I wish to inform you that the Division which included the Tyneside Irish covered itself with glory on July 1, but its losses were very heavy. Every one testifies to the magnificent work they did that day, and it is the admiration of all. I, their commander, will never forget their splendid advance through the German curtain of fire. It was simply wonderful, and they behaved like veterans.

Tyneside can well be proud of them; and although they will sorrow for all my brave and faithful comrades, it is some consolation to know they died not in vain, and that their attack was of the greatest service to the Army on that day.

Writing to his wife on July 3, 1916, Major-General Ingouville-Williams said:

My Division did glorious deeds. Never have I seen men go through such a hell of a barrage of artillery. They advanced as on parade and never flinched. I cannot speak too highly of them. The Division earned a great record, but, alas! at a great cost.

On July 20 he also wrote to his wife:

Never shall I cease singing the praises of my old Division, and I never shall have the same grand men to deal with again.

A few days later Major-General Ingouville-Williams died for his country.

Seventy-three officers and men of the Tyneside Irish received decorations. Four Distinguished Service Orders and twenty Military Crosses went to the officers, eight Distinguished Conduct Medals and forty Military Medals were received by the men, and a sergeant was awarded the high Russian decoration of the Order of St. George. Among the officers who received the Military Cross was Lieutenant T. M. Scanlan, whose father, Mr. John E. Scanlan, Newcastle-on-Tyne, took a prominent part in the raising of the Brigade. Lieutenant Scanlan states that only eight men were left out of his platoon after July 1, and six of them were awarded honours.

All honour to the Brigade! Those who helped to raise the battalions—Mr. Peter Bradley and Mr. N. Grattan Doyle, the chairmen of the committee; Mr. Gerald Stoney and Mr. John Mulcahy, the joint secretaries—have reason to be proud of the magnificent quality of the men who responded to their call. Let it stand as the last word of the story of their achievement that they overthrew and trampled down the proud Prussian Guards, and relaxed the grip which Germany had held for two years on a part of France.

CHAPTER 7

The Wearing of Religious Emblems at the Front

Nearly every man out here is wearing some sort of Catholic medallion or a rosary that has been given him, and he would rather part with his day's rations or his last cigarette than part with his sacred talisman. Extract from a letter written from the Front by a non-Catholic private in the Hussars.

The wearing of religious emblems by soldiers of the British Army is much talked of by doctors and nurses in military hospitals in France and at home. When wounded soldiers are undressed—be they non Catholic or Catholic—the discovery is frequently made of medals or *scapulars* worn around their necks, or sacred badges stitched inside their tunics. It is a psychological phenomenon of much interest for the light it throws upon human nature in the ordeal of war. It shows, too, how war is a time when supernatural signs and wonders are multiplied.

Testimony to the value of these religious favours as safeguards against danger and stimulants to endurance and heroism was given in a most dramatic manner by Corporal Holmes, V.C., of the King's Own Yorkshire Light Infantry, who also holds the highest French decoration, the *Medaille Militaire*. He visited the Catholic schools at Leeds. All the girls and boys were assembled to see him. One of the nuns told the children how Corporal Holmes won his honours during the retreat from Mons. He carried a disabled comrade out of danger, struggling on with his helpless human burden for three miles under heavy fire. Then taking the place of the driver, who was wounded, he brought a big gun, with terror-stricken horses, out of action, through lines of

German infantry and barbed wire entanglements.

At the crossing of the Aisne a machine-gun was left behind, as the bridge over which it was hoped to carry it was shelled by the enemy. Corporal Holmes plunged into the river with it, some distance below the bridge, and, amid shot and shell, brought it safely to the other bank. When the nun had finished recounting his deeds, Corporal Holmes unexpectedly turned back his tunic, and saying, "This is what saved me," pointed to his rosary and medal of the Blessed Virgin.

There is the equally frank and positive declaration made by Lance-Corporal Cuddy of the Liverpool Irish (the King's Liverpool Regiment), who was awarded the Distinguished Conduct Medal for gallantry in saving life after the great Battle of Festubert. He was in the trenches with his regiment. Cries for help came from some wounded British soldiers lying about fifteen yards from the German trenches. The appeal smote the pitying heart of Cuddy. He climbed the parapet of his trench, and, crawling forward on his stomach, discovered two disabled men of the Scottish Rifles.

One of them had a broken thigh. Cuddy coolly bound up the limb, under incessant fire from the German trenches, and crawled back to his trench, dragging the man with him. Then, setting out to bring in the second man, he was followed by Corporal Dodd of the same battalion, who volunteered to assist him. On the way a bullet struck Dodd on the shoulder and passed out through his leg. Cuddy bandaged him and carried him safely back. Once more he crawled over the fire-swept ground between the trenches to the second Scottish rifleman. This time he took an oil-sheet with him. He wrapped it round the wounded man and brought him in also.

All this was the work of hours. Not for a moment did this brave and simple soul flinch or pause in his humane endeavours. He seemed to be indifferent, or absolutely assured, as to his own fate. And he had the amazing good luck of going through the ordeal scathless, save for a slight wound in the leg. As is the way with soldiers, the comrades of Cuddy joked with him on his success in dodging the bullets of the bloody German snipers. "They were powerless to hit me. I carry the Pope's prayer about me, and I put my faith in that," he answered, in accordance with his simple theology. This prayer of Pope Benedict XV is one "*to obtain from the mercy of Almighty God the blessings of Peace.*"

Both soldiers were convinced, as Catholics, that, being under the special protection of the Heavenly Powers whose symbols they wore, they were safe and invincible until their good work was done. Psalm

104 speaks of God, "*who maketh the sweeping winds his angels, and a flaming sword His ministers.*" Why should He not work also through the agency of the religious emblems of His angels and saints? With this belief strong within them, Holmes and Cuddy leaped at the chance of bringing comfort to comrades in anguish, and help to those sorely pressed by the enemy.

There is another aspect of this question of the psychology of war. It is a boast of the age that we have freed ourselves from what is called the deadening influence of superstition. Nevertheless, since the outbreak of the war there has been an extraordinary revival of the secular belief in omens, witchcraft, incantations and all that they imply—the direct influence of supernatural powers, of some sort or other, on the fortunes of individuals in certain events. One amiable form of it is the enormously increased demand for those jewellers' trinkets called charms and amulets, consisting of figures or symbols in stone and metal which are popularly supposed to possess powers of bringing good fortune or averting evil, and which formerly lovers used to present to each other, and wear attached to bracelets and chains, to ensure mutual constancy, prosperity and happiness.

Even the eighteenth-century veneration of a child's *caul*—the membrane occasionally found round the head of an infant at birth—as a sure preservative against drowning is again rife among those who go down to the sea in ships. The menace of the German submarine has revivified the ancient desire of seafaring folk to possess a *caul*, which was laid dormant by the sense of security bred by years of freedom from piracy, and the article has gone up greatly in price in shops that sell sailors' requirements at the chief ports. Fortune-tellers, crystal-gazers, and other twentieth-century witches and dealers in incantations, who pretend to be able to look into the future and provide safeguards against misfortune, are being consulted by mothers, wives and sweethearts, anxiously seeking for some safe guidance for their nearest and dearest through the perils of the war.

So far as the Army is concerned, the belief that certain things bring good luck or misfortune has always been widely held by the rank and file. Formerly there were two talismans which were regarded as especially efficacious in warding off evil, and particularly death and disablement in battle. These were, in the infantry, a button off the tunic of a man, and, in the cavalry, the tooth of a horse, in cases where the man and the horse had come scathless through a campaign. A good many years ago the old words "charm," "talisman," "amulet," dropped out of use in the Army.

The French slang word "*mascot*," which originated with gamblers and is applied to any person, animal or thing which is supposed to be lucky, came into fashion; and some animal or bird—monkey, parrot, or goat, or even the domestic dog or cat—was appointed "the mascot of the regiment." But since the outbreak of the war the Army has returned to its old faith in the old talisman. A special charm designed for soldiers, called "Touchwood," and described as "the wonderful Eastern charm," has had an enormous sale. It was suggested by the custom, when hopes are expressed, of touching wood, so as to placate the fates and avert disappointment, a custom which is supposed to have arisen from the ancient Catholic veneration of the true Cross.

"Touchwood" is a tiny imp, mainly head, made of oak, surmounted by a khaki service cap, and with odd, sparkling eyes, as if always on the alert to see and avert danger. The legs, either in silver or gold, are crossed, and the arms, of the same metal, are lifted to touch the head. The designer, Mr. H. Brandon, states that he has sold 1,250,000 of this charm since the war broke out.

Not long ago there was a curious scene in Regent's Park. This was the presentation of "Touchwood" to each of the 1200 officers and men of a battalion of the City of London Regiments (known as "The Cast-Irons") by Mdlle. Delysia, a French music-hall dancer, before they went off for the Front. Never has there been such a public exhibition—uncontrolled and unashamed—of the belief in charms. Mr. Brandon has received numerous letters from soldiers on active service, ascribing their escape from perilous situations to the wearing of the charm. One letter, which has five signatures, says—

> We have been out here for five months fighting in the trenches, and have not had a scratch. We put our great good fortune down to your lucky charm, which we treasure highly.

Thus we see that mankind has not outgrown old superstitions, as so many of us thought, but, on the contrary, is still ready to fly to them for comfort and protection in danger. The truth is that the human mind remains at bottom essentially the same amid all the changes made by time in the superficial crust of things. Man is still the heir of all the ages. Some taint of "the old Popish idolatries" survives in the blood of most of us, no matter how Protestant and rationalistic we may suppose ourselves to be. And now that the foundations of civilisation are disrupted, and humanity is involved in the coils of the most awful calamity that has ever befallen it, is it to be wondered at that hands should be piteously stretched out on all sides, and in all sorts of ways—unorthodox as well as orthodox—groping in the dark for protective touch with the unseen Powers who rule our destinies.

It is in these circumstances that non-Catholic soldiers of the new Armies are turning from materialistic charms to holy emblems. It may be thought that this new cult is but a manifestation, in a slightly different form, of the same primal superstitious instinct of mankind as inspired the old, but as it has a religious origin and sanction and is really touched by spiritual emotion, it seems to me to be far removed from the other in spirit and intention. Non-Catholic soldiers appear to have been led into the new practice by the example of Catholic soldiers.

These religious objects, commemorative of the Blessed Virgin and other saints, have always been carried about their persons by Irish Catholic soldiers, to some extent, as well as by Catholics generally in civil life. The custom is now almost universal among Catholic officers and men at the Front. It resembles, in a way, the still more popular practice of carrying photographs of mother, wife and child. Will it be denied that the soldier, as he looks upon the likenesses of those who cherish him, and hold him ever in their thoughts, does not derive hope and consolation from his consciousness of their watchful and prayerful love?

There are several little breastplates thus worn by Catholics to shield them from spiritual evil and bodily calamity. The chaplet of beads, known as the rosary, is well known. The brown scapular of St. Mary of Mount Carmel is made of small pieces of cloth connected by long strings, and is worn over the shoulders in imitation of the brown habit of the Carmelite friars. Then there are the Medal of Our Lady of Perpetual Succour, a reproduction of the wonderful picture discovered by the Redemptorist Order in Rome; and the Miraculous Medal of Our Lady, revealed by the Immaculate Virgin to Catherine Labouré, Sister of Charity of St. Vincent de Paul, in Paris.

Another is the "*Agnus Dei*" ("Lamb of God"), a small disc of wax, impressed with the figure of a lamb supporting a cross, and blessed by the Pope, which is the most ancient of the sacramentals, or holy objects worn, used or preserved by Catholics for devotional purposes. But what is now perhaps the most esteemed of all is the Badge of the Sacred Heart. On an oval piece of red cloth is printed a picture of Jesus, standing before a cross, with His bleeding heart, encircled by thorns and flames, exposed on His breast. The badge is emblematical of the sufferings of Jesus for the love of and redemption of mankind. It is the cognisance of a world-wide league, known as the Apostleship of Prayer, conducted by the Society of Jesus, and having, it is said, a membership of 25,000,000 of all nations.

The promotion of these special devotions in the Catholic Church has been assigned to different Orders: such as the rosary to the Dominicans; the *scapular* to the Carmelites; the Way of the Cross to the Franciscans. So the spread of the devotion of the Sacred Heart is the work of the Jesuits. The headquarters of the Apostleship of Prayer in this country is the house of the Jesuits in Dublin, who publish as its organ a little monthly magazine called *The Messenger*. There has been so enormous a demand for the badge since the war broke out that the Jesuits have circulated a statement emphasising that it is not to be regarded as "a charm or talisman to preserve the wearer from bullets and shrapnel." To wear it in this spirit would, they say, be "mere superstition."

"What it stands for and signifies is something far nobler and greater," they also say.

"It is, in a sense, the exterior livery or uniform of the soldiers and clients of the Sacred Heart of Jesus, King of heaven and earth, just as the brown *scapular* is the livery of the servants and soldiers of Mary, heaven's glorious Queen. As such it procures for those who wear it in the proper spirit the grace and protection of God; and the scapulars the special protection of Mary, much more than the livery or uniform of a country procures for those who fight under its flag the help and protection of the nation to which they belong.

What is the attitude of the Irish Catholic soldier towards this religious movement as a means of preservation and grace in the trials and perils of war? I have read many letters from Irish Catholics on service in France, Flanders and the East in which the matter is referred to, and have discussed it with some of those who have been invalided home. All this testimony establishes beyond question that the mystical sense of the Irish nature, which has been developed to a high degree by the two tremendous influences of race and religion, leads the Irish Catholic soldier profoundly to believe that there is a supernatural interference often with the chances and fortunes of the battlefield in answer to prayers.

Michael O'Leary, V.C., a splendid type of the Irish soldier in body and mind, gave a brief but pointed statement of his views on the matter. "A shell has grazed my cheek and blown a comrade by my side to pieces," he said, "though there was no reason, so far as I could see, but the act of God, why the shell should not have knocked my head off and grazed my comrade's cheek."

The average Irish soldier probably knows nothing of the materialistic theory that Nature is a closed system; that the laws of the universe are fixed and immutable; that no wearing of holy objects, and no amount of praying even, will ever disturb their uniform mechanical working; and that the sole reason why any soldier on the battlefield escapes being hit by a bullet or piece of explosive shell is that he was not directly in its line of flight. Such a doctrine would be regarded, at least by the simple and instinctive natures in the Irish ranks, as the limit of blasphemy. Their belief in the reality and power of God is most profound. God is to them still the lord and master of all the forces of Nature; and the turning aside of a bullet or piece of explosive shell would be but the slightest manifestation of His almighty omnipotence.

Mystery surrounds the Irish Catholic soldier at all times. His realisation of the unseen is very vivid. The saints and angels are his companions, not the less real and potent because they are not visible to his eyes. But it is on the field of battle that he is most closely enveloped by these spiritual presences. He is convinced that he has but to call upon them, and that, if he be in a state of grace, they will come to his aid as the ministers of God. So he prays that God may protect and save him, and he wears next his heart the emblems of God's angels and saints. Thus he feels invincible against the powers of darkness in both the spiritual and material worlds. For these devotions have also the effect of putting him in train to receive submissively whatever fate God may will him. He knows that God can safeguard him in the fight if He chooses; and he believes that if God does not chose so to do it is because in His wisdom He does not deem it right.

"*Blessed be the holy will of God!*" The old, familiar Irish ejaculation springs to his lips, that variant of Job's unshakable trust in the Almighty: "Though He slay me, yet will I trust Him." Thus it is that the sight of his comrades lying around him, dead and wounded, who prayed like him and, like him, carried rosary beads or wore the badge of the Sacred Heart, has no effect in shaking his belief in his devotions and his holy emblems. So when the hour of direst peril is at hand he is found not unnerved and incapable of standing the awful test. There is an ancient Gaelic proverb which says: "What is there that seems worse to a man than his death? and yet he does not know but it may be the height of his good luck." Even if death should come, what is it but the shadowy gate which opens into life everlasting and blissful?

There are on record numerous cases of protection and deliverance ascribed by non-Catholics as well as Catholics to the wearing of religious emblems. The Sisters of Mercy, Dungarvon, Waterford, tell the story of the marvellous escape from death of Private Thomas Kelly, Royal Munster Fusiliers, at the first landing on the Gallipoli peninsula on April 25, 1915. Kelly had emerged with his comrades from the *River Clyde*—the steamer which had brought his regiment to the landing-place, Beach V—and was in the water wading towards the shore when this happened to him—

> A bullet struck him, passing through his left hand, which at the moment was placed over his heart. The bullet hit and shattered a shield badge of the Sacred Heart, which was sewn inside his tunic, then glanced aside and passed over his chest, tearing the skin. The mark of its passage across the chest can still be plainly seen. The bullet then passed through the pocket of his tunic at the right-hand side, completely destroying his pay-book. When wounded he fell into the water, where he lay for about two hours under a perfect hurricane of bullets and shrapnel. In all that time, while his companions were falling on every side, he received only one slight flesh wound. He is now in Ireland, loudly proclaiming, to all whom he comes in contact with, his profound gratitude to the Sacred Heart. He is quite recovered from his wounds, and expects soon to be sent to the Front. His trust in the Sacred Heart is unbounded, and he is fully convinced that the Sacred Heart will even work miracles for him, if they are necessary, to bring him safely home again.

Private Edward Sheeran, Royal Irish Rifles, relating his experiences in France, says—

> We were waiting in reserve, and were shelled heavily before the advance. Four of us were lying low in the traverse of a trench. Every time I heard a shell approaching I said, 'O Sacred Heart of Jesus, have mercy on us!' Just as I was reciting this ejaculation a shell burst in our midst. For a minute I was dazed, and when I surveyed the damage, imagine my surprise to find the man next

to me blown to pieces, parts of him over me. Another never moved again to my knowledge, while the remaining one had his arms shattered. As regards myself, my pack was blown off my back, but all the injury I received was a very slight wound in the left shoulder. Thanks to the mercy of the Sacred Heart I was able to rejoin my battalion two days afterwards.

"A very grateful sister," writing to the *Irish Messenger*, in thanksgiving for "a great favour obtained through Our Blessed Lady of Perpetual Succour," states—

My brother was ordered out to the war and was in the fighting line from the first. I sent him a miraculous medal of Our Blessed Lady and promised publication if he came back safe. He has been in twelve battles and got nine wounds, none dangerous, only on his hands and one leg badly broken. He was being carried off the field by his comrades and the shells were falling so fast that they had to leave him and fly for their lives. He lay there three hours, bleeding and faint, until he was picked up again, and, thanks to Our Blessed Lady's protection, he is now safe in a London hospital and making a speedy recovery.

The brother of an Irish Catholic nurse in a British military hospital in France writes to the *Irish Messenger*—

I was speaking lately to my sister, the nurse to whom you sent the parcel of badges, beads, etc. She says if every parcel of badges did as much good as hers has done and is doing, you will have a big reward in eternity. The poor Irish and English Catholic lads in their torments find the greatest comfort in their beads and badges, and put more trust in the Sacred Heart than in surgeons and nurses. One poor man said: 'I know I am dying, but, nurse, write to my poor wife and tell her that my beads and a sip of Holy Water was my consolation. Tell her I put my trust in the Sacred Heart and die confident. Send her this old badge which I wore all through the war.'

In Ireland there are tens of thousands of Catholic mothers, wives and sisters, ever praying for the safe return of their men from the Front, or else that they be given the grace of a happy death, and there is nothing that tends more to prevent them brooding when the day, the hour, the moment may come with a dread announcement from the War Office, than the consoling thought that these dear ones are faithful in all the dangers and emergencies of their life to the practices of their religion. That is why Private Michael O'Reilly, of the Connaught Rangers in France, writes to his mother:

> I have the Sacred Heart badge on my coat and three medals, a pair of rosary beads and father's *Agnus Dei* around my neck, so you see I am well guarded, and you have nothing at all to fear so far as I am concerned.

Even for the mother, death loses its sting when she gets news of her son which leaves her in no doubt as to his soul's eternal welfare. Here is a characteristic specimen of many letters from bereaved but comforted mothers which have been printed in *The Messenger*—

> Dear Rev. Father,—I beg to appeal to you for my dear good son who was killed in action on the 25th of March, and who died a most holy death. I have heard from Father Gleeson that he died with his rosary beads round his neck and reciting his rosary. He got a gunshot wound in the head and lived several hours after receiving the wound. I know perfectly well that it was owing to his having St. Joseph's Cord about him that he got such a happy death and had the happiness of receiving his Easter duty on Sunday the 21st. He also had the Sacred Heart Badge, a crucifix, and his Blue and Brown Scapulars on him, so that I am content about the way he died. He is buried in Bethune cemetery. I am a subscriber to *The Messenger*, and my son was in the Apostleship of Prayer and used to get the leaflets in his young days at the school he was going to, taught by the Christian Brothers. He was twenty-one years and seven months the day of his sad death. He belonged to the Royal Munster Fusiliers.

Some people, no doubt, will smile indulgently or mockingly-according to their natures—at what appears to them to be curious instances of human credulity. Others will cry out in angry protest against "Popish trumperies"; "idolatrous practices"; "fetishism." No religion can be truly understood from the outside. It must be lived in, within, to be apprehended. But surely those who are not altogether cursed with imperfect sympathies—those, at least, who take pleasure in the happy state of others, will shout aloud in joy to know that there is something left—no matter what—to sustain and console in this most terrible time of youth's agony and motherhood's lacerated heart.

It must not be supposed that the religious practices of the Irish

Catholic troops are confined to the wearing of *scapulars*, medals and *Agnus Deis*. There are among them, of course, many who attribute all kinds of phenomena to natural rather than to miraculous causes. By them, also, beads, medals and scapulars are venerated, and proudly displayed over their tunics—often, too, rosary beads are to be seen twisted round rifle barrels as outward symbols of the spirit of their religion, as aids to worship, as bringing more vividly before them the God they adore and the saints whose aid they invoke. But their faith gives, in addition, to the Catholic troops the Mass, which is celebrated by the Army chaplains up at the Front in wrecked houses or on the open, desolate fields, and attended by many hundreds of men in silent and intent worship, the sacraments of Confession and Communion, and makes possible that solemn spectacle of the priest administering the General Absolution, or forgiveness of sin, to a whole battalion, standing before him with bared and bowed heads, before going into action.

All these religious scenes have greatly impressed non-Catholic soldiers. They wonder at the consolation and inspiration which Catholic comrades derive from their services and their symbols. They feel the loneliness and the dread of things. They are impressed by the number of wayside shrines, with Crucifixes and Madonnas, which have survived the ravages of war. In their hearts they crave for spiritual companionship and help which the guns thundering behind them cannot give any more than the guns thundering in front; and they, too, put out their hands to grasp the supernatural presences, unseen but so acutely felt in the shadowy arena of war. If there was scoffing at a praying soldier in barracks, there is respect for him in the trenches. Non-Catholics join in the prayers that are said by Catholics.

"Plenty of shells were fired at our trenches, but, thank God, no harm was done," writes an Irish soldier. "When the shells came near us we used to pray. Prayers are like a double parapet to them, I think. Yesterday we were reciting the *Litany of the Sacred Heart* while the shells were annoying us. I was reading the beautiful praises and titles of the Litany, and both my Protestant and Catholic mates were answering me with great fervour. I was just saying *Heart of Jesus, delight of all the Saints, succour us,* when one shell hit our trench and never burst, and, furthermore, no shell came near us after that, for our opponents directed their attention elsewhere for the rest of the day." He adds that every night in the trenches the Rosary of the Blessed Virgin was recited; and the responses were given by non-Catholics as well as by

Catholics.

In like manner, non-Catholic soldiers are being weaned from the use of pagan charms and talismans, and are taking instead to the Catholic substitutes which have been blessed by the priest making over them the sign of the cross. Father Plater stated at a meeting of the Westminster Catholic Federation that, travelling in the south of England, he met in the train some soldiers of the Ulster Division, all Orangemen, and instead of consigning the holy father to other realms, as they probably would have done in other times and other circumstances, they actually asked him to bless their miraculous medals.

There is an ever-increasing desire among them for medals, rosaries, and for holy pictures, such as the little prints of saints and angels which Catholics carry in their prayer-books. At the convents in London where the Badge of the Sacred Heart is to be had, Protestant soldiers are constantly calling to get it, and they tell stories which they had heard of wonderful escapes by those who wore it. One nun told me they cannot keep the supply abreast of the demand. For instance, she said that on the day I saw her a private of the Royal Welsh Fusiliers got fifty badges for distribution in the regiment.

Religious emblems have a warmth and intimacy about them which secular charms lack. They are regarded as representing real spiritual beings, saints and angels. Secular charms, on the other hand, are devoid of association with any potentate or power known or believed to exist in the other world, and seem still to possess something of the mingled simplicity and grossness of the first dawning of superstition on the mind of the savage. The curiosity and interest of the non-Catholic soldier in these religious symbols being thus excited, the moment he handles one and examines its design, he feels a pleasant sensation of help and comfort, and a consequent increase in his vitality. He highly treasures his holy talisman. Should he pass unscathed through the constant yet capricious menace of an engagement, he ascribes his luck to supernatural protection.

As the English troops were passing through Hornu, near Mons, a young Belgian lady took a rosary from her neck and gave it to Private Eves of the West Riding Regiment, telling him to wear it as a protection against the bullets of the Germans. Eves, a non-Catholic Northumbrian, wore the rosary during the Battle of Mons.

"The air was thick with shells and machine-gun bullets," he says, "and how I escaped I don't know. A shell burst close to me. A piece of it struck my ammunition band and bent five cartridges out of shape;

but I escaped with only a bruise on the chest. I always say this rosary had something to do with it."

Many stories of the like might be told. A driver of the Royal Field Artillery says: "I think I owe all my luck to a mascot which I carry in my knapsack. It is a beautiful crucifix, given me by a Frenchwoman for helping her out of danger. It is silver, enamel and marble, and she made me take it."

Private David Bulmer of the Royal Engineers, an Ulster Presbyterian, returned home on furlough to his parents at Killeshandra, wearing a rosary. He declared it was the beads that saved his life on the battlefield, as he was the only man left in his company.

Sapper Clifford Perry has written to a Cardiff friend:

> Rosaries are very popular here. I think I can safely say that four out of every ten men one meets wear them around their necks. Strange to say, they are not all Catholics. Those who are not Catholics do not wear them as curios or ornaments either, as upon cases of inquiry they attach some religious value to them even though they cannot explain what it is. Still, no one could convince them to part with them.

Often the emblems and badges worn by non-Catholic soldiers are gifts from Catholic wives and children concerned for their spiritual and temporal well-being. "An Irish mother who trusts in the *Sacred Heart*" writes from Kensington in acknowledgment of the "wonderful escape" of her husband.

> He had only gone out from a stable when a German shell knocked the roof in, killing his two horses, and also killing one man and wounding five others. My husband, who is a Protestant, is wearing a Sacred Heart Badge and the Cross belonging to my rosary. He has been saved during many battles from the most awful dangers, having been fighting regularly since September 1914.

Father Peal, S. J., of the Connaught Rangers serving in France, relating some of his experiences as a chaplain after a battle, says:

> It was very solemn, creeping in and out among the wounded, finding who were Catholics. Some could not speak, others just able to whisper. One poor man lay on his face, with a hole in his back. He was actually breathing through this hole. I felt round his neck for his identification disc and found he had a medal and *Agnus Dei*. I naturally thought he was a Catholic, but he

whispered to me, 'Missus and the children did that.' We repeated an act of contrition, and I gave him conditional absolution.

So it has come to pass that rosaries, which were formerly a monopoly of the religious repositories in French towns and villages, may now be seen displayed in every shop window, so great is the demand for them, and that "The League of the Standard of the Cross"—an Anglican society—has, up to the end of 1916, sent out over 10,000 crucifixes to Protestant soldiers.

The wearing of Catholic emblems by the rank and file is encouraged by many officers who understand human nature, and make allowance for what some of them, no doubt, would call its inherent weaknesses. The practice has been proved to have on conduct a profound influence for good. It seems to incite and fortify the soldiers' courage. Man's will and resolution often prove to be weak and fickle things, especially on the field of battle, where they are put to the sternest and most searching of tests. Fear of death, which, after all, is but a manifestation of the primal instinct of self-preservation, often militates against the efficiency of the soldier.

It disorganises his understanding; it paralyses his power to carry out orders. The elimination of fear, or its control, is therefore part of the training of the soldier. How fortunate, then, is the soldier who can find such tranquillity in battle that he has passed beyond the fear of death. Psychologists tell us, such is the influence of the body upon the mind, that whether a man shall act the hero or the coward in an emergency depends largely on his physical condition at the time. The body of the soldier must, as far as possible, be made subordinate to his mind.

Religious sensibility and emotion, in whatever form it may manifest itself, tends to the exaltation of the mental mood; and as good officers know they cannot afford to neglect any means which promises to steady their men, calm them and give them confidence in action or under fire, they have enlisted this tremendous force on their side by favouring and promoting the Catholic custom of wearing holy objects.

A nun writing from a convent in South London says:

> The colonel at —— sent twenty-two medals to Father X—— to be blessed. The Father took the medals to the barracks himself, where the colonel informed him that he wanted them for Protestant officers who were going to France.

The girls of the Notre Dame Convent School, Glasgow, sent a parcel of 1 200 medals to a Scottish regiment. They received a letter of thanks from one of the officers, in which he says:

> You will be glad to know that most, if not all the men, Protestants though they be, have put your medals on the cord to which their identity discs are tied, so that Our Lady may help them.

Thus is the wearing of *scapulars* and medals in the Army welcomed as an aid to our arms, a reinforcement of our military power. In it may be found the secret of much of the dash and gallantry of the Irish troops. Up to the end of 1916, 221 Victoria Crosses have been awarded for great deeds done in the war. As many as twenty-four have been won by Catholics, of whom eighteen are Irish, a share out of all proportion to their numbers, but not—may I say?—to their valour. In order to appreciate adequately the significance of these figures it is necessary to remember the nature of the deed for which the Victoria Cross is given. It must be exceptionally daring, involving the greatest risk to life. It must be of special military value, or must lead to the saving of comrades otherwise hopelessly doomed.

Above all, it must be done not under orders but as a spontaneous act on the soldier's own motion. It is largely due to their religion and the emblems of their religion, and their views of fate and destiny, that Irish Catholic soldiers are so pre-eminently distinguished in the record of the highest and most noble acts of valour and self-sacrifice in war. There is the significant saying of Sergeant Dwyer, V.C., an Irishman and a Catholic, at a recruiting meeting in Trafalgar Square.

"I don't know what the young men are afraid of," said he. "If your name is not on a bullet or a bit of shrapnel it won't reach you, any more than a letter that isn't addressed to you." He, poor fellow, got a bullet addressed to him on the Somme. "'Twas the will of God," was the lesson taught him by his creed.

CHAPTER 8

The Irish Soldier's Humour and Seriousness

The memorable words of an Irish member, speaking in the House of Commons during the South African War, on the gallantry of the Irish regiments, come to my mind. "This war has shown," said he, "that as brave a heart beats under the tunic of a Dublin Fusilier as under the kilt of a Gordon Highlander."

The saying may be curiously astray as to the anatomy of the Scotch, but the truth of it in regard to Irish courage has been emphasised by the victories and disasters alike of the great world war. On all the fields of conflict east and west the Irish soldiers have earned the highest repute for valour. "They are magnificent fighters," says Lieutenant Denis Oliver Barnett, an English officer of a battalion of the Leinster Regiment, in letters which he wrote home to his own people. A public school boy, with a high reputation for scholarship, he became a soldier at the outbreak of war instead of going to Oxford. Courageous and high-minded himself—as his death on the parapet of the trenches, directing and heartening his men in bombing the enemy, testifies—his gay and sympathetic letters show that he was a good judge of character.

He also says of his men, "They are cheerier than the English Tommies, and will stand anything." Cheeriness in this awful war is indeed a most precious possession. It enhances the fighting capacity of the men. Where it does not exist spontaneously the officers take measures to cultivate it. As far as possible they try to remove all depressing influences, and make things bright and cheerful. I have got many such glimpses of the Irish soldier at the Front, and their total effect is the impersonation or bodying forth of an individual who provides his own gaiety, and has some over to give to others—whimsical, wayward, with a childlike petulance and simplicity; and yet very fierce withal.

I met at a London military hospital an Irish Catholic chaplain and an Irish officer of the Army Medical Corps back from French Flanders. They told Irish stories, to the great enjoyment and comfort of the wounded soldiers in the ward. "Be careful to boil that water before drinking it," said the doctor to men of an Irish battalion whom he found drawing supplies from a canal near Ypres.

"Why so, sir?" asked one of the men.

"Because it's full of microbes and boiling will kill them," answered the doctor.

"And where's the good, sir?" said the soldier. "I'd as soon swallow a menagerie as a graveyard any day."

Another example of a quick-witted Hibernian reply was given by the chaplain. He came upon a man of the transport service of his battalion belabouring a donkey which was slowly dragging a heavy load. "Why do you beat the poor animal so much?" remonstrated the priest; and he recalled a legend popular in Ireland by saying, "Don't you know from the cross on the ass's back that it was on an ass Our Lord went into Jerusalem?"

"But, Father," said the soldier, "if Our Lord had this lazy ould ass He wouldn't be there yet."

One of the inmates of the ward kept the laughter going by giving an example of Irish traditional blundering humour from the trenches"a humour due to an excited and over-active mind. "Don't let the Germans know we're short of powder and shot," cried an Irish sergeant to his men, awaiting the bringing up of ammunition; "keep on firing away like blazes."

Some of the flowers of speech that have blossomed from the Irish regiments at the Front are also worth culling. Speaking of the Catholic chaplain of his battalion, a soldier said, "He'd lead us to heaven; an' we'd follow him to hell."

As a loaf of bread stuck on a bayonet was passed on to him in the trenches another exclaimed, "Here comes the staff of life on the point of death."

The irregularity of the food supply in the trenches was thus described: "It's either a feast or a famine. Sometimes you drink out of the overflowing cup of fullness, and other times you ate off the empty plate."

"What have you there?" asked a nurse of an Irish private of the

Army Medical Corps, at a base hospital, as he was rummaging among the contents of a packing-case. Taking out a wooden leg, he answered: "A stump speech agin the war."

Good-humour at the Front is by no means an exclusively Irish possession. Happily the soldiers of all the nationalities within the United Kingdom are so light-hearted as to find even in the most dismal situation cause for raillery, pleasantry and laughter, and to derive from their mirth a more enduring patience of discomfort and trouble. The Irish form of humour, however, differs entirely from the English, Scottish or Welsh variety not only in quality but in the type of mind and character it expresses.

In most things that the Irish soldier says or does there is something racially individual. Perhaps its chief peculiarity, apart from its quaintness, is that usually there is an absence of any conscious aim or end behind it. The English soldier, and the Cockney especially, is a wag and a jester. He is very prone to satire and irony, deliberate and purposeful. Even his "grousing"—a word, by the way, unheard in the Irish regiments, unless it is somewhat incomprehensibly used by an English non-commissioned officer—is a form of caustic wit. Irish humour has neither subtlety nor seriousness. It is just the light and spontaneous whim, caprice or fancy of the moment. It is humour in the original sense of the word, that is the expression of character, habit and disposition.

The Munstermen have contributed to the vocabulary at the Front the expressive phrase, *Gone west,* for death; the bourne whence no traveller returns. In Kerry and Cork the word "west" or "wesht," as it is locally pronounced, expresses not only the mysterious and unknown, but is used colloquially for "behind," "at the back," or "out of the way." So it is also at the Front. A lost article is gone west as well as a dead comrade. "When I tould the Colonel," said an Irish orderly, "that the bottle of brandy was gone wesht, he was that mad that I thought he would ave me ate." As food and drink are sent west, perhaps the colonel had his suspicions.

The saying, "Put it wesht, Larry, an' come along on with you," may be heard in French *estaminets* as well as in Kerry public-houses.

At parade a subaltern noticed that one of his men had anything but a clean shave on the left side of his jaw. "'Twas too far wesht for me to get at, sir," was the excuse.

"Well," said the dentist to a Munster Fusilier, "where's this bad tooth that's troubling you?"

"'Tis here, sir," said the soldier, "in the wesht of me jaw."

Another Irish soldier told his quartermaster that he was in a very unpleasant predicament for want of a new pair of trousers. "The one I've on me is all broken wesht," said he. It is fairly obvious what part of the trousers the west of it was.

It would seem from the stories I have heard that odd escapes from death are an unfailing source of playfulness and laughter. A shell exploded in a trench held by an Irish battalion. One man was hurled quite twelve feet in the air, and, turning two somersaults in his descent, alighted on his back, and but little hurt, just outside the trench. He quickly picked himself up and rejoined his astonished comrades.

"He came down with that force," said an invalided Irish soldier who told me of the incident, "that it was the greatest wonder in the world he didn't knock a groan out of the ground."

No groan came from the man himself. "That was a toss and a half, and no mistake," he remarked cheerily when he got back to the trench; and in answer to an inquiry whether he was much hurt he said, "I only feel a bit moidhered in me head."

More comical still in its unexpectedness was the reply of another Irishman who met with a different misadventure from the same cause. A German 17-in. shell exploded on the parapet of a trench, and this Irishman was buried in the ruins. However, he was dug out alive, and his rescuers jokingly asked him what all the trouble was about. "Just those blessed snipers again," he spluttered through his mouth full of mud, "and may the divil fly away with the one that fired that bullet."

It is readily acknowledged at the Front that the Irish soldiers have a rich gift of natural humour. But, what is more—as some of my stories may show—they are never so exceedingly comic as when they do not intend to be comic at all. Is it not better to be funny without knowing it than to suffer the rather common lot of attempting to be funny and fail? It arises from an odd and unexpected way of putting things. How infinitely better it is than to be of so humdrum a quality as to be incapable of being comical even unconsciously in saying or in deed! Yet in this essentially Irish form of fun there is often a snare for the unwary. How can you tell that these laughable things are said and done by Irish soldiers without any perception of humour or absurdity? If you could look behind the face of that apparently simple-minded Irish soldier you might find that in reality he was "pulling your leg"—or "humbugging," as he would say himself—in a way that you would regard as most uncalled for and aggravating.

For instance, an Irish sentry in a camp in France was asked by a colonel of the Army Service Corps whether he had seen any of his officers about that morning. "Indeed, and I did, sir," was the reply. "'Twas only a while ago that two of the gintlemen came out of the office down there below, and passed by this way."

"And how did you know they were Army Service officers?"

"Aisy enough, sir. Didn't I see their swords stuck behind their ears?"

And in which category must be placed the equally amusing retort of another Irish sentry to his officer the naively simple, or the slyly jocular? The sentry looked so shy and inexperienced that the officer put to him the question, "What are you here for?" and got the stereotyped answer, "To look out for anything unusual."

"What would you call unusual?" asked the officer.

"I don't know exactly, sir, until I saw it," was the reply.

The officer became sarcastically facetious. "What would you do if you saw five battleships steaming across the field?" he said.

"Take the pledge, sir," was the sentry's answer.

These officers are, by all accounts, but two of many who have got unlooked-for but diverting answers from Irish soldiers. A sergeant who was sent out with a party to make observations fell into an ambuscade and returned with only a couple of men. "Tell me what happened," said the commanding officer, when the sergeant came to make his report; "were you surprised?"

"Surprised isn't the word for it, sir," exclaimed the sergeant. "It was flabbergasted entirely I was when, creeping round the end of a thick hedge, we came plump into the divil of a lot of Germans lying on their stomachs."

Then, seeing the officer smiling, as if in doubt, as he thought, he hastened thus to emphasise his wonder and astonishment at this sudden encounter. "I declare to you, sir, it nearly jumped the heart up out of me throat with the start it gave me."

Of a like kind for ingenuousness was the report made by another Irish non-com, who found himself all alone in a trench, with only a barrier of sandbags between him and the Germans. "I had nayther men, machine-gun or grenade," he wrote, expressing not only his temporal but his spiritual condition, for he added, "nothing, save the help of the Mother of God."

In Ireland domestic servants are noted for their forward manners and liberty of speech with the family, and the same trait is rather general in the relations between different social grades. An illustration of what it leads to in the Army was afforded at a camp concert attended by a large assembly of officers and men of a certain division, into which, at a solemn moment, an unsophisticated Irish soldier made a wild incursion. Lord Kitchener had been there that day and had inspected the division, and the general in command announced from the platform how greatly pleased the Secretary for War was with the soldierly fitness of the men. "I told Lord Kitchener," continued the general, speaking in grave and impressive tones, "that the division would see the thing through to the bitter end."

In the midst of a loud burst of cheering an Irish private rushed forward, and sweeping aside the attempt of a subaltern to stop him, jumped on to the platform, and seizing the aged general by the hand, exclaimed, "Glory to you, me vinerable friend! The ould division will stick to it to the last, and it's you that's the gran' man to lade us to victory and everlasting fame."

The general, greatly embarrassed, could only say, "Yes, yes, to be sure, my good fellow; yes, yes"; and the staff turned aside to hide their grins at this comic encounter between incongruities.

The colonel of an Irish battalion, after a harassing day in the trenches, got a pleasant surprise in the shape of a roast fowl served for dinner by his orderly. After he had eaten it and found it tender he recalled that complaints were rather rife among the inhabitants about the plundering of hen-roosts, and his conscience smote him. "I hope you got that fowl honestly," he said.

"Don't you be troubling your head about that, sir," replied the orderly, in a fine burst of evasion and equivocation. "Faith, 'twas quite ready for the killing, so it was, and that's the main thing." Then, as if to improve the occasion by a homily, he added, in a tone of religious fervour, "Ah, sure, if we wor all as ready to die as that hin, sir, we needn't mind a bit when the bullet came." The colonel was almost "fit to die" with quiet laughter.

It may well be that sometimes the English officers of Irish battalions are puzzled by the nature of their men—its impulsiveness, its glow, its wild imagery and over-brimming expression. It is easy to believe, too, that the changeful moods of the men, childlike and petulant, now jovial, now fierce, and occasionally unaccountable, may be a sore annoyance to officers who are very formal and precise in matters of discipline. I have heard from an Irish colonel of an Irish battalion that the English commander of the brigade of which the battalion was a unit came to him one day in a rage and asked him where his damned fools had been picked up. It appears the Brigadier-General, going the rounds alone, came suddenly upon one of the sentries of the battalion at a remote post. The sentry happened to be a wild slip of an Irish boy, not long joined and quite fresh from Mayo, and, taken by surprise, he challenged the Brigadier-General by calling out, "In the name of God, who the divil are you?"

The colonel told me his reply to the Brigadier-General was this: "Certainly, the challenge and the salute were not quite proper. But you can imagine what kind of a reception that simple but fearless lad would give to a German; and, after all, is not that the main thing just now?" Yes, the capacity of fighting well should, in war time, cover a multitude of imperfections in a soldier.

In order to get the best out of the Irish soldiers it is necessary to have a knowledge of their national habits and peculiarities, and a sympathetic understanding of their qualities and limitations. I am glad to be able to say that the most glowing tributes to the sterling character of the Irish soldiers that I have heard have come from their English or Scottish officers. These are true leaders, because they possess imagination and sympathy by which they can look into the hearts of men that are diverse from them in blood and temperament and nature.

I suppose there is nothing on earth, no matter how solemn or terrible, which may not be turned into a subject of irreverent humour in one or other of its aspects. English soldiers appear to have found that out even in regard to the war. An officer told me of a remarkable encounter on a Flanders high road between an Irish battalion coming back from the trenches and an English battalion going up for a turn at holding a section of the lines, which he thought presented a striking contrast in racial moods. The uniforms of the Irishmen were plastered with mud, and they had a week's grime on their unshaven faces. They had also suffered heavily in repelling a German attack. Yet they looked as proud as if they had saved Ireland by their exertions, and hoped to save the Empire by their example, and they sang from the bottom of their hearts, and at the top of their voices, the anthem of their national yearnings and aspirations, with its refrain—

Whether on the scaffold high, or the battlefield we die,
What matter when for Erin dear we fall.

The English battalion, spick and span, swung by to horrible discomforts, to wounds and death, as blithely as if they were on a route march at home. They also were singing, and if they were in the same mood as the Irishmen they would be rendering the chorus—

Land of Hope and Glory,
Mother of the Free,
How shall we extol thee
Who are born of thee?
Wider still and wider
Shall thy bounds be set;
God, who made thee mighty,
Make thee mightier yet.

But instead of that the chorus of their song, set to a hymn tune, was this—

Will you fight for England?
Will you face the foe?
And every gallant soldier
Boldly answered—NO!

It has been said, with general acceptance, that the spirit of a nation can best be studied in its songs. But can it really? How wrong would be the moral drawn from its application in this case! High patriotism is a solemn thing; but the average British soldier's attitude towards it is like that of Dr. Johnson when he took up philosophy—"somehow cheerfulness was always breaking in." The English soldier will not sing songs of a lofty type and deep purpose—songs which express either intimate personal feeling or deeply felt national convictions. These emotions he hides or suppresses, for he cannot give vent to them without feeling shamefaced or fearing that he may be regarded as insincere.

Yet he is by no means so inconsequential or cynical as he affects to be. He is animated—none more so—by the spirit of duty and sacrifice. When it comes to fighting he is in earnest, desperately and ferociously in earnest, as the Germans know to their cost. It seems to me that he has been misled by Kipling into supposing that the true pose of the British soldier is to be more concerned with the temporal than with the spiritual, to grumble about the petty inconveniences of his calling, to pretend to an indifference to its romantic side and its ideals, to die without thinking that the spirits of his national heroes are looking down upon him.

The Irish have the reputation of having a delight in fighting. It is supposed that "ructions" are the commonplace of their civic life.

Undoubtedly they have "a strong weakness"—as they would phrase it themselves—for distributing bloody noses and cracked crowns even among friends. It is true, also, that they find the grandest scope for their natural disposition in warfare. A war correspondent relates that he met a wounded Dublin Fusilier hobbling painfully back to the field dressing-station after a battle, and giving the man his arm to help him on, he was prompted to make the pitying remark: "It's a dreadful war."

"'Tis indeed, sir; a dreadful war enough," said the soldier; and then came the characteristic comment: "but, sure, 'tis far better than no war at all."

Still, individuals are to be found among the Irish soldiers who take quite a materialistic view of the Army, and fail to rise to the anticipation of glory in a pending action. An agricultural labourer who had become one of Kitchener's men was asked how he liked soldiering. "It's the finest life in the whole wide world," he exclaimed. "It's mate, drink, lodgin' and washin' all in one. Wasn't I working hard for ten long years for a farmer there beyant in Kerry, and never once in all that time did the ould boy say to me, 'Stand at aise.'"

It will be noticed that in this enthusiastic outburst there is nothing about the divarshion of fighting. Another story that I heard records the grim foreboding of an Irish soldier who was lagging behind on the march to the trenches for the first time. "Keep up, keep up," cried the officer; and, by way of encouragement, he added: "You know, we'll soon make a Field Marshal of you."

"You're welcome to your joke, sir," said the soldier; "but I know well what you'll make of me—a casualty, sure enough."

Another Irish soldier thought he saw a way of making money out of the fighting. The colonel of the battalion told his men, according to the story, that for every German they would kill he would give a sovereign. The next morning the men were told the Germans were coming.

"How many?"

"Thirty thousand at least."

"Wake up, Mike," said one to a sleeping comrade; "our fortune is made."

There is also a story told of a remark made by an Irish soldier regardless of the glory and romance of the highest distinction in the Army. The award of the Victoria Cross to Michael O'Leary was held up to a battalion for emulation. "Yerra," cried a voice, "I'd a great deal rather get the Victoria 'bus."

It may be that in this we have nothing more than an instance of the impish tendency in the Irish nature displaying itself at the spur of the moment, rather than the yearning for home, its ease, repose and comforts. It recalls an anecdote of the American Civil War. General Thomas Francis Meagher of the Irish Brigade was informed by an *aide-de-camp* in the course of a battle that the Federalists had carried an important strategic point and several colours belonging to Confederate battalions. "Here's good news for ye, boys," shouted Meagher. "Our troops have won the day and captured the enemy's colours."

"Yerra, Gineral," cried a private, looking up at Meagher, who was on horseback, "I'd rather have, this blessed minute, half a pint of Dinnis McGure's whisky than all the colours of the rainbow."

Then there is the story told by the colonel of an Irish regiment of an incident in the Battle of the Somme. He noticed that a private followed everywhere at his heels, and especially where the fighting was hottest. The colonel thought that perhaps the private was anxious to come to his aid should any harm befall him. At the end of the day, however, the private thus explained his conduct to the colonel: "My mother says to me, sir, 'Stick to the colonel, and you'll be all right. Them colonels never get hurt.'"

But, with all their playfulness and jocularity, there are no soldiers to whom the serious aspects of the war make a more direct appeal than to the Irish. This is seen in various ways. It is seen in their devotional exercises. The Irish Guards and other Irish regiments have been known frequently to recite the Rosary and sing hymns even in the trenches. It is seen also in their national fervour. They go into action singing their patriotic songs. From these qualities they derive support for their martial spirit, their endurance and their unconquerable courage. They never quail in the face of danger. No soldiers have risen to loftier heights of moral heroism, as the numerous records of their deeds on the roll of the Victoria Cross bear inspiring witness.

But their humour always remains. One of the injunctions to men at the Front is "Don't put your head above the parapet." The Irish soldiers are more apt than others to disregard it, however frequently its wisdom is brought home to them. I have heard only one that was convinced. "*Faix*," he remarked, as the bullets of the snipers soon stopped his survey of the prospect outside the trench, "it's aisy to understand that the more a man looks round in this war the less he's likely to see." They have a comforting philosophy that it takes many a ton of lead to kill a man.

An Irish soldier invalided home from France was asked what struck him most about the battles he took part in. "What struck me most?" said he. "Sure it was the crowd of bullets flying about that didn't hit me!"

CHAPTER 9

The Irish Brigade

Pride and sorrow struggle for mastery at the spectacle of troops returning to camp from the battle, their appearance telling of the intolerable strain which this war imposes, even in the case of victory, upon the human faculties. The thought of it alone is painful to the feelings of anyone who has the least imagination. They are all begrimed and careworn, and many have the distraught look of those who have seen and suffered terrible things. So the Irish Brigade came back from Guillamont and Guinchy, on the Somme, in the early days of September 1916, what time the Empire was resounding with the fame of their exploits. On a Sunday they carried Guillamont with a rush; on the following Saturday they literally pounced upon Guinchy, and in between they lay in open trenches under continuous shell fire.

I saw the Irish Brigade before they left for the Front, and noted in the ranks the many finely shaped heads and thoughtful faces of poets and leaders of men, interspersed with the lithe frames of athletes and the resolute, hard-bitten countenances of born fighters. At first I was moved to sorrow at the thought of the pass to which civilisation has come that the best use which could be made of all this superb youth and manhood in its valiancy was to send it forth into the devouring jaws of war.

Then I perceived that something like a radiance shimmered about the marching ranks. It came, I noticed, both from their muscular strength and their martial ardour, for the flush of battle already mantled their cheeks, and its light was in their dancing eyes; and at once I understood that if I saw but the mound surmounted by the little wooden cross in France, and in Ireland the desolate hearthstone, they, with the wider and more aspiring imagination of youth, rejoiced that they were going out to fight in liberty's defence, and saw only their bayonets triumphantly agleam in the fury of the engagement. Careless and gay, they captured the two villages on the Somme in a ding-dong, helter-skelter fashion. They maintained the reputation of the Irish infantry as "the finest missile troops in the British Army" (so they are described by Colonel Repington, the renowned military correspondent of *The Times*), by the spirit and dash of their charge, their eagerness to get quickly into touch with the foe, and the energy and dexterity with which they wield that weapon which finally decides the issue of battles—the bayonet.

As they emerged out of the cloud of smoke on the Somme, and marched back to camp in much diminished numbers—caked with mud, powdered with grey dust, very tired—across the ground their valour had won and their grit maintained against fierce counter attacks, they displayed quite another phase of the Irish nature—its melancholy and its mysticism. The piper that led them back began to play some old Irish rhapsodies having that wonderful blending of joy and grief which makes these airs so haunting. That was well. For the men were in so extreme a stage of exhaustion, physical and mental, that they lurched and reeled, and were overwhelmed with distress at missing many beloved comrades that fought with them, and officers that led them only a few days before. Then they heard the pipes, and their hearts were uplifted by the strains, plaintive and yearning, defiant and challenging, which expresses in music the history of their race. They seemed, indeed, to have caught even some of the jaunty, boastful swagger of the piper, as he strode before them, blowing into his reeds and working the bag with his left elbow.

The general of the brigade watched his troops go by, and in his eyes they were all the grander for the horrid disarray of their torn, muddy and bloody uniforms, and their haggard faces blackened with sweat and smoke and soil. "I am proud of you," he called out in a voice surging with emotion. "Ye did damned well, boys." A handful of men, once a company, was led by a sergeant. Every officer was gone.

"Bravo, Dublins!" exclaimed the general; but 'for the moment his heart was heavy within him as he recalled to mind the dashing, gallant young lads, so hearty and joyous, buried now round about the ruins of the villages from which the Germans had been driven at the bayonet-point by the splendid rank and file at whose head they fell. Quickly the thoughts of the general came back to the survivors. "Ireland is proud of you, boys," he cried in exultant tones. He knew that would stir them. Ireland is their glory; and they lifted up their heads a little more as they caught the import of their commander's words.

This Irish Brigade, officially known as the Irish Division, was the outcome of the meeting in Dublin addressed by Mr. Asquith, shortly after the outbreak of the war, in the course of his tour of the country as Prime Minister to explain the origins and aims of the conflict. Lord Wimborne, the Viceroy, presided. The Lord Mayor of Dublin and mayors of most of the chief towns of Ireland, the chairmen of county councils and representatives of all shades of political and religious opinions were present. Mr. John Redmond proposed, at the meeting, the formation of an Irish Brigade.

While "Irish Division" sounds meaningless to young Irishmen, "'Irish Brigade" at once arouses thrilling memories of the battlefields of Europe during the eighteenth century. For a hundred years, from the fall of the Stuarts to the French Revolution, there was an Irish Brigade in the service of France. It was regularly recruited from Ireland through that long span of time, though to join it was a penal offence. As the young men stole secretly away to France in smuggling crafts from the west of Ireland, they were popularly known as "the wild geese." *Everywhere and always Faithful* was the motto bestowed on the brigade by the King of France. That being so, there was a hearty response to the call for a new Irish Brigade to serve again in France, and for causes more worthy than the old.

Just as the Ulster Division was composed of Unionists and Protestants, the Irish Division was recruited mainly from the Nationalist and Catholic sections of the population. The Nationalist Volunteers, supporters of the policy and aims of the Irish Parliamentary Party, provided most of the rank and file. Like another Irish Division, the first of Ireland's distinctive contributions to the New Armies, which perished in the ill-starred expedition to Gallipoli, the Irish Division was composed of the youth of Ireland at its highest and best—clean of soul and strong of body, possessing in the fullest measure all the brightest qualities of the race, the intellectual and spiritual, not less than the political and humorous.

One of the first to join was Mr. William Redmond, M.P. for East Clare, younger brother of the Irish Leader, though he was well over the military age. He was appointed Captain in the Royal Irish Regiment—the premier Irish regiment—in which he had served thirty-three years previously, before his election to the House of Commons. Speaking at an early recruiting meeting, he said that, should circumstances so demand, he would say to his countrymen "Come" instead of "Go." He was as good as his word. For his services at the Front he was promoted to the rank of Major, and has been mentioned by Field-Marshal Haig in despatches.

Other nationalist Members of Parliament who were officers of the Brigade were Captain W. Archer Redmond, Dublin Fusiliers, son of Mr. John Redmond, Captain Stephen Gwynn, well known as a man of letters, who joined the Connaught Rangers as a private and was promoted to the rank of Captain in the battalion; Captain J. L. Esmonde, Dublin Fusiliers, and Captain D. D. Sheehan, Munster Fusiliers, who also gave his two boys to the Brigade. General Sir Lawrence Parsons, son of the Earl of Rosse—scion of a distinguished Irish family resident for centuries at Birr, King's Co.—was appointed to the command of the division.

Sir Francis Vane, an eminent Irish soldier of Nationalist sympathies, who was appointed by the War Office to supervise the recruiting for the Division, says that never in his life did he witness so extraordinary a scene as that presented at Buttevant and Fermoy, Co. Cork, where the men first assembled in September and October 1914. "It reminded me," he says, "of the pages of Charles Lever in the variety of Irish types answering to the call. There were old men and young sportsmen, students, car drivers, farm labourers, Members of Parliament, poets, *litterateurs*, all crowding into barracks which were totally incapable of housing decently the half of them." They were dressed in all sorts of clothes, from the khaki, red and blue of the Services, to "the latest emanation of the old clo' merchants."

That curious assortment of all types and classes was the rough material out of which was fashioned, by training and discipline, a superb military instrument. The soldierly essentials were there in abundance. Within two years they came successfully through ordeals that would have tried the nerves of the toughest veterans of the Old Guard of Napoleon.

In the course of 1915 the division was removed to camps at Aldershot to complete their training. The men were visited there, in November, by Cardinal Bourne, Archbishop of Westminster, who gave them his benediction, and said he was sure they would do their duty at the Front "as good children of Ireland and good sons of the Catholic Church." Early in December they were reviewed by the Queen. It was originally arranged that the review should be held by the King, but his Majesty, on a visit to the Front, had been flung from his horse, and was not sufficiently recovered from the accident to be able to be present.

Among those in the reserved enclosure surrounding the saluting-base that day were Mr. John Dillon, M.P., and Mr. T. P. O'Connor, M.P. In the march past the Queen they were led off by the South Irish Horse, a body of Yeomanry. Each of the three infantry brigades was headed by one of the Irish wolfhounds which Mr. John Redmond presented to the division as mascots. At the conclusion of the review her Majesty sent for General Parsons and the three Brigadier-Generals, and congratulated them upon the appearance and efficiency of the troops.

Shortly afterwards the division left for the Front, under the command of Major-General William Bernard Hickie, C.B., an Irishman and a Catholic, who has had a very brilliant military career. Born on May 21, 1865, the eldest son of the late Colonel J. F. Hickie of Slevoyre, Borrisokane, Co. Tipperary, he was educated at Oscott and Sandhurst. At the age of nineteen he joined his father's old regiment, the 1st battalion of the Royal Fusiliers, of which in due course he became Colonel. In the South African War he served on the Staff, in command of a mounted infantry corps and of a mobile column.

On his return home he became Deputy Assistant Quartermaster-General to the 8th Division. In 1912 he was appointed Assistant Quartermaster-General of the Irish Command. On the outbreak of the war General Hickie became Deputy Assistant Quartermaster-General of the Second Army, and is stated to have particularly distinguished himself maintaining good order during the retreat from Mons. The Irish Brigade was most fortunate in having such a man as commander. Thoroughly understanding the Irish character, its weak points as well as its strong ones its good-humoured and careless disposition; its impatience often of the restraints and servitude of military life; its eagerness always for a fight or any sort of enterprise with a spice of danger in it—he was able to get the most out of his men.

One of his happy thoughts was the institution of a system of rewards in the division apart from but supplementary to the usual military honours. Any company officer or man who, in the opinion of the commander of his regiment, has given proof of exceptional good conduct and devotion to duty in the field, is presented by General Hickie with a Parchment Certificate at a parade. The certificate has been specially prepared in Ireland, having the words "The Irish Brigade" in Gaelic letters enwreathed with shamrocks at the top, setting out the name of the recipient, the nature and date of his achievement, and the signature of the general. The men send these certificates home, where they are preserved as precious mementoes. An Honours Book of the Irish Brigade is also kept in which these presentations and the military honours won are recorded.

The first experience which the Irish Brigade had of the trenches was in the Loos-Hullock line. It is the most desolate of the war-stricken regions, one bare, black, open plain, where everything has been blown to pieces and levelled to the ground, save here and there some wire entanglements; where there is no sign of human life, except when parties of the thousands upon thousands of combatants who burrow beneath its surface, emerge in the darkness of the night for stealthy raids on each other's positions. The front line trenches of both sides run close together. At one point they are no more than sixteen yards apart. They are notoriously of the worst type, nothing more, indeed, than shallow and slimy drains, badly provided with dugouts, and much exposed to fire. Under such conditions the craving of the body for food and rest could be satisfied only at the bare point of existence.

Major William Redmond, in a letter to Dr. Fogarty, Bishop of Killaloe, dated February 3, 1916, says: "Our first spell in the trenches was for twelve days, and in that time we had no change of clothing, just stayed as we were all the time. The shelling was terrific, and the division suffered some losses. The day before we came out the enemy began to celebrate the *Kaiser's* birthday, January 27, and we were shelled without ceasing for twenty-four hours. The men of our division behaved very well, and received good reports; so the general said." Testimony to the excellent way in which the Irishmen passed through the ordeal comes from quite independent and impartial sources. Here, for example, is an extract from a letter written by the Rev. H. J. Collins, chaplain to a battalion of the Black Watch—

> Our Division had the privilege of introducing the Irish battalions to the trenches, when they arrived out here; and they were our guests for a week or so before taking over on their own account. They made a great impression on our lads by their cheerfulness and their eagerness to be 'up and at' the Hun. The Connaughts arrived one evening just as our line was being heavily shelled, and although they were our visitors they at once took charge of the situation. They had never been in the trenches in their lives before; they were experiencing shell fire for the first time; and before they had had time to get their packs off and settle down, one impatient sergeant was over the

parapet, crying out in a rich and musical brogue: 'Come on, the Connaughts!'

As is well known, the men of one regiment are not greatly disposed to praise those of another. In fact, some bitter regimental feuds exist in the British Army, or used to among the old Regulars. It is, therefore, all the more remarkable to find in the *Glasgow Herald* of February 24, 1916, a letter signed "Jock," proclaiming in the warmest terms the fine qualities of the new Irish soldiers.

"Your readers may like to hear that we Scotsmen, who have been tried and not found wanting, have a great admiration for the new Irish Division that came out some time ago," says "Jock." "We have lived in the trenches side by side with them, and find them as keen as a hollow-ground and as ardent as a young lover. At a recent attack when the Germans were advancing the excitement became unbearable, and one sergeant got up on the parapet with the shout of: 'Come on, bhoys, get at them.' One of them, too, was heard to grumble, 'Here we've been in th' trenches fur two weeks an' niver wance over th' paradise.' It is to be feared they will outvie even the kilts."

Yet during this instructional period, when the various battalions of the brigade were attached to other regiments for preliminary practice in the trenches, some high military honours were won. Sergeant J. Tierney, of the Leinster Regiment; Lance-Corporal A. Donagh, and Private P. F. Duffy, of the Connaught Rangers, gained the Distinguished Conduct Medal. Donagh and Duffy, in response to a call for volunteers, undertook to carry messages forward under heavy fire, as all telephone communication had been cut.

The task was one of extreme danger, but the men succeeded in accomplishing it unhurt, and were awarded the D.C.M. for their coolness and bravery. Corporal Timoney, of the Munster Fusiliers, was especially mentioned in Army Orders for an act of courage in picking up and throwing away a live Mills-grenade which had fallen among some men under instruction. By this act he undoubtedly saved the lives of several men, and if it had happened in the field instead of at practice he would have been eligible for recommendation for a higher honour.

CHAPTER 10

Irish Replies to German Wiles and Poison Gas

It was from the Germans that the Irish Brigade got the first intimation of the troubles in Dublin at Easter, 1916. The Germans, heedless of their failure to induce the Irish soldiers in their captivity to forswear allegiance and honour, availed themselves of the Rebellion to try their wiles on the Irish soldiers in the field. Both sides in the trenches often become acquainted, in curious ways, with the names and nationality of the regiments opposed to them. But in regard to a particular section of the British line, between Hulluch and Loos, in April 1916, the Germans might easily know it was held by Irish troops. The fact was proclaimed by the green banner with the golden harp which the boys of the brigade hoisted over the breastworks-the flag which, in their eyes, has been consecrated in the great cause of liberty by the deeds and sacrifices of their forefathers, the flag for whose glorified legend they were proud to die.

So it happened that one morning these Irish troops were surprised to see two placards nailed to boards on the top of poles, displayed by the Germans, on which the following was written in English—

Irishmen! In Ireland's revolution English guns are firing on your wives and children. The English Military Bill has been refused. Sir Roger Casement is being persecuted. Throw away your arms; we give you a hearty welcome.
We are Saxons. If you don't fire, we won't.

The Irish Brigade and the Irish Volunteers who rose in rebellion in Dublin were alike recruited from the same class. Such are the unhappily wayward circumstances of Irish life that the tremendous fact whether this lad or that was to fight for England in Flanders or against her in Dublin was in many cases decided by mere chance or accident. At any rate, the kith and kin of numbers of men of the Irish Brigade were among the Sinn Feiners.

A widowed mother in Dublin had, in consequence, a most tragic experience. The post on Easter Monday morning brought her a letter from a company officer of a battalion in the Irish Brigade announcing that her son had been killed in action. "He died for Ireland," said the officer, knowing that it was true and that it would help to soften her maternal grief. Before the day was out her other son, wearing the green uniform of the Irish Volunteers, staggered home mortally wounded, and as he lay gasping out his life on the floor he, too, used the same phrase of uplifting memories: "Mother, don't fret. Sure, I'm dying for Ireland."

The effect of the German placards on the battalion of Munster Fusiliers, then holding the British line, was very far astray from that which their authors hoped for and intended. A fusillade of bullets at once bespattered the wheedling phrases. What fun to make a midnight foray on the German trenches and carry off the placards as trophies! No sooner was the adventure suggested than it was agreed to. In the darkness of night a body of twenty-five men and two officers of the Munsters crawled out into No Man's Land. They were discovered when about half-way across by a German searchlight, and then the flying-bullets of two machine-guns commenced to splutter about them.

Some of the men were killed; some were wounded. The others lay still for hours in the rank grass before they resumed their stealthy crawl, like the Indians they used to read of in boyhood stories, and, having noiselessly cut their way under the enemy entanglements, they sprang, with fixed bayonets and terrifying yells, into the trench. The Germans, startled out of their senses by this most unexpected visit, scurried like rabbits into the nearest dugouts. The notice-boards were then seized and borne in triumph to the Irish trenches, to the unbounded delight and pride of the battalion; and they are now treasured among the regiment's most precious spoils of vanquished enemies.

A few days later, on the morning of April 27, the Germans tried what blows could do where lying blandishments had failed; and the Irish Brigade had to face, for the first time, an infantry attack in force. The enemy began their operations by concentrating a bombardment of great intensity upon trenches held by Dublin Fusiliers. Then, shortly after five o'clock, there came on the light breeze that blew from the German lines a thick and sluggish volume of greenish smoke. "Poison gas! On with your helmets!" Surely, the hearts of the most indomitable might well have quailed at the thought of the writhing agony endured by those who fall victims to this new and most terrible agency of war.

Instead of that, the flurry and excitement of putting on the masks was followed by roars of laughter as the men looked at one another and saw the fantastic and absurd beings, with grotesque goggle-eyes, into which they had transformed themselves. But they were not the only monsters in the uncanny scene. Like grey spectres, sinister and venomous, the Germans appeared as they came on, partly screened by the foul vapour which rolled before them. Not one of them reached the Irish trenches. The Dublins, standing scathless in the poison clouds which enveloped them, poured out round after round of rifle fire, until the Germans broke and fled, leaving piles of their dead and wounded at the wire entanglements, and the body of the officer who had led them caught in the broken strands.

Two hours later, that same morning, there was another sally from the German trenches, under cover of gas, against a different section of the Irish. The parapets here had been so demolished by shell fire that the Germans gained a footing in the trenches. But they were hardly in before they were out again. "The time during which the Germans were in occupation of our trenches was a matter of minutes only," says the war correspondent of *The Times*. They were put to rout by the Inniskillings, who came up from the reserve trenches at the double.

"Never was a job more cleanly and quickly done," adds *The Times* correspondent. On the next occasion that the Germans launched an attack with gas, they had themselves to drink, so to speak, the poison cup they had prepared for the Irish. That was two days subsequently, on April 29. "Providence was on our side," writes Major William Redmond, "for the wind suddenly changing, the gas blew back over the German trenches where the Bavarians had already massed for attack. Taken by surprise, they left their front line and ran back across the open under the heavy and well-directed fire of our artillery. In one battalion of that Bavarian Infantry Regiment the losses from their own gas and from our fire on that day were stated to be, by a deserter, over eight hundred; and the diary of a prisoner of another battalion captured on the Somme in September states that his regiment also had about five hundred gassed cases, a large number of whom died."

The Irish Division continued to hold the Hulluch-Loos sector of the line until the end of August 1916. They were subjected to severe bombardments. It was a common occurrence for the enemy to send from two to five thousand 5.9 shells a day into their trenches. What fortitude and grim determination must they not have had at their command to enable them to pass unshaken through these terrible ordeals. They retaliated in the way they love best, with many a dashing raid on the German positions.

For conspicuous gallantry in these operations the Military Cross was awarded to several of the officers. In the cases of Captain Victor Louis Manning and Lieutenant Nicholas Joseph Egan of the Dublin Fusiliers, the official record says that "by skilful and determined handling of their bombing parties they drove off three determined bomb attacks by the enemy in greatly superior numbers," and that "they continued to command their parties after they had both been wounded," gives but a faint idea of the daring nature of their deed. A small counter-mine was exploded under a German mine at a point between the opposing lines, but nearer to those of the Germans. The Germans were able to occupy the mound first and establish a machine-gun on it, with which they dominated the Dublin trenches.

Volunteers being called for to clear them out, Lieutenant Egan and a small party of privates, armed with bombs, rushed out and carried the position. Then they had to hold it against German counter-attacks which were launched during the next three days. Lieutenant Egan was wounded in the wrist early in the fight, but he and six men, being plentifully supplied with bombs, held their ground doggedly. Instead of waiting for the Germans to reach the mound, in what threatened to be the worst of the counter-attacks, the party of Dublins advanced to meet them and drove them back, thus conveying the impression that they were in greater strength than was really the case.

On the night of the third day another party, under Captain Manning, came to their support. After a further series of encounters had ended in favour of the Dublins, the Germans abandoned the hope of recapturing the post, which was subsequently strongly consolidated by the victors. On the fourth day, when the struggle had definitely ended in favour of the Dublins, and Lieutenant Egan was about to return to the lines, a bomb fell at his feet. He was blown a distance of fifteen yards, and was picked up seriously wounded in the thigh. Lieutenant Egan is a grandson of Mr. Patrick Egan of New York, well known in the stormy agrarian agitation in Ireland under Parnell and Davitt as the treasurer of the Land League. Previous to the war Lieutenant Egan was in business in Canada.

Another fine exploit standing to the credit of the Irish Brigade was that of Lieutenant Patrick Stephen Lynch of the Leinsters, who got the Military Cross "for conspicuous gallantry when successfully laying and firing a torpedo under the enemy's wire." It was an uncommon deed, and just as uncommon is the very remarkable tribute with which the official record ends: "His cool bravery is very marked and his influence over his men very great."

The Brigadier-General, George Pereira, D.S.O., in a letter of congratulation to Lieutenant Lynch, dated July 1, 1916, says: "Your leading the attack along the parapet was splendid, but you must be more careful another time." Before the month was out Lieutenant Lynch got a bar to his Military Cross—in other words, he had won the distinction twice over—an honour which, as General Hickie wrote to him, was well deserved, and likely to be very rare. This young Waterford man—a fine type of the fearless and dashing Irish officer, made out of a civilian in two years—was promoted captain in the Leinsters, and was killed on his birthday and the completion of his twenty-fifth year, December 27, 1916. The battalion was plunged into grief by the loss of Captain Lynch.

"'Paddy'—the name we all knew him by from the C.O. down to the youngest sub.—was considered the most efficient officer in this battalion, and he was certainly the most popular," writes Lieutenant H. W. Norman, an officer of the Captain's company. "Everybody mourns his death, and when the news got to his men they could not believe that such a brave and daring officer could be killed, but the news was only too true; and when it was confirmed I saw many the officer and man crying like children. He lost his life to save his men, who were in a trench that was being heavily shelled. He went up with a sergeant, in spite of danger and certain death, to get them out, and on the way up a shell landed in the trench where they were, killing both instantaneously."

Another noble deed was that for which Lieutenant John Francis Gleeson, Munster Fusiliers, won the Military Cross. "Under heavy rifle fire and machine-gun fire, he left his trench to bring in a wounded man lying within ten yards of the enemy entanglements."

It was also in connection with these raids on the German trenches that the Irish Division gained the first of its Victoria Crosses. The hero is Captain Arthur Hugh Batten-Pooll of the Munster Fusiliers—a

Somerset man, and he got the V.C. "for most conspicuous bravery whilst in command of a raiding party." At the moment of entry into the enemy's lines," the official record continues, "he was severely wounded by a bomb, which broke and mutilated all the fingers of his right hand. In spite of this he continued to direct operations with unflinching courage, his voice being clearly heard cheering on and directing his men. He was urged, but refused, to retire. Half an hour later, during the withdrawal, whilst personally assisting in the rescue of other wounded men, he received two further wounds. Still refusing assistance, he walked unaided to within a hundred yards of our lines, when he fainted, and was carried in by the covering party." Captain D. D. Sheehan of the Munster Fusiliers supplies the following spirited account of the raid—

> Our men got into the enemy's trenches with irresistible dash. They met with a stout resistance. There was no stopping or stemming the sweep of the men of Munster. They rushed the Germans off their feet. They bombed and they bludgeoned them. Indeed, the most deadly instrument of destruction in this encounter was the short heavy stick, in the shape of a shillelagh, the use of which, we are led to believe, is the prescriptive and hereditary right of all Irishmen. The Munster Fusiliers gave the Huns such a dressing and drubbing on that night as they are not likely to have since forgotten. Half an hour in the trenches and all was over. Dugouts and all were done for. Of the eight officers, four were casualties, two, unhappily, killed, and two severely wounded, of whom one was Batten-Pooll.

For months the Irish Brigade had on their right the renowned Ulster Division. Thus the descendants of the two races in Ireland who for more than two centuries were opposed politically and religiously, and often came to blows under their rival colours of "Orange" and "Green," were now happily fighting side by side in France for the common rights of man. Though born and bred in the same tight little island, the men themselves had been severed by antagonisms arising out of those hereditary feuds, and thus but imperfectly understood each other.

"When they met from time to time," says Major William Redmond, M.P., "the best of good feeling and comradeship was shown as between brother Irishmen."

Evidence of these amicable relations is afforded by a letter written by Private J. Cooney of the Royal Irish Regiment.

"The Ulster Division are supporting us on our right," he says. "The other morning I was out by myself and met one of them. He asked me what part of Ireland I belonged to. I said a place called Athlone, in the county Westmeath. He said he was a Belfast man and a member of the Ulster Volunteers. I said I was a National Volunteer, and that the National Volunteers were started in my native town. 'Well,' said he, 'that is all over now. We are Irishmen fighting together, and we will forget all these things.' 'I don't mind if we do,' said I; 'but I'm not particularly interested. We must all do our bit out here, no matter where we come from, north or south, and that is enough for the time.'"

Private Cooney adds:

> This young Belfast man was very anxious to impress me with the fact that we Irish were all one; that there should be no bad blood between us, and we became quite friendly in the course of a few minutes.

Meeting thus in the valley of darkness, blood and tears, the fraternity born of the dangers they were incurring for the same great ends, united them far more closely than years of ordinary friendship could have done. To many on both sides the cause of their traditional hostility appeared very trivial; and there were revealed to them reasons, hitherto obscured by prejudice and convention, for mutual loving-kindness and even for national unification.

But it was not the first time that north and south fought together in the Empire's battle. There is an eloquent passage on the subject in Conan Doyle's *Great Boer War*. It refers to the advance of Hart's "Irish Brigade"—consisting of the 1st Inniskillings, 1st Connaughts and 1st Dublins—over an open plain to the Tugela River, at the Battle of Colenso, under heavy fire from front and flank, and even from the rear, for a regiment in support fired at them, not knowing that any of the line was so far advanced—

> Rolling on in a broad wave of shouting, angry men, they never winced from the fire until they swept up to the bank of the river. Northern Inniskillings and Southern men of Connaught, orange and green, Protestant and Catholic, Celt and Saxon, their only rivalry now was who could shed his blood most freely for the common cause. How hateful those provincial politics and narrow sectarian creeds which can hold such men apart!

On July 1 the Ulster Division won immortal renown on the Somme. It was now the turn of the Irish Brigade to uphold the martial fame of the race on the same stricken field. They were done with trench raids for a while, and in for very big fighting.

CHAPTER 11

Storming of Guillamont by the Irish Brigade

At the end of August the Irish Brigade was ordered to the Somme. The civil authorities of the district, headed by the mayor and cure, called upon General Hickie to express their appreciation of the good conduct and religious devotion of his troops. The general was a proud man that day. Nothing pleased him more than praise of his soldiers. In return, they gloried in him. As an example of his fatherly solicitude for them, he had established a divisional laundry under the care of the nuns, in which 25,000 shirts a week and 5000 pairs of socks per day are washed for them, and every day's rations sent to the men in the trenches was accompanied by a dry pair of socks. The result was that "trench feet"—feet benumbed with the cold and the wet—were almost unknown in the division. He also provided for a thousand baths a day being given to his men in a specially constructed bath-house.

The marches of the brigade to their new station was done to the accompaniment of patter, drip, trickle, ripple, splash—all the creepy sounds of continuous rain, and across the sodden and foul desolation that was once the fair fields of France. Up to the firing line swung a battalion of the Munster Fusiliers, gaily whistling and singing in the rain. They carried a beautiful banner of the Sacred Heart, the gift of the people of the city of Limerick, from which many of the men came.

Miss Lily Doyle of Limerick, who made the presentation to Major Lawrence Roche of the battalion, tells me that the idea of the banner originated with the Reverend Mother of the Good Shepherd's Convent, Limerick, who had read, in what are termed the *Extended Revelations*, that a promise was given by Jesus to Blessed Margaret Mary that, inasmuch as soldiers derided His Sacred Heart when He hung upon the Cross, any soldiers who made reparation by carrying His standard would have victory with them. The cost of the banner (£10) was mainly raised by penny subscriptions. It was worked by the Good Shepherd nuns on crimson poplin. On one side is a beautiful piece of embroidery representing Our Lord with His Heart exposed on His breast to Blessed Margaret Mary, with the inscriptions, "*Tu Rex Gloria Christi*" and "*Parce Domine, parce populo tuo.*" On the other side are the words of the Archangel Michael: "*Quis ut Deus*," surrounded with monograms of "Royal Munster Fusiliers" and "God save Ireland."

"You could not have sent us a more suitable gift," the Rev. J. Wrafter, S. J., chaplain of the battalion, wrote to Miss Doyle, "or one which would give more pleasure to the men. I believe they prefer it to any material comforts that are sent to them." This is the third religious banner borne by soldiers since the Crusades. The first was the standard of Joan of Arc, and the second that of the Pontifical *Zouaves*, when Rome was an independent state.

As the Munsters thus marched to battle a cry of "Look!" was suddenly raised in the ranks, and as all eyes turned in the direction indicated a wonderful sight was seen. The great tower of Albert Cathedral appeared through the mist of rain, and the sun shone on the great copper statue of the Blessed Virgin and the Child, which dominated the countryside for miles around, and, laid prostrate by German gunners, was now lying out level with the top of the tower. Thus that symbol of faith, though fallen, was not overthrown. Its roots in the pedestal were firm and strong. The Virgin Mother, facing downwards, still held the Infant Jesus scathless in her outstretched hands, as if showing Him the devastation below, ready to be uplifted again on the day of Christianity's victory.

The piety of the battalion was kindled by that strange and moving spectacle. Quickly responsive always to things that appeal to the imagination, the men felt as if they were witnesses of a miracle, and with one accord they took off their helmets and cheered and cheered again.

Though it is an unusual thing for the commander-in-chief to give in his dispatches the names of the troops who took part in a particular engagement, Sir Douglas Haig makes special mention of the Irish Brigade in his message announcing that Guillamont had fallen. "The Irish regiments which took part in the capture of Guillamont on September 3 behaved," he says, "with the greatest dash and gallantry, and took no small share in the success gained that day."

September 3 was a Sunday. On the night before the battle the Irish troops selected for the attack on Guillamont bivouacked on the bare side of a hill. They were the Connaughts, the Royal Irish, the Munsters and the Leinsters. The rain had ceased, but the ground was everywhere deep in mud, the trenches were generally flooded and the shell holes full of water. It was a bleak and desolate scene, relieved only here and there by the sparkle of the little fires around which the platoons clustered. Just as the men of one of the battalions were preparing to wrap themselves in their greatcoats and lie down for the rest which they might be able to snatch in such a situation, the Catholic chaplain came over the side of the hill and right to the centre of the camp.

"In a moment he was surrounded by the men," writes Major Redmond. "They came to him without orders—they came gladly and willingly, and they hailed his visit with plain delight. He spoke to them in the simple, homely language which they liked. He spoke of the sacrifice which they had made in freely and promptly leaving their homes to fight for a cause which was the cause of religion, freedom and civilisation. He reminded them that in this struggle they were most certainly defending the homes and the relations and friends they had left behind them in Ireland. It was a simple, yet most moving address, and deeply affected the soldiers."

Major Redmond goes on to say:

When the chaplain had finished his address he signed to the men to kneel, and administered to them the General Absolution given in times of emergency. The vast majority of the men present knelt, and those of other faith stood by in attitudes of reverent respect. The chaplain then asked the men to recite with him the Rosary. It was most wonderful the effect produced as hundreds and hundreds of voices repeated the prayers and recited the words, 'Pray for us now and at the hour of our death. Amen.' At the dawn Masses were said by the chaplains of all the battalions in the open, and most of the officers and men received Holy Communion.

The attack was timed to begin at noon. All the morning the warpipes of these Leinsters, Munsters and Connaughts gave out inspiring Irish tunes "Brian Boru's March," that was played at the Battle of Clontarf in the eleventh century when the Danish invaders were driven from Ireland; "The White Cockade," the Jacobite marching tune of the first Irish Brigade in the service of France; "The Wearin' o' the Green," one of the finest expressions of a country's devotion to an ideal; and "A Nation Once Again," thrilling with the hopes of the future. The pipers strode up and down, green ribbons streaming from their pipes, sending forth these piercing invocations to ancient Irish heroes, to venerable saints of the land, to the glories and sorrows of Ireland, to the love of home, to the faith and aspirations of the race, to come to the support of the men in the fight. And what of the men as they waited in the assembly trenches for the word? The passage from Shakespeare's *Henry V* best conveys their mood: "*I see ye stand like greyhounds in the leash straining upon the start.*"

At twelve o'clock the battalions emerged from the trenches. Numbers of the men had tied to their rifles little green flags with the yellow harp. Like the English infantry associated with them, the Irish advanced in the open snaky lines in which such attacks are always delivered. But there was a striking difference—noted by the war correspondents—in the pace and impetus of the Irish and the English. Mr. Beach Thomas of the *Daily Mail* says:

> It gives, I think, a satisfying sense of the variety and association of talent in the new Army to picture these dashing Irish troops careering across the open while the ground was being methodically cleared and settled behind them by English riflemen.

"The English riflemen who fought on their right had more solidity in their way of going about the business," says Mr. Philip Gibbs of the *Daily Chronicle*, "but they were so inspired by the sight of the Irish dash and by the sound of the Irish pipes that those who were in support, under orders to stand and hold the first German line, could hardly be restrained from following on." The English advance was calm, restrained, deliberate, infused by a spirit of determination that glowed rather than flamed. A breath of fire seemed to sweep through the Irish. From first to last they kept up a boisterous jog-trot charge. "It was like a human avalanche," was the description given by the English troops who fought with them.

The country across which this dash was made was pitted with innumerable shell holes, most of them of great width and depth and all full of water and mud. A Munster Fusilier graphically likened the place to a net, in his Irish way—"all holes tied together." So the men, as they advanced, stumbled over the inequalities of the ground, or slipped and tripped in the soft, sticky earth. It was a scene, too, of the most clamorous and frightful violence. The shells were like fiends of the air, flying with horrid shrieks or moans on the wings of the wind, ignoring one another and intent only on dropping down to earth and striking the life out of their human prey. Blasts of fire and flying bits of metal also swept the plain.

There is a loud detonation, and when the smoke clears away not a trace is seen of the ten or dozen comrades that a moment before were rushing forward like a Rugby pack after the ball. They have all been blown to the four winds of heaven. "Jim, I'm hit," cries a lad, as if boastingly, on feeling a blow on his chest. He twirls round about like a spinning top and then topples face downward. His body has been perforated by a rifle bullet. A shell explodes and a man falls. He laughs, thinking he has been tripped up by a tree root or piece of wire. Both his legs are broken. Another shell bursts.

A Leinsterman sees a companion lifted violently off his feet, stripped of his clothes, and swept several yards before he is dashed violently to the ground. He goes over to his friend and can see no sign of a wound on the quite naked body. But his friend will never lift up his head again. The blasting force of the high explosive, the tremendous concussion of the air, has knocked the life out of him. "Goodbye, Joe, and may God have mercy on your soul," the Leinsterman says to himself, and, as he dashes on again he thinks, "Sure, it may be my own turn next." It is that which assuages the grief of a soldier for a dead comrade, or soon ousts it altogether from his mind.

Khaki and grey-clad forms were lying everywhere in the frightfully distorted postures assumed by the killed in action arms—twisted, legs doubled together, heads askew. Some had their lips turned outward, showing their teeth in a horrible sneer. Their mouths had been distended in agony. Others had a fixed expression of infinite sadness, as if in a lucid moment before death there came a thought of home. More horrifying still was the foul human wreckage of former battles—heads and trunks and limbs trodden under foot in the mud, and emitting a fearful stench.

The priests followed in the wake of the troops to give the consolations of religion to the dying. They saw heartrending sights. One of them, describing his experiences, says:

> I was standing about a hundred yards away, watching a party of my men crossing the valley, when I saw the earth under their feet open, and twenty men disappear in a cloud of smoke, while a column of stones and clay was shot a couple of hundred feet

into the air. A big German shell, by the merest chance, had landed in the middle of the party. I rushed down the slope, getting a most unmerciful whack between the shoulders. I gave them all a General Absolution, scraped the clay from the faces of a couple of buried men who were not wounded, and then anointed as many of the poor lads as I could reach. Two of them had no faces to anoint, and others were ten feet under the clay, but a few were living still. By this time half a dozen volunteers had run up, and were digging the buried men out. We dug like demons for our lads' lives, and our own, to tell the truth, for every few minutes another 'iron pill' from a Krupp gun would come tearing down the valley.

Another priest says:

Many of the wounded were just boys, and it was extraordinary how they bore pain, which must have been intense. Very few murmurings were heard. One young man said to me, 'Oh, father, it is hard to die so far from home in the wilds of France.' Certainly the fair land of France just here did seem wild, with the trees all torn and riven with shot, and the earth on every side ploughed with huge shell holes.

But the Irish troops swept on. Nothing could stop them—neither their fallen comrades, nor the groans of the wounded, nor the abominably mangled dead; and the blasts of fire and iron and steel which the enemy let loose beat in vain against their valour and resolution. "'Tis God's truth I'm telling you," a Leinsterman remarked to me, "when I say we couldn't stop ourselves in the height of our hurry, we were that mad." In fact, they had captured Guillamont before they were aware of it. "Where's that blessed village we've got to take? "they shouted, as they looked round and saw not a stick or a stone. "We're in it, boys," replied a captain of the Munsters as he planted a green flag with a yellow harp on the dust heap which his map indicated was once the centre of Guillamont, and the Irishmen, mightily pleased with themselves, raised a wild shout.

CHAPTER 12

The Brigade's Pounce on Guinchy

Guinchy fell within the same week as Guillamont. It was stormed on the following Saturday, September 9. The village had been taken two or three times previously—some accounts say four—by the British and recaptured each time by the Germans. But the grip of the Irish Brigade could not be relaxed. Standing on a hill 500 feet high, Guinchy was one of the most important enemy strongholds on the Somme, particularly for artillery. It had been fortified with the accumulated skill of eighteen months' labour by the German engineers. It was well protected by guns. Picked troops—the Bavarians—defended it. The Germans, according to a captured officer, believed that Guinchy could not be taken. "But," he added, "you attacked us with devils, not men. No one could withstand them." The capture of the place was therefore a good day's work. It stands solely to the credit of the Irish Brigade. They did it all by themselves.

The attack was mainly delivered from the direction of Guillamont. All through the week, for five days and nights, most of the Irish battalions had lain in the trenches—connected shell craters for the most par—under heavy artillery fire. In these circumstances they could get nothing hot to eat. They subsisted mainly on the iron rations of bully beef and biscuit, which formed part of each man's fighting equipment, and a little water. As for sleep, they were unable to get more than disturbed and unrefreshing snatches. Yet they were as full of spirit and had nerves as unshaken as if they had come fresh from billets, and they were as eager for a fight as ever.

In preparation for the advance, a thunderstorm of British fire and steel broke over the German trenches. The splitting, tearing crashes of the mighty "heavies" lying miles back; their firing accuracy, the penetrating power of their shells, had a heartening influence on the men.

"Ah, those guns," said an officer of the Royal Irish Regiment—"their effect, spiritual and temporal, is wonderful. Your own makes you defiant of the very devil; the enemy's put the fear of God into you." The German lines were blotted out by smoke and flying soil. The ground rocked and swayed. It was like a heavy sea, only the waves were of earth.

The whistle sounded at four o'clock, and up and over went the men in a mass. Like the country before Guillamont, the country before Guinchy was slashed and gouged and seared, and the air had the sickening taste of gunpowder, poison gas and the corruption of the body. The men walked or ran, in broken array, in and out of the shell holes or over the narrow ledges that separated them. Soon the enemy got the range. Severed limbs, heads, arms and legs, and often the whole body, were flung high into the air. It was a dreadful scene. The noise, too, was appalling, what with the roaring of the guns, the bursting of the shells, and, not less, the frenzied yells of the charging masses. There is no shout in the *mêlée* of battle so fierce as the Irish shout. Every man is like "*Stentor of the brazen voice,*" whose shout, as Homer says in the *Iliad*, "*was as the shout of fifty men.*"

So the Irish shouted as they dashed forward, partly in relief of their feelings, and partly in the hope of confusing and dismaying their adversaries. It was an amazing martial feat, that charge of the Irish Brigade at Guinchy. Within just eight minutes they had overrun the intervening ground and captured the village. Nothing stopped nor stayed them. They did not pause to lie down for a while and let the bullets and shrapnel fly over them. Many were seen, as the advance proceeded, lying huddled on the ground as if taking shelter. They had taken shelter, indeed, but it was behind a stronger thing than a mound of earth—and that is death.

The most graphic and thrilling narrative of the engagement is given in a letter written home by a second lieutenant of one of the Irish battalions. They were in reserve, five or six hundred yards behind the first line, who were in occupation of the rising slope nearer to Guinchy. It was about four o'clock when they were ordered to move up so as to reinforce the first line. They got up in the nick of time, just as the great charge had begun, and they saw a sight which the officer says stirred and thrilled them to the depths of their souls.

"Mere words," he says, "must fail to convey anything like a true picture of the scene, but it is burned into the memory of all those who were there and saw it. Between the outer fringe of Guinchy and the front line of our own trenches is No Man's Land, a wilderness of pits so close together that you could ride astraddle the partitions between any two of them. As you look half right, obliquely down along No Man's Land, you behold a great host of yellow-coated men rise out of the earth and surge forward and upward in a torrent—not in extended order, as you might expect, but in one mass. There seems to be no end to them. Just when you think the flood is subsiding, another wave comes surging up the bend towards Guinchy. We joined in on the left. There was no time for us any more than the others to get into extended order. We formed another stream converging on the others at the summit."

He goes on to give a wonderful impression of the spirit of the men—their fearlessness and exuberance which nothing could daunt:

> By this time we were all wildly excited. Our shouts and yells alone must have struck terror into the Huns. They were firing their machine-guns down the slope. Their shells were falling here, there and everywhere. But there was no wavering in the Irish host. We couldn't run. We advanced at a steady walking pace, stumbling here and there, but going ever onward and upward. That numbing dread had now left me completely. Like the others, I was intoxicated with the glory of it all. I can remember shouting and bawling to the men of my platoon, who were only too eager to go on.

The officer mentions a curious circumstance which throws more light on that most interesting subject—the state of the mind in battle. He says the din must have been deafening—he learned afterwards that it could be heard miles away and yet he had a confused remembrance only of anything in the way of noise. How Guinchy was reached and what it was like is thus described:

> How long we were in crossing No Man's Land I don't know. It could not have been more than five minutes, yet it seemed much longer. We were now well up to the Boche. We had to clamber over all manner of obstacles—fallen trees, beams, great mounds of brick and rubble—in fact, over the ruins of Guinchy. It seems like a nightmare to me now. I remember seeing comrades falling round me. My sense of hearing returned to me, for I became conscious of a new sound—namely, the *pop, pop, pop, pop* of machine-guns, and the continuous crackling of rifle fire. By this time all units were mixed up, but they were all Irish-

men. They were cheering and cheering like mad. There was a machine-gun playing on us nearby, and we all made for it.

Through the centre, of the smashed and battered village ran a deep trench. It was occupied by about two hundred Germans, who continued to fire rifle and machine-gun even after the Irish had appeared on all sides, scrambling over the piles of masonry, bent and twisted wood and metal and broken furniture.

"At this moment we caught our first sight of the Huns," the officer continues. "They were in a trench of sorts, which ran in and out among the ruins. Some of them had their hands up. Others were kneeling and holding their arms out to us. Still others were running up and down the trench, distracted, as if they didn't know which way to go, but as we got closer they went down on their knees, too."

In battle the Irish are fierce and terrible to the enemy, and in victory most magnanimous.

"To the everlasting good name of the Irish soldiery," the officer says, "not one of these Huns, some of whom had been engaged in slaughtering our men up to the very last moment, was killed. I did not see a single instance of a prisoner being shot or bayoneted. When you remember that our men were worked up to a frenzy of excitement, this crowning act of mercy to their foes is surely to their eternal credit. They could feel pity even in their rage." He adds: "It is with a sense of pride that I can write this of our soldiers."

Many incidents in which smiles and tears were commingled took place in the nests of dugouts and cellars among the ruins of the village. The Dublin Fusiliers lost most of their officers in the advance. Many of them were the victims of snipers. In the village the direction of affairs was in the hands of young subalterns. The manliness and decision of these boys were wonderful. One of them captured, with the help of a single sergeant, a German officer and twenty men whom they had come upon on rounding the corner of a trench. The German officer surrendered in great style. He stood to attention, gave a clinking salute, and said in perfect English, "Sir, myself, this other officer and twenty men are your prisoners."

The subaltern said, "Right you are, old chap! "and they shook hands.

Hundreds of the defenders of Guinchy had fled. "An' if they did itself, you couldn't blame them," said a wounded Dublin Fusilier to me. "We came on jumping mad, all roaring and bawling, an' our bayonets stretched out, terribly fierce, in front of us, that maybe 'tis ourselves would get up and run like blazes likewise if 'twere the other way about."

Hot and impulsive in all things, the Irishmen were bent on advancing into the open country beyond Guinchy in chase of the retreating Germans. The officers had frantically to blow their whistles and shout and gesticulate to arrest this onward rush of the men to destruction in the labyrinth of the enemy supports which had escaped bombardment. "Very frankly the men proclaimed their discontent," says the special correspondent of *The Times*, "with what they called the 'diplomacy' which forbade them to go where they wanted—namely, "to hell and beyond, if there are any Germans hiding on the other side."

The only cases of desertion in the Irish Division occurred on the night before the storming of Guinchy. It is a deliciously comic incident. Three servants of the staff mess of one of the brigades disappeared. They left a note saying that, as they had missed Guillamont, they must have a hand in the taking of Guinchy. "If all right, back tomorrow. Very sorry," they added. Sure enough they were found in the fighting line.

CHAPTER 13

Honours and Distinctions for the Irish Brigade

Many decorations and rewards were won by the Irish Brigade. The Honours Book of the Brigade contained, at the end of 1916, about one thousand names of officers and men, presented by Major- General Hickie with the parchment certificate for gallant conduct and devotion to duty in the field. Over three hundred military decorations were gained. Two high Russian honours were also awarded—the Cross of St. George, Second Class, to Lance-Corporal T. McMahon, Munster Fusiliers, and the Cross of St. George, Fourth Class, to Lance-Sergeant L. Courtenay, Dublin Fusiliers. The list of decorations is so long that only a select few of those won by officers of the Brigade for gallant conduct in the capture of Guillamont and Guinchy can be given. Father Maurice O'Connell, the senior chaplain of the Brigade, got the Distinguished Service Order. Father Wrafter, S.J., and Father Doyle, S.J., got the Military Cross. All the Chaplains of the Division were indeed splendid. The others are: Fathers Browne, S.J., Burke, Cotter, O'Connor, and FitzMaurice, S. J. The official records show that the D.S.O. was also awarded to the following—

> Temporary Captain (temporary Major) Robert James Abbot Tamplin, Connaught Rangers.—He led his company with the greatest courage and determination, and was instrumental in capturing the position. He was wounded.
>
> Second-Lieutenant Cyril Paxman Tiptaft, Connaught Rangers, Special Reserve.—With his platoon he consolidated and held for fourteen hours a strong point, thus preventing the enemy from getting behind our advanced positions, which they tried

to do again and again. He set a fine example to his men, and kept up their spirits in spite of heavy casualties.

Temporary Lieutenant-Colonel George Alexander McLean Buckley, Leinster Regiment.—He led his battalion with the greatest courage and determination. He has on many occasions done very fine work.

Temporary Lieutenant-Colonel Edwin Henry Charles Patrick Bellingham, Royal Dublin Fusiliers.—He took command of the two leading battalions when the situation was critical, and displayed the greatest determination under shell and machine-gun fire. The success of the operation was largely due to his quick appreciation of the situation, and his rapid consolidation of the position.

Temporary Captain John Patrick Hunt, Royal Dublin Fusiliers.—He formed and held a defensive flank for ten hours, until relieved, under heavy machine-gun and rifle fire, thus frustrating the enemy's attempt to turn the flank.

Major Walter McClelland Crosbie, Royal Munster Fusiliers.—He led two companies with the greatest courage and initiative. Later, he organised the position with great skill, displaying great coolness throughout. He was wounded.

The Military Crosses won included the following—

Captain William Joseph Rivers Reardon, Royal Irish Regiment, Special Reserve.—He led his men with great dash, and during a counter-attack, though wounded, stayed with a party of men in a most exposed position, till he could carry on no longer.

Lieutenant Edward Alexander Stoker, Royal Irish Regiment, Special Reserve.—With two or three men he went under heavy shell fire, and captured some enemy snipers. During the enemy counter-attack he brought a party of men across the open to the threatened flank, under heavy fire.

Temporary Second-Lieutenant Thomas Adams, Royal Inniskilling Fusiliers.—For conspicuous gallantry when leading a raid. He entered the enemy's trenches, and it was largely due to his skill and determination that the raid was successful.

Temporary Second-Lieutenant Hugh Abbot Green, Royal Inniskilling Fusiliers.—When two senior company commanders had become casualties, he took command and led the men forward, capturing a portion of the final objective, which had been missed by the first attacking troops. He then advanced eighty yards, and, though himself wounded, consolidated his position.

Temporary Captain Victor Henry Parr, Royal Inniskilling Fusiliers.—He rallied men of different units in a wood during an enemy counter-attack, and, though wounded, led them forward and beat off the attack.

Temporary Second-Lieutenant Charles Lovell Naylor, Royal Irish Fusiliers.—He took command of his company when the other officers had become casualties, and showed great pluck when driving off a counter-attack. He then advanced and reoccupied one of our advanced posts.

Temporary Captain Thomas Francis O'Donnell, Royal Irish Fusiliers.—In the attack he dashed forward and led the battalion the whole way. He was first into the enemy's position, where he did fine work consolidating the defences.

Lieutenant Valentine Joseph Farrell, Leinster Regiment, Special Reserve.—When the senior officers of two companies had become casualties in the firing line he took command, and. by his fine example, kept his men together under intense fire.

Captain Charles Carleton Barry, Leinster Regiment, Special Reserve.—For conspicuous gallantry and devotion to duty when returning with another officer from reconnaissance. The latter officer was severely wounded. Although wounded in the arm, Captain Barry succeeded in pulling his comrade into a shell hole, and dressing his wound. He finally succeeded in getting the officer back to our trench. These actions were carried out under heavy machine-gun and snipers' fire.

Temporary Second-Lieutenant Nicholas Hurst, Royal Dublin Fusiliers.—He organised a party to rush two machine-guns, which were holding up the advance, and, when the first party failed, he organised a second, which succeeded. The strong point was captured and two officers and thirty men made prisoners.

Temporary Second-Lieutenant Harold Arthur Jowett, Royal Dublin Fusiliers.—For conspicuous gallantry during an attack, moving up and down his line under heavy fire, encouraging his men and setting a fine example to all ranks. He displayed considerable coolness and skill in maintaining his position until the line was re-established.

Temporary Lieutenant William Kee, Royal Dublin Fusiliers.—Although twice wounded, he continued to lead his men during an attack until ordered back to the dressing station. He has several times carried out reconnaissance work most efficiently.

Temporary Lieutenant Eugene Patrick Quigley, Royal Dublin Fusiliers.—Though wounded, he brought a machine-gun into action against some enemy who were collecting to repel our attack. Not finding a suitable rest for one of his guns, he had it placed on his shoulder, where it opened fire.

Temporary Second-Lieutenant Dennis Joseph Baily, Royal Munster Fusiliers.—When all the officers round him had become casualties he took command and led the men forward with great dash and ability.

Temporary Lieutenant Labouchere Hillyer Bainbridge-Bell, Royal Munster Fusiliers.—He continually repaired breaks in the line during several days of heavy shelling, never hesitating to go out when the wires were cut. He was several times smothered in debris, and was much bruised.

Temporary Captain Cecil William Chandler, Royal Munster Fusiliers.—Although wounded, he led his men and beat off repeated enemy attacks, displaying great courage and initiative throughout.

Temporary Captain Maurice Fletcher, Royal Munster Fusiliers.—He directed a working party, close to the enemy's line, and completed his task under continuous shelling and rifle fire. He has done other fine work.

Temporary Lieutenant Fabian Strachan Woodley, Royal Munster Fusiliers.—By his skill and determination he beat off three counter-attacks of the enemy, who were endeavouring to reach his trench. Four days later he led his men in two attacks with great pluck.

Captain Place, Royal Irish Regiment, was awarded bar to Cross he had already won.

These official records, brief and coldly phrased though they be, cannot be read without a thrill of pride in the race which produced the men. There is one other account of the winning of a Military

Cross that must be specially given, for it describes the feats of "the boy hero of Guinchy," Second-Lieutenant James Emmet Dalton, of the Dublin Fusiliers. He joined the Army in January 1916, and was only eighteen years of age when he took command and proved himself a born leader of men at Guinchy. The following is the official record, which, happily, is more extended than usual—

> At the capture of Guinchy, on the 9th of September, 1916, he displayed great bravery and leadership in action. When, owing to the loss of officers, the men of two companies were left without leaders, he took command and led these companies to their final objective. After the withdrawal of another brigade and the right flank of his battalion was in the rear, he carried out the protection of the flank, under intense fire, by the employment of machine-guns in selected commanding and successive positions. After dark, whilst going about supervising the consolidation of the position, he, with only one sergeant escorting, found himself confronted by a party of the enemy, consisting of one officer and twenty men. By his prompt determination the party were overawed and, after a few shots, threw up their arms and surrendered.

The Irish Brigade also got a second Victoria Cross at the Battle of the Somme. It was won by Lieutenant John Vincent Holland of the Leinster Regiment for most conspicuous bravery. He was born at Athy, Co. Kildare, the son of John Holland, a past President of the Royal College of Veterinary Surgeons of Ireland, was educated at the Christian Brothers' Schools, and Clongowies Wood College. At the outbreak of war he was employed in the chief mechanical engineers' department of the Central Argentine Railway at Rosario, and, hastening home, got his commission in the Leinster Regiment. For his services at the Front he received the Certificate of the Irish Brigade. It was at Guillamont that Leiutenant Holland won the Victoria Cross. The official account of his exploits is as follows—

> For most conspicuous bravery during a heavy engagement, when, not content with bombing hostile dugouts within the objective, he fearlessly led his bombers through our own artillery barrage and cleared a great part of the village in front. He started out with twenty-six bombers and finished up with only five, after capturing some fifty prisoners. By this very gallant action he undoubtedly broke the spirit of the enemy, and thus

saved us many casualties when the battalion made a further advance. He was far from well at the time, and later had to go to hospital.

As proof of Lieutenant Holland's dash it is related that the night before the engagement he made a bet of five pounds with a brother officer that he would be first over the parapet when the order came. He won the bet, the V.C., and, in addition, he was made a Chevalier of the Legion of Honour and of St. George of Russia.

CHAPTER 14

The Wooden Cross

For all this glory and renown the Irish Brigade had to pay a bitter price. Many a home in Ireland was made forlorn and desolate. The roads of the countryside by which the men went off to the war will be lonely and drear for ever to womenfolk, for never again will they be brightened by the returning footsteps of son or husband.

One of the most grievous losses which the brigade sustained was the death of Lieutenant-Colonel Lenox-Conyngham of the Connaught Rangers. He came of an Ulster soldier family. He was the son of Colonel Sir W. Fitzwilliam Lenox-Conyngham of Springhill, co. Derry, was born in 1861, and three of his brothers were also serving in the Army with the rank of Colonel. He fell at the head of his battalion, which was foremost in the rush for Guillamont.

"I cannot imagine a more fitting death for him," writes Captain Stephen Gwynn, M.P., who served under Colonel Lenox-Conyngham since the days the battalion was formed at Fermoy. "He was never in doubt as to how his men would acquit themselves. To us officers he said things in private which would sound a little arrogant if I quoted them—and yet they have been made good." The welfare of the men was always his first concern.

Captain Gwynn relates that on the return of the battalion one night, after a dreary day of field operations at home, the company officers, feeling very miserable, were gathered about the door of their mess-room, waiting for dinner, when the colonel called out that their proper place was in the cook-house, seeing that the men were first served. The incident greatly rejoiced the heart of Captain Gwynn, for, having served in the ranks, he knew that the officer who is best served by the men is he who places their comfort and well-being before his own. In France, whenever any compliment was paid to Colonel

Lenox-Conyngham, he could not be content until, with frank generosity, he passed it on to the company officers. "It is you who have done it," he would say. "He was right too," says Captain Gwynn. "We did the work, and no men were ever less interfered with; but we did it as we had been taught to do it, and because we were kept up to it at every point."

I can only mention a few typical cases of the officers of the Irish Brigade killed at Guillamont and Guinchy. Lieutenant E. R. F. Becher, of the Munster Fusiliers, was but nineteen, and the only child of E. W. Becher, Lismore, co. Waterford. He was descended in direct line from Colonel Thomas Becher, who was *aide-de-camp* to King William at the Battle of the Boyne, and was on that occasion presented by the King with his watch, which is still an heirloom in the family. Captain H. R. Lloyd of the Royal Irish Regiment was descended from the ensign who carried the colours of the Coldstream Guards at Waterloo. He was educated at Drogheda Grammar School, and was at business in Brazil when the war broke out.

Lieutenant J. T. Kennedy of the Inniskillings was editor of the *Northern Standard*, Monaghan. Lieutenant Charles P. Close of the Dublin Fusiliers was a native of Limerick, and conducted a teaching academy in that city. At the time he volunteered he was the commanding officer of the City Regiment of National Volunteers. Another officer of the National Volunteers was Lieutenant Hugh Maguire, son of Dr. Conor Maguire of Claremorris. He was a university student when he volunteered for service in response to the national call, and got a commission in the Connaught Rangers, but was temporarily attached to the Inniskillings when he was killed.

Another gallant youth was Lieutenant Thomas Maxwell, Dublin Fusiliers, son of Surgeon Patrick W. Maxwell of Dublin, who was in his twenty-first year when he fell while in temporary command of the leading company of his battalion in the taking of Guinchy. Then there is Second-Lieutenant Bevan Nolan. He was the third son of Walter Nolan, Clerk of the Crown for South Tipperary. When the war broke out he was in Canada, and, returning at once, obtained a commission in the Royal Irish Regiment. He was a very gallant young officer, and most popular with his comrades.

In the camp the general verdict was: "Nolan is destined for the V.C., or to die at the head of his platoon." He was only twenty-one years of age, and a splendid type of young Tipperary. The greatest loss in individual brain-power which Ireland suffered was through the death of that brilliant man of letters and economist, Lieutenant T. M. Kettle of the Dublin Fusiliers. He was a son of Andrew J. Kettle, a Dublin farmer, one of the founders of the Land League, and a member of the executive who in 1881, on the arrest of the leaders, Parnell, Davitt and Dillon, signed the No-Rent Manifesto addressed to the tenants.

In the House of Commons, where he sat as a Nationalist from 1906 to 1910, young Kettle made a reputation for eloquence and humour of quite a fresh vein. He resigned on his appointment as Professor of National Economics in the National University of Ireland. He was married to Margaret, daughter of David Sheehy, M.P., whose sister is the widow of Sheehy Skeffington, shot by the military in the Dublin Rebellion.

In public life Kettle was a vivid figure, and very Irish. At first he belonged to the extreme, or irreconcilable section of Nationalists, noted for a cast of thought or bias of reasoning which finds that no good for Ireland can come out of England. When England was fighting the Boers he distributed anti-recruiting leaflets in the streets of Dublin. To his constituents in East Tyrone he once declared that Ireland had no national independence to protect against foreign invasion. "I confess," he added, referring to the over-taxation of Ireland, "I see many reasons for preferring German invasion to British methods of finance in Ireland."

But increased knowledge brought wider views. As a result of his experiences in Parliament, where he found in all parties a genuine desire to do what was best for Ireland according to their lights, he approached the consideration of Irish questions with a remarkably tolerant, broad-minded and practical spirit. When the war broke out there was no more powerful champion of the Allies. The invasion of Belgium, which he had witnessed as a newspaper correspondent, moved him to an intense hatred of Germany, and, throwing himself with all his energy into the recruiting campaign in Ireland, he addressed no fewer than two hundred meetings, bringing thousands of his countrymen to the Colours. One of his epigrammatic and pointed sayings—suggested by the ill-favour of absentee landlordism of old in Ireland—was: "*Nowadays the absentee is the man who stays at home.*"

In a letter written to a friend on the night his battalion was moving up to the Somme, Kettle said he had had two chances of leaving—one on account of sickness and the other to take a Staff appointment. "I have chosen to stay with my comrades," he writes. "The bombardment, destruction and bloodshed are beyond all imagination. Nor did

I ever think that valour of simple men could be quite as beautiful as that of my Dublin Fusiliers."

On the eve of his death he wrote to his wife another fine tribute to his battalion. "I have never," he says, "seen anything in my life so beautiful as the clean and, so to say, radiant manner of my Dublin Fusiliers. There is something divine in men like that."

Kettle fell in the storming of Guinchy. His friend and comrade, Lieutenant James Emmet Dalton, M.C., states that they were both in the trenches in Trones Wood opposite Guillamont, on the morning of September 8th, discussing the loss of two hundred men and seven officers which the battalion had sustained the day before from German shell fire, when an orderly arrived with a note for each of them, saying, "Be in readiness. Battalion will take up A and B position in front of Guinchy tonight at 12 midnight." Lieutenant Dalton continues:

> I was with Tom when he advanced to the position that night, and the stench of the dead that covered our road was so awful that we both used some foot-powder on our faces. When we reached our objective we dug ourselves in, and then, at five o'clock p.m. on the 9th, we attacked Guinchy. I was just behind Tom when we went over the top. He was in a bent position, and a bullet got over a steel waistcoat that he wore and entered his heart. Well, he only lasted about one minute, and he had my crucifix in his hands. Then Boyd took all the papers and things out of Tom's pockets in order to keep them for Mrs. Kettle, but poor Boyd was blown to atoms in a few minutes. The Welsh Guards buried Mr. Kettle's remains. Tom's death has been a big blow to the regiment, and I am afraid that I could not put in words my feelings on the subject.

In another letter Lieutenant Dalton says:

> Mr. Kettle died a grand and holy death—the death of a soldier and a true Christian.

Lieutenant Kettle left his political testament in a letter to his wife and in verses addressed to his little daughter. The letter, written a few days before his death, with directions that it was to be sent to Mrs. Kettle if he were killed, says—

> Had I lived I had meant to call my next book on the relations of Ireland and England *The Two Fools; A Tragedy of Errors*. It has needed all the folly of England and all the folly of Ireland to produce the situation in which our unhappy country is now

involved. I have mixed much with Englishmen and with Protestant Ulstermen, and I know that there is no real or abiding reason for the gulfs, salter than the sea, that now dismember the natural alliance of both of them with us Irish Nationalists. It needs only a Fiat Lux of a kind very easily compassed to replace the unnatural by the natural. In the name, and by the seal, of the blood given in the last two years I ask for Colonial Home Rule for Ireland, a thing essential in itself, and essential as a prologue to the reconstruction of the Empire. Ulster will agree. And I ask for the immediate withdrawal of martial law in Ireland, and an amnesty for all Sinn Fein prisoners. If this war has taught us anything it is that great things can be done only in a great way.

The lines, *To my daughter Betty—The Gift of Love*, were written in the field before Guillamont, Somme, September 4, 1916—

In wiser days, my darling rosebud, blown
To beauty proud as was your mother's prime—
In that desired, delayed, incredible time
You'll ask why I abandoned you, my own,
And the dear breast that was your baby's throne,
o dice with death, and, oh! they'll give you rhyme
And reason; one will call the thing sublime,
And one decry it in a knowing tone.
So here, while the mad guns curse overhead,
And tired men sigh, with mud for couch and floor,
Know that we fools, now with the foolish dead,
Died not for Flag, nor King, nor Emperor,
But for a dream, born in a herdsman shed
And for the secret Scripture of the poor.

These young leaders have won the wooden cross—the symbol of the supreme sacrifice they made that others might live; the symbol, also, of eternal peace for themselves—the wooden cross which marks their graves. From north, south, east and west of Ireland, of differing creeds, of opposing political opinions—these men of the Irish Brigade and the Ulster Division—they lie, as they fought, side by side, comrades in a noble cause. It is sad to think of the many rare intelligences, ardent and glowing spirits, which are quenched forever in the little cemeteries that have sprung up along the Allied Front. The loss to Ireland is incalculable. But gain might come from it, which, weighed in the balance, would not be found wanting, if only the solemn lesson which it teaches were brought home to all: that one in Irish name, as one in Irish fame, are the northerners and southerners who died in France for the liberation of humanity.

Major-General Hickie—as mindful of the memories of those of his men who have fallen as of the well-being of those still in the fighting ranks—erected as a memorial to the dead of the Irish Brigade a statue in white marble of Our Lady of Victories in a town of the district. Another striking proof of his esteem for the men is afforded by the following Order which he issued on December 18, 1916—

> Today is the anniversary of the landing of the Irish Division in France. The Divisional Commander wishes to express his appreciation of the spirit which has been shown by all ranks during the past year. He feels that the Division has earned the right to adopt the motto which was granted by the King of France to the Irish Brigade, which served in this country for a hundred years: '*Everywhere and always faithful.*' With the record of the past, with the memory of our gallant dead, with this motto to live up to, and with our trust in God, we can face the future with confidence.
>
> God Save The King.

CHAPTER 15

More Irish Heroes of the Victoria Cross

In this war Victoria Crosses are being won in remarkably large numbers, despite dangers and sufferings immeasurably greater than were ever conceived of in any war of the past. It would seem, indeed, as if human nature is capable of withstanding any test to which it can conceivably be put. "Man," said Mr. Lloyd George, "is the bravest animal that God has made; and, in comparison with him, the lion is an arrant coward."

Up to the end of 1916 the war has contributed 221 additional names to that golden chronicle of valorous deeds The Roll of the Victoria Cross. Of these as many as thirty-five are Irishmen. That is a most glorious achievement, having regard to the proportion of Irishmen in the Army. The number, taking the Irish regiments, the Irishmen in English and Scottish regiments and in the forces of the different Dominions, is altogether about 500,000; and estimating the entire strength of the Army to be 5,000,000, it will be seen that if the other nationalities won Victoria Crosses in the same ratio to their numbers as the Irish, the Roll of the present war would contain not 221, but 350 names. To put it in another way, the Irish on a basis of numbers would be entitled only to twenty-two of the 221 Victoria Crosses that have actually been awarded.

But however that may be, the Irish part of the Roll, as it stands, will be found to be a very thrilling record of the gallantry of Irish officers and men in the various theatres of war. Twenty of the thirty-five Irish heroes of the Victoria Cross are dealt with in the first series of *The Irish at the Front*. Of the remaining fifteen, the deeds of four are recounted in the exploits of the Ulster Division; one, in the story of the Irish

Brigade—the second Cross that fell to the Brigade having been won by an English officer—and the other ten are dealt with here.

Sub-Lieutenant Arthur Walderne St. Clair Tisdall, V.C., of the Royal Naval Volunteer Reserve, was another of the many gallant Irishmen who distinguished themselves at the memorable first landing at Gallipoli on April 25, 1915, when the Munsters and the Dublins won imperishable renown. The announcement of the award of the Victoria Cross to Sub-Lieutenant Tisdall was not made until March 31, 1916. The following official statement explains the delay—

> During the landing from the ss. *River Clyde* at V Beach, in the Gallipoli Peninsula, on April 25, 1915, Sub-Lieutenant Tisdall, hearing wounded men on the beach calling for assistance, jumped into the water, and, pushing a boat in front of him, went to their rescue. He was, however, obliged to obtain help, and took with him on two trips Leading Seaman Malin, and on other trips Chief Petty Officer Perring and Leading Seamen Curtiss and Parkinson. In all Sub-Lieutenant Tisdall made four or five trips between the ship and the shore, and was thus responsible for rescuing many wounded men under heavy and accurate fire. Owing to the fact that Sub-Lieutenant Tisdall and the platoon under his orders were on detached service at the time, and that this officer was killed in action on May 6, it has now only been possible to obtain complete information as to the individuals who took part in this gallant act.

Sub-Lieutenant Tisdall came of a well-known Irish family, the Tisdalls of Charlesfort, who have been established in co. Meath since the year 1668. The late head of the family, Major Tisdall of the Irish Guards, fell guarding the retreat of the British Army in France in September 1914. The volume of *Memoirs and Poems of A. W. St. C. Tisdall, V.C.*, by Mrs. M. L. Tisdall, states that among his ancestors and relatives on both sides were "Crusaders, Royalists, who lost everything-even their family name—for King Charles I; Scotch Covenanters and French Huguenots, who had been driven from their own countries for their faith's sake; Irish patriots who fought at the Battle of the Boyne, a Danish Diplomatist who had danced with Queen Marie-Antoinette; an ancestress who is said to have fired the first cannon at the siege of Gibraltar; a famous Attorney-General for Ireland; a brilliant and versatile Cathedral Chancellor, a Bishop, three missionaries, and many university, military and naval men."

He was born at Bombay on July 21, 1890, his father—the Rev. Dr. St. Clair Tisdall (now of St. George's Vicarage, Deal)—being then in charge of the Mohammedan mission of the Church Missionary Society. He was educated at Bedford School from 1900 to 1909, when he left as Scholar of Trinity College, Cambridge, where he had a distinguished career, culminating in the winning of the Chancellor's Gold Medal in the university in 1913, after which he entered the Home Civil Service. On the outbreak of war he was called to the Colours as an A.B. of the Royal Naval Volunteer Reserve, of which he had been a member for some time previously. He served in the ranks in the Antwerp expedition, and was afterwards given a commission. By this time, the memoirs tell us, "he had acquired great self-control, and had practically conquered two of his Irish handicaps—*viz*. a hot temper and a certain carelessness, or casualness, in business. Latterly, the 'Tisdall temper,' as it is called in the family, only flashed out in the presence of what he considered wrong or unjust."

The following extract from a letter by an officer of the Royal Navy who took part in the landing in Gallipoli was published in *The Times* on December 6, 1916—

> It has been, unfortunately, my sad lot to write of the ending on this earth of many heroes, for I have been through much since August 1914; but I sincerely assure you that I have never seen more daring and gallant deeds performed by any man, naval or military, than those performed by the man I now know to have been Sub-Lieutenant A. W. St. Clair Tisdall, Anson Battalion, R.N.V.R., at the landing from the *River Clyde* on that terrible 'V' Beach. Throughout the afternoon of April 25 a boat containing an officer (unknown to all) and three bluejackets, one of them a petty officer, was very prominent.
>
> The officer and the petty officer did the most daring of things, and were seen by very many. Time after time they visited that awful beach and brought back wounded officers and men. Darkness came on and that officer was nowhere to be found. All the petty officer and bluejackets could say was, 'He's one of those Naval Division gents.' Days and weeks passed away, and I and others never ceased trying to find out if we could who and where the unknown hero was. Over and over we discussed in the *River Clyde* and in dugouts on the beach how those two had escaped.

It was not till June 15, 1915, that the writer of the letter learned who the hero was. He adds: "His very saving of the wounded and the handling of them was in itself the work of an artist, and a very great one."

The end of this gallant officer is told by an A.B. of the Anson Battalion, who, writing to Mrs. Tisdall, says:

On May 6 the Naval Division got orders to make an advance, which we did, and advanced about a mile. When we got nicely settled in the enemy trench your son stood up on the parapet, looking for the enemy, but was not there long before he was shot through the chest, and he never said one word.

This was at the first Battle of Achi Baba. Tisdall was buried on the night of May 7, a few yards from where he fell. It was a glorious death, but far from the kind of death he had dreamt of. In a poem, *Love and Death*, written in 1910, he says—

Be love for me no hoarse and headstrong tide,
Breaking upon a deep-rent, sea-filled coast,
But a strong river on which sea-ships glide,
And the lush meadows are its peaceful boast.

Be death for me no parting red and raw
Of soul and body, even in glorious pain,
But while my children's children wait in awe,
May peaceful darkness still the toilsome brain.

Corporal William Richard Cotter, an Irishman serving in the East Kent Regiment, got the V.C. for an act of unexampled courage and endurance. It was a deed which showed to what heights the bravery of Irish soldiers can soar. On the night of March 6, 1916, in the course of a raid made by his company along an enemy trench, his own bombing party was cut off owing to heavy casualties in the centre of the attack. The situation was so serious that Cotter went back under heavy fire to report and bring up more bombs. On the return journey his right leg was blown off close below the knee, and he was wounded in both arms.

By a kind of miracle, the miracle of human courage, he did not drop down and die in the mud of the trench mud—so deep that unwounded men found it hard to walk in it—but made his way for fifty yards towards the crater where his comrades were hard pressed. He came up to Lance-Corporal Newman, who was bombing with his sector to the right of the position. Cotter called to him and directed him to bomb six feet towards where help was most needed, and worked his way forward to the crater against which the Germans were making a violent counter-attack. Men fell rapidly under the enemy's bomb fire, but Cotter, with only one leg, and bleeding from both arms, took charge.

The enemy were repulsed after two hours' fighting, and only then did Cotter allow his wounds to be bandaged. From the dugout where he lay while the bombardment still continued he called out cheery words to the men, until he was carried down, fourteen hours later. He died of his wounds. A wonderful story of gallantry, endurance and fortitude, it would seem almost incredible were it not established by official record of the awarding of the V.C. to Corporal Cotter—

> For most conspicuous bravery and devotion to duty. When his right leg had been blown off at the knee, and he had also been wounded in both arms, he made his way unaided for fifty yards to a crater, steadied the men who were holding it, controlled their fire, issued orders, and altered the dispositions of his men to meet a fresh counter-attack by the enemy. For two hours he held his position, and only allowed his wounds to be roughly dressed when the attack had quieted down. He could not be moved back for fourteen hours, and during all this time had a cheery word for all who passed him. There is no doubt that his magnificent courage helped greatly to save a critical situation.

Cotter was born at Sandgate, near Folkestone, of Irish parents who came from Limerick, and was thirty-four years of age. He was educated at the Catholic School, Folkestone. Always fond of adventure, he ran away to sea as a boy. He then enlisted in the Army, and, after twelve years in the Buffs, came out on the Reserve in 1914, and was employed by the Sandgate Council. He was called up at the outbreak of war. He had lost an eye as the result of an accident, but nevertheless was sent on active service, and this disability enhances the extraordinary heroism of his deed. He was the eldest of six sons, one of whom was killed in France, one was in the Navy, one in Salonika, and another died after serving in the South African War. The chaplain of his regiment wrote to his parents informing them of his death, and said his last words were "Goodbye, God bless them all." Cotter was previously recommended for the Distinguished Conduct Medal in December 1915.

Thomas Hughes, of the Connaught Rangers, got the V.C. for most conspicuous bravery and determination. The official record adds:

He was wounded in an attack, but returned at once to the firing line after having his wounds dressed. Later, seeing a hostile machine-gun, he dashed out in front of his company, shot the gunner, and single-handed captured the gun. Though again wounded, he brought back three or four prisoners.

He was born at Corravoo, near Castleblayney, Co. Monaghan, his father being a farmer, and was at the Curragh, employed as a jockey in a racing stable, until, on the outbreak of war, he joined the Connaught Rangers.

"Come on, the Dubs." This slogan was heard at a critical moment during one of the pushes on the Somme in the summer of 1916. It was shouted by Sergeant Robert Downie of the Dublin Fusiliers, and his coolness and resource in danger saved the situation and got him the Victoria Cross. The Dublins have been through many memorable campaigns and battles and have won many honours, but Sergeant Downie is the first of his regiment to win the most prized of all distinctions. The following is the official record of the award—

> For most conspicuous bravery and devotion to duty in attack. When most of the officers had become casualties, this non-commissioned officer, utterly regardless of personal danger, moved about under heavy fire and reorganised the attack, which had been temporarily checked. At the critical moment he rushed forward alone, shouting, 'Come on, the Dubs.' This stirring appeal met with immediate response, and the line rushed forward at his call. Sergeant Downie accounted for several of the enemy, and in addition captured a machine-gun, killing the team. Though wounded early in the fight, he remained with his company, and gave valuable assistance, whilst the position was being consolidated. It was owing to Sergeant Downie's courage and initiative that this important position, which had resisted four or five previous attacks, was won.

Sergeant Downie is twenty-three years of age. He was born in Glasgow of Irish parents, both his father and mother being natives of Laurencetown, Co. Down, and received his education at St. Aloysius' Catholic Schools, Springburn, Glasgow. He is one of a family of sixteen, of whom thirteen are alive. His father was employed for thirty years in the Hydepark Locomotive Works, Glasgow, as an oiler and beltman. After leaving school young Downie served for some time in the same works as his father, and at the age of eighteen he enlisted in the Dublin Fusiliers. He went to France with the Expeditionary Force. He is married, and his wife lives with her two children at Springburn.

A wounded officer of the Dublins thus describes how Downie won the V.C.—

> For coolness and resource under danger, it would be impossible to beat Downie. The ordeal we had to go through that day was one of the most severe we have struck since the present war, and, as you know, the 'Dubs' have been in many tight corners. We had orders to advance against a position that had so far resisted all efforts of our men to take. We knew it had to be taken this time, be the cost what it might. We went over with a good heart. The men were magnificent. They faced their ordeal without the slightest sign of wavering. The enemy's fire was ploughing through our ranks. We lost heavily.
>
> In a short time there was not an officer left capable of giving directions. It was only then that the attack began to falter. At that moment the enemy fire increased its intensity. It was many times worse than any hell I have ever heard of. The machine-gun fire of the enemy swept across the ground like great gusts of wind, and the finest troops in the world might have been pardoned for a momentary hesitation in face of such fire. Downie took the situation in. He ran along the line of shell holes in which the men were sheltering and cried out, 'Come on, the Dubs.'
>
> The effect was electrical. The men sprang from their cover, and under his leadership dashed to the attack on the enemy position. Their blood was now up, and there was no stopping them until the goal was reached. The immediate approach to the part of the trench they were attacking was swept by the fire of one machine-gun that galled the attacking party a lot. Downie made straight for that. Using alternately bomb, bayonet, and rifle, he wiped out the entire crew, and captured the gun, which he quickly turned on the enemy. The effect of this daring exploit was soon felt. The enemy resistance weakened, and the Dublin lads were soon in possession of the trench.
>
> It was later on, when the attack was being pressed home, that Downie was wounded. It was severe enough to justify any man in dropping out, but Downie was made of better stuff. He stuck to his men, and for the rest of the day he directed their opera-

tions with a skill and energy that defeated repeated attempts of the enemy to win back the lost ground. Throughout the very difficult operations his cheery disposition and his eye for discerning the best thing to do in given circumstances, were as good as a reinforcement to the hard-pressed Irishmen.

Captain John A. Sinton, Indian Medical Service, was awarded the Victoria Cross, after the action at Shaikh Saad in Mesopotamia. The official record is as follows—

> For most conspicuous bravery and devotion to duty. Although shot through both arms and through the side he refused to go to hospital, and remained as long as daylight lasted attending to his duties under very heavy fire. In three previous actions Captain Sinton displayed the utmost bravery.

Captain Sinton was born in Lisburn, Co. Antrim, and is thirty-one years of age. He is a member of a well-known Quaker family. As a boy he went to the Memorial School in Lisburn, named after the heroic Brigadier-General, John Nicholson, of the Indian Mutiny, and afterwards attended the Royal Belfast Academical Institution. He had a brilliant career in the Medical School at Queen's University, Belfast. He took first place at the examination for the Indian Medical Service at the School of Tropical Medicine in Liverpool. He went to India in 1912, and was attached to the 31st Duke of Connaught's Own Lancers at Kohat. At the outbreak of war he transferred to the Dogras, in order to take part in the operations of the Indian Expeditionary Force in the Persian Gulf.

Private Henry Kenny of the Loyal North Lancashire Regiment is another London Irishman, and the third of the name of Kenny who have gained the coveted V.C. The stories of the other two Kennys are told in the first series of *The Irish at the Front*. Private Kenny's father is a native of Limerick, where all his people belonged to, and from where he moved to England with his parents. Private Kenny himself was born in Hackney, London, and enlisted, at the age of eighteen, in 1906. On the outbreak of war he was recalled to the Colours as a reservist, and took part in many famous engagements. The official record of his gallantry is as follows—

> For most conspicuous bravery. Private Kenny went out on six different occasions on one day under a very heavy shell, rifle and machine-gun fire, and each time succeeded in carrying to a place of safety a wounded man who had been lying in the

open. He was himself wounded in the neck whilst handing the last man over the parapet.

When Kenny was invalided home on account of the wounds he received in performing the noble action for which he won the Victoria Cross, he made no reference to his achievement. The sixth man whom he rescued was his own colonel, and it was while he was bearing his commanding officer into safety that he was himself wounded. On his return home for a holiday after the announcement of the award he visited the House of Commons, and was introduced to Sir E. Carson, Lord and Lady Pirrie, Mr. and Mrs. Redmond, Lord Wimborne and Colonel Churchill, and had tea on the terrace.

There was much rejoicing amongst the pupils and staff of the Royal Hibernian Military School, Phoenix Park, Dublin, when it became known that the greatest honour that can be bestowed upon a soldier—the Victoria Cross—had been won by a former pupil of the school in the person of Private Frederick Jeremiah Edwards, of the Middlesex Regiment. There are three Royal Military Schools in the United Kingdom (the Duke of York's School, near London, the Queen Victoria School in Scotland, and the Royal Hibernian School), and naturally there was keen anxiety amongst them as to which would be the first to place a V.C. to its credit in the present war.

The Irish school has won, thanks to Private "Jerry" Edwards. He is the second "old boy" of the Hibernian School to win the V.C., the previous occasion on which the distinction was gained being during the Crimean War. Private Edwards was born at Queenstown, co. Cork, the son of a soldier. He entered the Hibernian School at seven years of age. He is spoken of as a bright, intelligent and plucky lad by the schoolmasters, to whom his lively spirits were oftentimes a source of worry—and, perhaps, of trouble for "Jerry." When he was fourteen he left the school to join the Army. The circumstances under which he won the V.C. in his twenty-first year are thus officially described—

> For most conspicuous bravery and resource. His part of the line was held up by machine-gun fire, and all officers had become casualties. There was confusion and indication of retirement. Private Edwards, grasping the situation, on his own initiative dashed out towards the gun, which he knocked out with his bombs. This very gallant act, coupled with great presence of mind and a total disregard of personal danger, made further advance possible and cleared up a dangerous situation.

A former schoolmate of Private Edwards, and a comrade in the Middlesex Regiment, gives the following more specific particulars of the hero's courage and determination in carrying along the wavering men by the force of his example—

> The day our regiment went over there was some wild work. The enemy concentrated on our part of the line a furious fire. There was absolutely no cover for a great part of the way. One by one our officers were picked off. Young Lieutenant —— was the last to go. As he fell he called to the men to go right on. They did so for a time, but things got worse, and finally the men seemed to lose heart. 'Jerry' Edwards declared that he wasn't going back. He sprang forward into the thick hail of machine-gun bullets, in full view of the taunting Huns on their parapet. 'This way, Die-hards,' he cried, and at the sound of the glorious old nickname the men recovered from their panic. Gradually order was restored, and the men followed Edwards up to the enemy parapet. This was stormed in a few minutes. Edwards himself bowled over a machine-gun and its crew. He picked up a couple of bombs and threw them. Privates behind him handed up more, and from an exposed position on the enemy parapet he kept raining bombs on the foe. The gun and crew were blown to bits, and the rest of the enemy bolted to their next position. Edwards saw what they were up to, and, leading some of the men by the near cut, he intercepted the flying enemy. Then a great bombing match began. Our lads won, thanks to the way the team was handled by Edwards. Though the position was dangerous for some time afterwards, we held on, and finally consolidated the ground.

The finest quality in gallantry is that which impels a soldier to leave a place of safety voluntarily, and, though he is not under the excitement of battle, to plunge with cool calculation into some danger which he knows and has estimated to its full extent. For a deed of valour of that character the Victoria Cross was given to Private William Young, East Lancashire Regiment. The official record says—

> On seeing that his sergeant had been wounded he left his trench to attend to him under very heavy fire. The wounded non-commissioned officer requested Private Young to get under cover, but he refused, and was almost immediately very seriously wounded by having both jaws shattered. Notwithstanding

his terrible injuries, Private Young continued endeavouring to effect the rescue upon which he had set his mind, and eventually succeeded with the aid of another soldier. He then went unaided to the dressing-station, where it was discovered that he had also been wounded by a rifle bullet in the chest. The great fortitude, determination, courage, and devotion to duty displayed by this soldier could hardly be surpassed.

Private Young was born in Glasgow of Irish parents, and joined the East Lancashire Regiment in May 1899, when about twenty-one years of age. He was transferred to the Army Reserve in August 1902, and joined Section D, Army Reserve, in May 1911. He responded to the mobilisation call on August 5, 1914, and went to France on September 14, going all through the fighting until wounded at the battle of Ypres in November 1914, by a bullet in the thigh. Returning to the Front, he was "gassed," and the resulting injuries to his eyes laid him up for three weeks in hospital. On going back to the trenches the second time he performed his heroic deed on December 22, 1915.

Young's home was at Preston, where he had a wife and nine children, the youngest of whom was born while the father was at the war. In the following letter to his wife Private Young told how the news of his distinction was received by him in a military hospital in England, where he underwent an operation for the complete removal of his lower jaw and the fitting of an artificial one in its place.

> Of course, long enough before you get this letter you will see by the papers that I have received the greatest honour that any Britisher can get, namely, the V.C., and, of course, I am naturally very proud of the great honour, both for my sake and the sake of you and the kiddies and the good old regiment I have the honour to belong to, and the old proud town of Preston. I was shaving when the news came through, and the matron and sisters, nurses and patients have the hands wrung off me, and I can see I could do with another pair of hands. There are telegrams coming every two or three minutes, so I have a busy time in front of me. I have another soldier from Lancashire helping me to answer them.

Young's indomitable spirit was finely evidenced in a second letter to his wife—

> I feel all right, seeing what I have gone through; in fact it was the grace of God, careful nursing, and a grand constitution that

pulled me through. . . . You know the old saying, '*Fools rush in where Angels dare not tread*,' and if I was in the same place tomorrow I would do exactly the same thing. I knew that if I went over the wife and the kiddies would be well looked after. I am very glad to say that the sergeant I carried out is all right, and I expect in about a fortnight's time he will be at home on sick leave with his young wife, as he only got married just after the war broke out, so you see it's an ill wind that blows nobody good.

Young was able in April 1916 to visit Preston, where he was given a public welcome. But he had to return to hospital again, and died in August 1916. A local fund was raised, and so generously responded to that it was possible to invest a sum of over £500 for the family.

Captain Henry Kelly of the Duke of Wellington's West Riding Regiment got the V.C. for deeds which are thus officially described—

For most conspicuous bravery in attack. He twice rallied his company under the heaviest fire, and finally led the only three available men into the enemy trench, and there remained bombing until two of them had become casualties and enemy reinforcements had arrived. He then carried his company sergeant-major, who had been wounded, back to our trenches, a distance of seventy yards, and subsequently three other soldiers. He set a fine example of gallantry and endurance.

Captain Kelly was born in Manchester of Irish parentage. His father was from Wicklow and his mother from Limerick. He is twenty-eight years of age, and joined the Manchester "Pals" with his younger brother on September 4, 1914. He was promoted to the rank of Sergeant-Major two months later, and in the following May was gazetted Second Lieutenant to the West Riding Regiment. Prior to joining the Army he was employed at the General Post Office in Manchester as a sorting clerk and telegraphist. He was a prominent member of the Ancient Order of Hibernians, and also of the city branch of the United Irish League. He could speak the Irish language before he ever spent a holiday in Ireland. A detailed account of the circumstances in which Captain Kelly won the V.C. is given by a soldier in his company—

The enemy had pounded us unmercifully with their big guns, and the strain put on our men was so great that they began to waver. Captain Kelly sprang forward and urged his men to the attack under a blistering hot fire. They responded with cheers, and under his direction they held a very exposed position for hours. Later, things looked black once more. So he up again and called on his lads to hold fast for all they were worth. To show his contempt for the danger to which we were exposed he led the way towards another position.

He decided to have a cut in at the enemy's trench. He got hold of a non-com, and two privates belonging to the bombing section. With these he entered the enemy trench and started to bomb the *Boches* out. They got a good way along, driving before them an enemy more than big enough to eat up the whole company. Then Fritz was reinforced, and under the direction of a very brave officer the enemy began to push our party back. The two privates were knocked out, and Captain Kelly had to make for home. He picked up the sergeant-major and carried him out of the German trench.

The enemy had. many a pot shot at him, and the shell fire continued as well. It is a miracle how he escaped. The *Boches* were close on his heels. The captain just laid down his burden for a few minutes and threw a bomb or two at them. They skulked back. Then he picked up his burden and came marching back to us. All the way he was under heavy fire. After taking a look round to see how things were shaping he found that three of our chaps were out in the open, wounded. Immediately he set off to find them. One by one he carried them into safety, in spite of the furious fire kept up by the enemy.

Australia is proud of Private Martin O'Meara, V.C., of the Australian Infantry. So also is Tipperary. He comes of an old Tipperary family, and has well sustained the splendid traditions of the fighting race. The official record of the award of the V.C. is as follows—

> For most conspicuous bravery. During four days of very heavy fighting he repeatedly went out and brought in wounded officers and men from 'No Man's Land' under intense artillery and machine-gun fire. He also volunteered and carried up ammunition and bombs through a heavy barrage to a portion of the trenches which was being heavily shelled at the time. He showed throughout an utter contempt of danger and undoubtedly saved many lives.

Private O'Meara, V.C., is thirty-two years of age. He is the youngest son of Mr. Thomas O'Meara, Rathcabbin, Birr, and is one of a family of nine children. Before he left Ireland, in 1911, Private O'Meara worked as a tree-feller, and in Australia he continued to labour in the woods, being engaged in making railway sleepers at Collie in West Australia. In the August of 1915 he answered the call to arms, and entered the Blackboy Training Camp as a member of the 12th reinforcements of the Australian Infantry.

Before embarking from Australia a friend vouches that O'Meara said: "As I am going I will do the best I can to bring back the Victoria Cross." To achieve the highest award in the British Army was evidently strongly before his mind. He was two months in France before going up to the trenches, where he remained five days in all, covering himself with glory and winning the V.C. in this short period. Private O'Meara got a fortnight's leave in October 1916—two months after he had won the V.C.—and availed himself of it to visit his native place. The modesty of the man is to be seen in the mode of his home-coming. His family expected him, but did not know the exact date of his arrival. He got off the train at Birr Station and walked home—about five miles—in the darkness, along the disused Birr and Portumna railway line, which passes close to his home. No one recognised him at the station or along the way. He opened the door and walked in, surprising his brother and sister inside.

At the end of his leave he returned almost as quietly as he had come. A fund to make him a presentation was raised locally, and a considerable sum was invested in War stock, and a gold watch was bought. Advantage was taken of the presence of General Hickie, commanding an Irish Division, on a short visit from France to his home at Selvoir, North Tipperary, to have him present the gold watch to O'Meara. But O'Meara, like the genuine fighting man that he is, had immediately volunteered for active service on his return to London from home, after recovering from his wounds, and it was found exceedingly difficult to get into touch with him.

In fact, but for the interest taken by General Hickie it would have been impossible. Ultimately his exact whereabouts were learned through the War Office, and arrangements were made for his return. Even so, O'Meara could not get home in time for the presentation, and it was made to his brothers and sisters. Physically, he is a fine type of manhood, and in disposition is most lovable.

CHAPTER 16

Relations Between Enemy Trenches

In the trenches one evening a battalion of the Leinster Regiment held a "kailee" (*ceilidh*), or Irish sing-song, at which there was a spirited rendering of the humorous old ballad, "Bryan O'Lynn," sung to an infectiously rollicking tune. The opening verse runs—

Bryan O'Lynn had no breeches to wear,
So he bought a sheep-skin to make him a pair,
With the woolly side out, and the skinny side in,
Faix, 'tis pleasant and cool, says Brian O'Lynn.

The swing of the tune took the fancy of the Germans in their trenches, less than fifty yards away. With a "*rumpty-tum-tumty-tum-tumty-tum-tum*," they loudly hummed the air of the end of each verse, all unknowing that the Leinsters, singing at the top of their voices, gave the words a topical application

With the woolly side out and the skinny side in,
Sure, We'll wallop the Gerrys, said Brian O'Lynn.

Hearty bursts of laughter and cheers arose from both trenches at the conclusion of the song. It seemed as if the combatants gladly availed themselves of the chance opportunity of becoming united again in the common brotherhood of man, even for but a fleeting moment, by the spirit of good-humour and hilarity.

Lieutenant Denis Oliver Barnett, a young English officer of a different battalion of the same Leinster Regiment (whose letters from the Front have been published as a memorial by his parents), tells of a more curious incident still, which likewise led to a brief cessation of hostilities. Two privates in his company had a quarrel in the trenches, and nothing would do them but to fight it out on No Man's Land. The Germans were most appreciative and accommodating. Not only did they not molest the pugilists, but they cheered them, and actually fired the contents of their rifles in the air by way of a salute. The European War was, in fact, suspended in this particular section of the lines while two Irishmen settled their own little differences by a contest of fists.

"Who will now say that the Germans are not sportsmen?" was the comment of the young English officer. There is, however, another and perhaps a shrewder view of the episode. It was taken, I have been told, by a sergeant of the company. "Yerra, come down out of that, ye pair of born fools," he called out to the fighters. "If ye had only a glimmer of sense ye'd see, so ye would, that 'tis playing the Gerrys' game ye are. Sure, there's nothing they'd like better than to see us all knocking blazes out of each other."

But as regards the moral pointed by the officer, there must be, of course, many "sportsmen" among the millions of German soldiers; though the opinion widely prevailing in the British Army is that they are more often treacherous fighters. Indeed, to their dirty practices is mainly to be ascribed the bitter personal animosity that occasionally mark the relations between the combatants, when the fighting becomes most bloody and desperate, and—as happens at times in all wars—no quarter is given to those who allow none.

In the wars of old between England and France, both sides were animated by a very fine sense of chivalry. Barère, one of the chief popular orators during the worst excesses of the French Revolution, induced the Convention to declare that no quarter was to be given to the English. "Soldiers of Liberty," he cried, "when victory places Englishmen at your mercy, strike!" But the French troops absolutely refused to act upon the savage decree. The principle upon which both French and English acted during the Peninsular War was that of doing as little harm to one another as possible consistently with the winning of victory.

Between the rank and file friendly feelings may be said, without any incongruity, to have existed. They were able, of their own accord, to come to certain understandings that tended to mitigate, to some extent, the hardships and even the dangers to which they were both alike exposed. One was that sentries at the outposts must not be fired on or surprised. Often no more than a space of twenty yards separated them, and when the order to advance was given to either Army the sentries of the other were warned to retire. Once a French sentry helped a British sentry to replace his knapsack so that he might more quickly fall back before the firing began.

A remarkable instance of signalling between the opposing forces is mentioned by General Sir Charles Napier in his *History of the Peninsular War*. Wellington sent a detachment of riflemen to drive away some French troops occupying the top of a hill near Bayonne, and as they approached the enemy he ordered them to fire. "But," says Napier, "with a loud voice one of those soldiers replied, 'No firing,' and holding up the butt of his rifle tapped it in a peculiar way." This was a signal to the French and was understood by them—probably as a result of a mutual arrangement—to mean, "We must have the hill for a short time."

"The French, who, though they could not maintain, would not relinquish the post without a fight if they had been fired upon, quietly retired," Napier writes; "and this signal would never have been made if the post had been one capable of a permanent defence, so well do veterans understand war and its proprieties."

Throughout that long campaign the British and French recognised each other as worthy foemen, and they were both solicitous to maintain unstained the honour and dignity of arms. As the opposing forces lay resting before Lisbon for months, the advanced posts got so closely into touch that much friendly intercourse took place between them. French officers frequently asked for such little luxuries as cigars, coffee and stationery to be brought to them from Lisbon, which was held by the British, and their requests were always readily complied with.

At the Battle of Talavera, on July 28, 1809, the possession of a hill was fiercely contested all day. The weather was so intensely hot that the combatants were parched with thirst. At noon there was an almost entire cessation of artillery and rifle fire, as if an informal truce had been suddenly come to, by a flash of intuition, and with one accord French and British rushed down to the rivulet at the foot of the hill to moisten their burning throats.

The men crowded on each side of the water's edge," says Napier. "They threw aside their caps and muskets, and chatted to each other in broken French and still more fragmentary English across the stream. Flasks were exchanged; hands shaken. Then the bugle and the rolling drum called the men back to their colours, and the fight awoke once more."

Such amenities between combatants are very ancient—the Greeks and Trojans used to exchange presents and courtesies, in the intervals of fighting—and the early stages of this war seemed to afford a promise that they would be revived. The fraternising of the British and Germans at their first Christmas under arms, in 1914, will, perhaps, always be accounted as the most curious episode of the war. It was quite unauthorised by the higher command. The men themselves, under the influence of the great Christian festival, brought about a suspension of hostilities at several points of the lines, and they availed themselves of the opportunity to satisfy their natural curiosity to see something more of each other than they could see through the smoke of battle with deadly weapons in their hands and hatred in their eyes.

Each side had taken prisoners; but prisoners are "out of it," and therefore reduced to the level of non-combatants. The foeman in being appears in a very different light. He has the power to strike. You may have to kill him or you may be killed by him. So the British and the Germans, impelled in the main by a common feeling of inquisitiveness, met together, unarmed, in No Man's Land. There was some amicable conversation where they could make themselves understood to each other, which happened when a German was found who could speak a little English. Cigarettes and tunic-buttons were freely exchanged. But, for the most part, British and Germans stood, with arms folded across their breasts, and stared at each other with a kind of dread fascination.

It never happened again. How could it possibly be repeated? The introduction of the barbaric elements of "frightfulness," hitherto confined to savage tribes at war, the use of such devilish inventions as poison gas and liquid fire, are due to the malignant minds of the German high command, and for them the German soldiers cannot be held accountable. But the native lowness of morality shown by so many of the German rank and file, their apparent insensitiveness to ordinary humane instincts, the well-authenticated stories of their filthy and cruel conduct in the occupied districts, inevitably tended to harden and embitter their adversaries against them too. Of the instances of their treachery to Irish soldiers which have been brought to my notice, I will mention only two. One arose out of the "truce" of Christmas Day, 1914, despite the goodwill of the occasion. The victim, Sergeant Timothy O'Toole, Leinster Regiment, first mentions that he took part in a game of football with the Germans, and then proceeds—

> I was returning to my own trench unaccompanied about 12.15 p.m. When I reached within fifteen paces I was sniped by a Hunnish swine, the bullet entering my back, penetrating my

intestines. Following the example of Our Lord, I instantly forgave him, concluding he was only a black sheep, characteristic of any army or community, but I was labouring under a delusion. Within five minutes of being hit, I had quite a number around me, including officers and clergymen. I was so mortally wounded that the *'Padre'* administered the last rite of the Church on the spot.

Four stretcher bearers came out for me. I noticed the white band and Red Cross on their arms. Immediately I was lifted up on the stretcher. Though I was semi-unconscious I remember the bullets beating the ground like hailstone on a March day. I was wounded again, this time the bullet going through the lower part of my back. Here two of my bearers got hit, Privates Melia and Peters. The former died in hospital immediately after. Naturally the two bearers instantly dropped the stretcher. I fell violently to the ground—nice medicine for a man wounded in the abdomen.'

"Thank Providence, I am still living," Sergeant O'Toole adds, "but a living victim of German atrocity and barbarism." In the other case a very gallant young officer of the Dublin Fusiliers, Lieutenant Louis G. Doran, lost his life on the Somme, October 23, 1916, through the guile and falsehood of German soldiers. The circumstances are told in a letter written by Captain Louis C. Byrne to the father of Lieutenant Doran, Mr. Charles J. Doran of Blackrock, Co. Dublin—

Believe me, Mr. Doran, I sympathise fully with you in your loss because I was your son's company commander and by his death I have lost one of the best officers in my company. We attacked a certain position and we had just got to it when some Germans put up their hands to surrender. Your son went out to take their surrender and they shot him through the heart and he died at once. My other three officers were also knocked out, and only myself and thirty-six men returned to headquarters after the battle. Still, we took the position owing to gallantry of men like your son. He died a noble and heroic death—no man could possibly wish for a better one.

He told me he had just had a brother wounded, so your loss is double and words cannot express my sympathy with you. Your son was buried with the men in the position we took. It was impossible to bring his body down owing to heavy fire. I think it is what he would have liked best.

The lady to whom Lieutenant Doran was engaged to be married kindly sent me a few extracts from his letters which convey something of his care and thought for his men. "Those I have seen from the men," she says, "amplify this from their own experience in ways which he would never dream of mentioning, he was always so modest about all he did."

"I'm going to tell you what I would really love to get now and again," Lieutenant Doran wrote in one letter. "You see, we officers are never very hard up for grub, and I would much prefer to receive something for my men, who get very little in the way of luxuries or dainties. As you know, a platoon is split into four sections, and anything that I could divide into four parts amongst them would be most acceptable. For instance, four small tins of butter would be a great luxury, or a big cake—anything that gives them a change."

In another he said: "As you say, there are always hungry soldiers to be found, and I often wish some of the presents I receive would only come together, as one cake is a useless thing among forty hungry men. The poor fellows have fairly rough fare as a rule, and sometimes not even much of that. One wonders how it is they keep so cheerful."

The men, in turn, were most devoted to Lieutenant Doran. They would do anything to prevent a hair of his head being hurt.

Generally speaking, feeling in the British Army is, however, extraordinarily devoid of that vindictiveness which springs from a deep sense of personal injury, and evokes, in turn, a desire for revenge which, were it shown, would, however lamentable, be not unnatural in many circumstances of this war. The Germans, in the mass, are regarded as having been dehumanised and transformed into a process of ruthless destruction. In any case, they are the enemy. As such, there is a satisfaction—nay, a positive delight—in sweeping them out of existence.

That is war. But the rage for killing them is impersonal. Against the German soldier individually it may be said that, on the whole, there is no rancour. In fact, the British soldiers have a curiously detached and generous way of regarding their country's enemies. When the German soldier is taken prisoner, or picked up wounded, the British soldier is disposed, as a hundred thousand instances show, to treat him as a "pal"—to divide his food and share his cigarettes with him as he passes to the base.

It is very noticeable how all the war correspondents, in their accounts of the taking of the village of Guinchy on the Somme by the

Irish Division, dwelt on the chivalrous way in which the Irish treated their vanquished foes. Once the spirit of combativeness is aroused in the Irish soldiers they hate the enemy like the black death to which they strive to consign them. But when the fury of battle has died down in victory there are none so soft and kindly to the beaten enemy. Surrender should always, of course, disarm hostility. No true soldier would decline to lower his bayonet when a foeman acknowledges defeat and places his life in his keeping. That is, after a fair and gallant fight on the part of the foeman. It was because the Germans at Guinchy were vindictive in combat, and despicable when overthrown, that the Irish acted with rare magnanimity in accepting their submission and sparing their lives.

In that engagement the Irish made a characteristically headlong dash for the enemy positions. Rifle and machine-gun fire was poured into them by the Germans up to the very last moment until, in fact, they had reached the trenches; and then, as they were about to jump in and bayonet and club their bloodthirsty foemen, they found them on their knees, with hands uplifted. The Irish were enraged at the sight. To think that men who had been so merciless should beg for mercy when their opponents were on top of them! Were their comrades slain only a moment since to go unavenged? These thoughts passed rapidly through the minds of the Irish. As swiftly came the decision, worthy of high-souled men. An enemy on his knees is to them inviolable, not to be hurt or injured, however mean and low he may have proved himself to be. So the Irish bayonet, at the very breasts of the Germans, was turned aside; that was the right and proper thing to do, and it would not call for notice but that it shines with the light of chivalry in comparison with the black meanness and treachery of the Germans.

In the gladiatorial fights for the entertainment of the people in ancient Rome the defeated combatant was expected to expose his throat to the sword of the victor, and any shrinking on his part caused the arena to ring with the angry shouts of the thousands of spectators: "Receive the steel." The way of the Irish at Guinchy was different, and perhaps the renunciation of their revenge was not the least magnificent act of a glorious day.

"If we brained them on the spot, who could blame us? 'Tis ourselves that would think it no sin if it was done by anyone else," said a private of the Dublin Fusiliers. "Let me tell you," he went on, "what happened to myself. As I raced across the open with my comrades, jumping in and out of shell holes, and the bullets flying thick around us, laying many the fine boy low, I said to myself, this is going to be a fight to the last gasp for those of us that get to the Germans. As I came near to the trenches I picked a man out for myself. Straight in front of me he was, leaning out of the trench, and he with a rifle firing away at us as if we were rabbits. I made for him with my bayonet ready, determined to give him what he deserved, when—what do you think?—didn't he notice me and what I was up to.

"Dropping his rifle, he raised himself up in the trench and stretched out his hands towards me. What could you do in that case, but what I did? Sure you wouldn't have the heart to strike him down, even if he were to kill you. I caught sight of his eyes, and there was such a frightened and pleading look in them that I at once lowered my rifle. I could no more prod him with my bayonet than I could a toddling child. I declare to the Lord the state of the poor devil almost made me cry. I took him by the hand, saying, 'You're my prisoner.' I don't suppose he understood a word of what I said, but he clung to me, crying, '*Kamerad! kamerad!*'

"I was more glad than ever then that I hadn't the blood of him on my soul. 'Tis a queer thing to say, maybe, of a man who acted like that; but, all the same, he looked a decent boy every bit of him. I suppose the truth of it is this: we soldiers, on both sides, have to go through such terrible experiences that there is no accounting for how we may behave. We might be devils, all out, in the morning, and saints, no less, in the evening."

The relations between the trenches include even attempts at an exchange of repartee. The wit, as may be supposed, in such circumstances, is invariably ironic and sarcastic. My examples are Irish, for the reason that I have had most to do with Irish soldiers, but they may be taken as fairly representative of the taunts and pleasantries which are often bandied across No Man's Land. The Germans holding part of their line in Belgium got to know that the British trenches opposite them were being held by an Irish battalion. "Hello, Irish," they cried; "how is King Carson getting on? and have you got Home Rule yet?"

The company sergeant-major, a big Tipperary man, was selected to make the proper reply, and in order that it might be fully effective he sent it through a megaphone which the colonel was accustomed to use in addressing the battalion on parade. "Hello, Gerrys," he called out. "I'm thinking it isn't information ye want, but divarshion; but 'tis information I'll be after giving ye, all the same. Later on we'll be sending ye some fun that'll make ye laugh at the other side of ye'r mouths. The last we heard of Carson he was prodding the Government like the very devil to put venim into their blows at ye, and more power to his elbow while he's at that work, say we. As for Home Rule, we mean to have it, and we'll get it, please God, when ye' re licked. Put that in ye're pipes and smoke it."

Of all the horrible features of the war, surely the most heartrending is the fate of the wounded lying without succour in the open between the opposing lines, owing to the inability of the higher command on both sides to agree to an arrangement for a short suspension of hostilities after an engagement so that the stricken might be brought in. Prone in the mud and slush they lie, during the cruel winter weather, with the rain pouring down upon them, their moans of agony in the darkness of the night mingling with the cold blasts that howl around them. But, thanks to the loving kindness of man for his fellow, even in war, these unfortunate creatures are not deserted. British soldiers without number have voluntarily crept out into No Man's Land to rescue them, often under murderous fire from the enemy. Many of the Victoria Crosses won in this war have been awarded for conspicuous gallantry displayed in these most humane and chivalrous enterprises.

One of the most uplifting stories I have heard was told me by a captain of the Royal Irish Fusiliers. Out there in front of the trench held by his company lay a figure in khaki writhing in pain and wailing for help. "Will no one come to me? "he cried in a voice broken with anguish. He had been disabled in the course of a raid on the German trenches the night before by a battalion which was relieved in the morning. These appeals of his were like stabs to the compassionate hearts of the Irish Fusiliers. Several of them told the captain they could stand it no longer, and must go out to the wounded man. If they were shot in the attempt, what matter?

It happened that a little dog was then making himself quite at home in both the British and German trenches at this part of the lines. He was a neutral; he took no sides; he regularly crossed from one to the other, and found in both friends to give him food and a kind word, with a pat on the head. The happy thought came to the captain to make a messenger of the dog. So he wrote, "May we take our wounded man in?," tied the note to the dog's tail, and sent him to the German trenches. The message was in English, for the captain did not know German, and had to trust to the chance of the enemy being able to read it.

In a short time the dog returned with the answer. It was in English, and it ran: "Yes; you can have five minutes." So the captain and a man went out with a stretcher and brought the poor fellow back to our lines.

Some of these understandings are come to by a sort of telepathic suggestion inspired by the principle of *live and let live,* however incongruous that may seem in warfare. As an instance, recuperative work, such as the bringing up of food to the firing lines is often allowed to go on in comparative quietude. Neither side cares to stand on guard in the trenches with an empty stomach. Often, therefore, firing is almost entirely suspended in the early hours of the night, when it is known that rations are being distributed. That is not the way everywhere and always.

A private of the Royal Irish Regiment told me that what he found most aggravating in the trenches was the fusillading by the Germans when the men were getting ready a bit to eat. "I suppose," he remarked, "'twas the smell of the frying bacon that put their dandher up." But even defensive work has been allowed to proceed without interference, when carried on simultaneously by both sides. Heavy rain, following a hard frost, turned the trenches in the Ypres district into a chaos of ooze and slime.

"How deep is it with you?" a German soldier shouted across to the British.

"Up to our knees, bedad," was the reply.

"You are lucky fellows. We're up to our belts in it," said the German.

Driven to desperation by their hideous discomfort, the Germans soon after crawled up on to their parapets and sat there to dry and stretch their legs, calling out, "*Kamerads*, don't shoot; don't shoot, *kamerads!*" The reply of the Irish was to get out of their trenches and do likewise. On another occasion, in the broad daylight, unarmed parties of men on both sides, by a tacit agreement, set about repairing their respective barbed-wire entanglements. They were no more than fifteen or twenty yards apart.

The wiring-party on the British side belonged to the Munster Fusiliers. Being short of mallets, one of the Munsters coolly walked across to the enemy and said, "Good-morrow, Gerrys. Would any of ye be so kind as to lend me the loan of a hammer?" The Germans received him with smiles, but as they did not know English they were unable to understand what he wanted until he made it clear by pantomimic action, when he was given the hammer "with a heart and a half," as he put it himself. Having repaired the defences of his own trench, he brought back the hammer to the Germans, and thought he might give them "a bit of his mind," without offence, as they did not know what he was saying. "Here's your hammer, and thanks," said he. "High hanging to the man that caused this war—ye know who I mean—and may we be all soon busily at work hammering nails into his coffin."

Many touching stories might be told of the sympathy which unites the combatants when they find themselves lying side by side, wounded and helpless, in shell holes and copses, or on the open plain after an engagement. The ruling spirit which animates the soldier in the fury of the fight is, as it seems to me, that of self-preservation. He kills or disables so that he may not be killed or disabled himself. Besides that, each side are convinced they are waging a purely defensive war. So it is that hostility subsides, once the sense of danger is removed, and each side sees in its captives not devils or barbarians, but fellowmen. Especially among the wounded, British and German, do these sentiments prevail, as they lie together on the field of battle. In a dim way they pitifully regard each other as hapless victims caught in the vortex of the greatest of human tragedies, or set against each other by the ambitions of rulers and statesmen in which they have no part. They try to help each other, to ease each other's sufferings, to stanch each other's wounds, to give each other comfort in their sore distress.

"Poor devil, unnerved by shell shock," was the comment passed as a wounded German was being carried by on a stretcher sobbing as if his heart would break. It was not the roar of the artillery and the bursting of high explosives that had unnerved him, but the self-sacrifice of a Dublin Fusilier, who, in succouring him, lost his own life. At the hospital the German related that, on recovering his senses after being shot, he found the Dublin Fusilier trying to stanch the wound in his shattered leg, from which blood was flowing profusely. The Irishman undid the field-dressing, consisting of bandage and antiseptic preparation, which he had wrapped round his own wound, and applied it to the German, as he appeared to be in danger of bleeding to death. Before the two men were discovered by a British stretcher party, the Dublin Fusilier had passed away. He developed blood-poisoning through his exposed wound. The German, on hearing the news, broke down and wept bitterly.

Reconciliation between wounded foemen is happily a common

occurrence on the stricken plain. The malignant roar of the guns may still be in their ears, and they may see around them bodies battered and twisted out of all human shape. All the more are they anxious to testify that there is no fury in their hearts with each other, and that their one wish is to make the supreme parting with words of reconciliation and prayers on their lips. I have had from a French officer, who was wounded in a cavalry charge early in the war, an account of a pathetic incident which took place close to where he lay.

Among his companions in affliction were two who were far gone on the way to death. One was a private in the *Uhlans*, and the other a private in the Royal Irish Dragoons. The Irishman got, with a painful effort, from an inside pocket of his tunic a rosary beads which had a crucifix attached to it. Then he commenced to mutter to himself the invocations to the Blessed Virgin of which the Rosary is composed:

Hail, Mary! full of grace, the Lord is with thee; blessed art thou among women, and blessed is the fruit of thy womb, Jesus.

The German, lying huddled close by, stirred with the uneasy movements of a man weak from pain and loss of blood on hearing the murmur of prayer, and, looking round in a dazed condition, the sight of the beads in the hands of his fellow in distress seemed to recall to his mind other times and different circumstances family prayers at home somewhere in Bavaria, and Sunday evening devotions in church, for he made, in his own tongue, the response to the invocation:

Holy Mary, Mother of God, pray for us sinners now at the hour of our death. Amen.

So the voices intermingled in address and prayer—the rapt ejaculations of the Irishman, the deep guttural of the German—getting weaker and weaker, in the process of dissolution, until they were hushed on earth for evermore.

War has outwardly lost its romance, with its colour and pageantry. It is bloody, ugly and horrible. Yet romance is not dead. It still survives, radiant and glowing, in the heroic achievements of our soldiers, and in the tender impulses of their hearts.

LEONAUR
ALSO FROM LEONAUR
AVAILABLE IN SOFTCOVER OR HARDCOVER WITH DUST JACKET

THE RELUCTANT REBEL by William G. Stevenson—A young Kentuckian's experiences in the Confederate Infantry & Cavalry during the American Civil War..

BOOTS AND SADDLES by Elizabeth B. Custer—The experiences of General Custer's Wife on the Western Plains.

FANNIE BEERS' CIVIL WAR by Fannie A. Beers—A Confederate Lady's Experiences of Nursing During the Campaigns & Battles of the American Civil War.

LADY SALE'S AFGHANISTAN by Florentia Sale—An Indomitable Victorian Lady's Account of the Retreat from Kabul During the First Afghan War.

THE TWO WARS OF MRS DUBERLY by Frances Isabella Duberly—An Intrepid Victorian Lady's Experience of the Crimea and Indian Mutiny.

THE REBELLIOUS DUCHESS by Paul F. S. Dermoncourt—The Adventures of the Duchess of Berri and Her Attempt to Overthrow French Monarchy.

LADIES OF WATERLOO by Charlotte A. Eaton, Magdalene de Lancey & Juana Smith—The Experiences of Three Women During the Campaign of 1815: Waterloo Days by Charlotte A. Eaton, A Week at Waterloo by Magdalene de Lancey & Juana's Story by Juana Smith.

TWO YEARS BEFORE THE MAST by Richard Henry Dana. Jr.—The account of one young man's experiences serving on board a sailing brig—the Penelope—bound for California, between the years 1834-36.

A SAILOR OF KING GEORGE by Frederick Hoffman—From Midshipman to Captain—Recollections of War at Sea in the Napoleonic Age 1793-1815.

LORDS OF THE SEA by A. T. Mahan—Great Captains of the Royal Navy During the Age of Sail.

COGGESHALL'S VOYAGES: VOLUME 1 by George Coggeshall—The Recollections of an American Schooner Captain.

COGGESHALL'S VOYAGES: VOLUME 2 by George Coggeshall—The Recollections of an American Schooner Captain.

TWILIGHT OF EMPIRE by Sir Thomas Ussher & Sir George Cockburn—Two accounts of Napoleon's Journeys in Exile to Elba and St. Helena: Narrative of Events by Sir Thomas Ussher & Napoleon's Last Voyage: Extract of a diary by Sir George Cockburn.

AVAILABLE ONLINE AT www.leonaur.com
AND FROM ALL GOOD BOOK STORES

ALSO FROM LEONAUR
AVAILABLE IN SOFTCOVER OR HARDCOVER WITH DUST JACKET

ESCAPE FROM THE FRENCH by Edward Boys—A Young Royal Navy Midshipman's Adventures During the Napoleonic War.

THE VOYAGE OF H.M.S. PANDORA by Edward Edwards R. N. & George Hamilton, edited by Basil Thomson—In Pursuit of the Mutineers of the Bounty in the South Seas—1790-1791.

MEDUSA by J. B. Henry Savigny and Alexander Correard and Charlotte-Adélaïde Dard —Narrative of a Voyage to Senegal in 1816 & The Sufferings of the Picard Family After the Shipwreck of the Medusa.

THE SEA WAR OF 1812 VOLUME 1 by A. T. Mahan—A History of the Maritime Conflict.

THE SEA WAR OF 1812 VOLUME 2 by A. T. Mahan—A History of the Maritime Conflict.

WETHERELL OF H. M. S. HUSSAR by John Wetherell—The Recollections of an Ordinary Seaman of the Royal Navy During the Napoleonic Wars.

THE NAVAL BRIGADE IN NATAL by C. R. N. Burne—With the Guns of H. M. S. Terrible & H. M. S. Tartar during the Boer War 1899-1900.

THE VOYAGE OF H. M. S. BOUNTY by William Bligh—The True Story of an 18th Century Voyage of Exploration and Mutiny.

SHIPWRECK! by William Gilly—The Royal Navy's Disasters at Sea 1793-1849.

KING'S CUTTERS AND SMUGGLERS: 1700-1855 by E. Keble Chatterton—A unique period of maritime history-from the beginning of the eighteenth to the middle of the nineteenth century when British seamen risked all to smuggle valuable goods from wool to tea and spirits from and to the Continent.

CONFEDERATE BLOCKADE RUNNER by John Wilkinson—The Personal Recollections of an Officer of the Confederate Navy.

NAVAL BATTLES OF THE NAPOLEONIC WARS by W. H. Fitchett—Cape St. Vincent, the Nile, Cadiz, Copenhagen, Trafalgar & Others.

PRISONERS OF THE RED DESERT by R. S. Gwatkin-Williams—The Adventures of the Crew of the Tara During the First World War.

U-BOAT WAR 1914-1918 by James B. Connolly/Karl von Schenk—Two Contrasting Accounts from Both Sides of the Conflict at Sea During the Great War.

AVAILABLE ONLINE AT **www.leonaur.com**
AND FROM ALL GOOD BOOK STORES

ALSO FROM LEONAUR
AVAILABLE IN SOFTCOVER OR HARDCOVER WITH DUST JACKET

IRON TIMES WITH THE GUARDS by An O. E. (G. P. A. Fildes)—The Experiences of an Officer of the Coldstream Guards on the Western Front During the First World War.

THE GREAT WAR IN THE MIDDLE EAST: 1 by W. T. Massey—The Desert Campaigns & How Jerusalem Was Won---two classic accounts in one volume.

THE GREAT WAR IN THE MIDDLE EAST: 2 by W. T. Massey—Allenby's Final Triumph.

SMITH-DORRIEN by Horace Smith-Dorrien—Isandlwhana to the Great War.

1914 by Sir John French—The Early Campaigns of the Great War by the British Commander.

GRENADIER by E. R. M. Fryer—The Recollections of an Officer of the Grenadier Guards throughout the Great War on the Western Front.

BATTLE, CAPTURE & ESCAPE by George Pearson—The Experiences of a Canadian Light Infantryman During the Great War.

DIGGERS AT WAR by R. Hugh Knyvett & G. P. Cuttriss—"Over There" With the Australians by R. Hugh Knyvett and Over the Top With the Third Australian Division by G. P. Cuttriss. Accounts of Australians During the Great War in the Middle East, at Gallipoli and on the Western Front.

HEAVY FIGHTING BEFORE US by George Brenton Laurie—The Letters of an Officer of the Royal Irish Rifles on the Western Front During the Great War.

THE CAMELIERS by Oliver Hogue—A Classic Account of the Australians of the Imperial Camel Corps During the First World War in the Middle East.

RED DUST by Donald Black—A Classic Account of Australian Light Horsemen in Palestine During the First World War.

THE LEAN, BROWN MEN by Angus Buchanan—Experiences in East Africa During the Great War with the 25th Royal Fusiliers—the Legion of Frontiersmen.

THE NIGERIAN REGIMENT IN EAST AFRICA by W. D. Downes—On Campaign During the Great War 1916-1918.

THE 'DIE-HARDS' IN SIBERIA by John Ward—With the Middlesex Regiment Against the Bolsheviks 1918-19.

ALSO FROM LEONAUR
AVAILABLE IN SOFTCOVER OR HARDCOVER WITH DUST JACKET

FARAWAY CAMPAIGN *by F. James*—Experiences of an Indian Army Cavalry Officer in Persia & Russia During the Great War.

REVOLT IN THE DESERT *by T. E. Lawrence*—An account of the experiences of one remarkable British officer's war from his own perspective.

MACHINE-GUN SQUADRON *by A. M. G.*—The 20th Machine Gunners from British Yeomanry Regiments in the Middle East Campaign of the First World War.

A GUNNER'S CRUSADE *by Antony Bluett*—The Campaign in the Desert, Palestine & Syria as Experienced by the Honourable Artillery Company During the Great War .

DESPATCH RIDER *by W. H. L. Watson*—The Experiences of a British Army Motorcycle Despatch Rider During the Opening Battles of the Great War in Europe.

TIGERS ALONG THE TIGRIS *by E. J. Thompson*—The Leicestershire Regiment in Mesopotamia During the First World War.

HEARTS & DRAGONS *by Charles R. M. F. Crutwell*—The 4th Royal Berkshire Regiment in France and Italy During the Great War, 1914-1918.

INFANTRY BRIGADE: 1914 *by John Ward*—The Diary of a Commander of the 15th Infantry Brigade, 5th Division, British Army, During the Retreat from Mons.

DOING OUR 'BIT' *by Ian Hay*—Two Classic Accounts of the Men of Kitchener's 'New Army' During the Great War including *The First 100,000* & *All In It*.

AN EYE IN THE STORM *by Arthur Ruhl*—An American War Correspondent's Experiences of the First World War from the Western Front to Gallipoli-and Beyond.

STAND & FALL *by Joe Cassells*—With the Middlesex Regiment Against the Bolsheviks 1918-19.

RIFLEMAN MACGILL'S WAR *by Patrick MacGill*—A Soldier of the London Irish During the Great War in Europe including *The Amateur Army*, *The Red Horizon* & *The Great Push*.

WITH THE GUNS *by C. A. Rose & Hugh Dalton*—Two First Hand Accounts of British Gunners at War in Europe During World War 1- Three Years in France with the Guns and With the British Guns in Italy.

THE BUSH WAR DOCTOR *by Robert V. Dolbey*—The Experiences of a British Army Doctor During the East African Campaign of the First World War.

AVAILABLE ONLINE AT **www.leonaur.com**
AND FROM ALL GOOD BOOK STORES

ALSO FROM LEONAUR
AVAILABLE IN SOFTCOVER OR HARDCOVER WITH DUST JACKET

THE 9TH—THE KING'S (LIVERPOOL REGIMENT) IN THE GREAT WAR 1914 - 1918 *by Enos H. G. Roberts*—Mersey to mud—war and Liverpool men.

THE GAMBARDIER *by Mark Severn*—The experiences of a battery of Heavy artillery on the Western Front during the First World War.

FROM MESSINES TO THIRD YPRES *by Thomas Floyd*—A personal account of the First World War on the Western front by a 2/5th Lancashire Fusilier.

THE IRISH GUARDS IN THE GREAT WAR - VOLUME 1 *by Rudyard Kipling*—Edited and Compiled from Their Diaries and Papers—The First Battalion.

THE IRISH GUARDS IN THE GREAT WAR - VOLUME 1 *by Rudyard Kipling*—Edited and Compiled from Their Diaries and Papers—The Second Battalion.

ARMOURED CARS IN EDEN *by K. Roosevelt*—An American President's son serving in Rolls Royce armoured cars with the British in Mesopatamia & with the American Artillery in France during the First World War.

CHASSEUR OF 1914 *by Marcel Dupont*—Experiences of the twilight of the French Light Cavalry by a young officer during the early battles of the great war in Europe.

TROOP HORSE & TRENCH *by R.A. Lloyd*—The experiences of a British Lifeguardsman of the household cavalry fighting on the western front during the First World War 1914-18.

THE EAST AFRICAN MOUNTED RIFLES *by C.J. Wilson*—Experiences of the campaign in the East African bush during the First World War.

THE LONG PATROL *by George Berrie*—A Novel of Light Horsemen from Gallipoli to the Palestine campaign of the First World War.

THE FIGHTING CAMELIERS *by Frank Reid*—The exploits of the Imperial Camel Corps in the desert and Palestine campaigns of the First World War.

STEEL CHARIOTS IN THE DESERT *by S. C. Rolls*—The first world war experiences of a Rolls Royce armoured car driver with the Duke of Westminster in Libya and in Arabia with T.E. Lawrence.

WITH THE IMPERIAL CAMEL CORPS IN THE GREAT WAR *by Geoffrey Inchbald*—The story of a serving officer with the British 2nd battalion against the Senussi and during the Palestine campaign.

AVAILABLE ONLINE AT **www.leonaur.com**
AND FROM ALL GOOD BOOK STORES

www.ingramcontent.com/pod-product-compliance
Lightning Source LLC
Chambersburg PA
CBHW031618160426
43196CB00006B/176